
Starting Your Career
as a
FREELANCE WRITER

Starting Your Career

as a

FREELANCE WRITER

MOIRA ANDERSON ALLEN

ALLWORTH PRESS

NEW YORK

09 08 07 06 05   7 6 5 4 3 2

Published by Allworth Press
An imprint of Allworth Communications, Inc.
10 East 23rd Street, New York, NY 10010

Cover design by Derek Bacchus
Interior design and page composition/typography by Sharp Des!gns, Lansing MI

ISBN: 1-58115-304-X

LIBRARY OF CONGRESS CATALOGING-IN-PUBLICATION DATA
Anderson Allen, Moira.
Starting your career as a freelance writer / Moira Anderson Allen.
p. cm.
ISBN 1-58115-304-X (pbk.)
1. Authorship—Vocational guidance. 2. Authorship—Marketing. I. Title.
PN151.A49 2003
808'.02'023—dc21
2003013234

Printed in Canada

Table of Contents

Part IV: Queries and Submissions

Part V: Rights and Contracts

Acknowledgments

irst and foremost, this book is dedicated to my husband, Patrick, who said, "Why don't you work on that writing book you always wanted to publish?"

Second, it is dedicated to my furry feline friends (Nani, Brisco, and Puff), without whose keyboard antics the book would have been written a bit faster. . . .

Finally, it is dedicated to everyone who has ever wanted to become a writer, and wondered, "Do I dare?" May you find the answer here!

Introduction

*T*his is the book I've always wanted to write. As a writer and writing instructor, I've searched in vain for a book that, to me, fully answers the questions writers ask about launching a freelance career. A book that explains in clear detail what to do first, what to do next, what to do after that.

It's not that there aren't any books on freelance writing on the market. Indeed, there are dozens. So, what makes me think I can write one that covers the topic better than the rest?

The answer is: While I'm a writer, I'm not *just* a writer. I'm also an editor. I've sat on both sides of the desk. I know what it's like to send out queries and submissions and wait, seemingly forever, for a response; but I also know what it's like to *receive* those queries and submissions, and what makes the good ones stand out from the rest. I know how to *get* an acceptance, and I also know what inspires me to *give* one.

In addition, through my association with the now-defunct writers' Web site Inkspot, and more recently Writing-World.com, I've answered literally hundreds of questions from writers about nearly every aspect of the writing business. Consequently, I know what questions writers ask about launching a successful career.

This book will guide you through the steps needed to start freelancing—and the steps needed to make your career successful. Whether you want to freelance as a sideline to your day job or while taking care of a home and family, or whether you're interested in going "full-time" and supporting yourself as a writer, this book will give you the tools for success.

You may want to read this book more than once as you progress in your career. But whether you read it once or a dozen times, there is one even more important thing you must do to become a successful writer. And that is: Put the book down and *start writing!*

MOIRA ALLEN
moirakallen@writing-world.com; www.writing-world.com

Starting Your Career
as a
FREELANCE WRITER

PART I

GETTING STARTED

CHAPTER 1

So You Want to Be a Freelance Writer

Writing for publication is one of the most rewarding careers I can think of. It offers the opportunity for independence, creativity, and the occasional moment of fame. It allows you to speak to others—to entertain, to educate, to inspire, to motivate. It gives you a chance to earn an income by doing something you love. It may even give you a chance to change the world, or at least to improve one small corner of it, by giving your readers the tools they need to make their lives better. And there's nothing quite like the thrill of seeing your name in print—not just the first time, but *every* time!

It's also one of the easier careers to break into. You don't need any special qualifications to become a freelance writer: no special degrees or educational background, no certification, no business license, no "permission." All you really need to do to get started is to sit down and *write*. Plus, thanks to the magic of the Internet, you can launch a successful writing career from just about anywhere in the world; you're no longer limited by problems of international language differences, postage, and currencies.

As a *creative* career, freelance writing can be far more lucrative than many other creative or artistic outlets. I enjoy crafts, for example, but when I have a choice between spending an hour making an item that might sell for $25, or spending two hours writing a how-to crafts article that might sell for $500, the decision is a no-brainer!

At the same time, freelance writing can be arduous and frustrating. It takes time to get a writing career launched, and even longer to become "successful." The publishing marketplace is becoming an increasingly hostile environment for writers, as many publications are run by corporations that are interested only in the bottom line. Rejection is an inevitable part of this business—a part every writer must learn to accept gracefully.

And make no mistake: freelance writing *is* a business. Writing for publication isn't simply an exercise in creativity; it is a process of developing a *product*. The business side of freelancing includes determining what types of markets are available to you, and the types of materials you can sell to those markets. As a business, freelance writing also has its mundane side—handling correspondence, keeping records and financial accounts, and so forth.

The good news is that a writing career is remarkably flexible. It adjusts to your hours, enabling you to invest as few or as many hours as you wish. Most freelancers begin as moonlighters, writing in their "spare" time while handling a day job or taking care of a family. Moonlighting gives you a chance to develop your skills, build a portfolio or client base, and build a nest-egg against the day that you decide to go full-time. It also gives you a chance to determine, *before* you make that jump, whether this is the career for you. Indeed, many writers never do go full-time, but freelance to supplement their regular income.

What Is a Freelancer?

A freelance writer is, by definition, a writer who is self-employed. As a freelancer, you do not draw a paycheck but work independently, writing what you want and when you want, and offering your work to any market that will buy it. If you enter into a more formal relationship with a publisher (e.g., by becoming a columnist for a magazine), you may become an "independent contractor" for that publication, but you will not be an employee. This independence is what many freelancers cherish most about the business.

Beyond that, the term "freelancer" can be applied to a variety of writing activities and markets. This book covers the following types of freelance writing:

❖ *Writing for magazines.* Nonfiction magazines represent the largest, most accessible, and highest-paying market for freelancers. There are literally thousands of print magazines that accept freelance material in the United States alone, and hundreds of other potential markets internationally. Though many predicted that the Internet would cause the "death" of print periodicals, readers still prefer them, and advertisers still find them the best way to reach customers. Hence, they remain a strong market for writers. The downside of magazines, however, is that they work months in advance; when you sell a piece to a magazine, you often won't see it in print for six months to a year.

❖ *Writing for online periodicals.* Web zines, e-mail newsletters, and sites associated with offline entities (such as stores, catalogs, and media) offer an attractive market for freelancers. Most online markets do not pay as well as print markets, however, as they generally attract less advertising and subscriber revenues. This marketplace is also shrinking in the aftermath of the dot-com boom. The good news is that online markets work on a faster schedule, so your material may get published within weeks (or even days) of submission. Despite what many experts predicted, writing for online markets is little different from writing for print: Publications still want solid, information-packed pieces with a beginning, middle, and end.

✤ *Writing for newspapers.* There are at least as many newspapers in the U.S. as magazines, if not more, and many are open to freelance contributions. As Sue Lick explains in chapter 15, however, newspapers generally look for both a local angle and a "news" angle (i.e., what makes an article timely?). Most local and regional papers pay less than magazines, but it's often possible to sell the same piece to several noncompeting papers. Newspapers also work on a much shorter schedule than magazines, usually publishing material within weeks of acceptance.

✤ *Writing nonfiction books.* Few freelancers *start* their careers by writing nonfiction books, but many find this a logical "next step," particularly when they've written a number of articles or columns in a particular topic area, or when they have a particular area of expertise. An agent is generally not needed to sell a nonfiction book, and you can usually obtain an advance before you begin writing.

✤ *Writing and editing for businesses.* Writing business and corporate materials can provide a steadier workflow and income than writing for periodicals. The key difference, however, is that when writing for business customers, you will not be producing your own material but creating and editing materials (such as brochures, reports, sales literature, documentation, etc.) as dictated by your customer. This type of freelancing requires good editing skills and (sometimes) some business or technical expertise. Fortunately, thanks to the Internet, it's now possible to write for businesses outside your local area. Peter Bowerman discusses business writing in chapter 30.

Other freelance activities not covered in the book include editing (such as developmental editing, technical editing, copyediting, and proofreading); speechwriting; teaching and speaking; writing educational and curriculum materials; writing humor, essays, and poetry; writing fiction (both short stories and novels); and even illustrating and cartooning. For most freelance writers, nonfiction and/or business writing tends to be the primary source of income.

How Much Can You Earn?

One of the first questions would-be freelancers ask is, "How much can I earn?" The answer, of course, is, "It depends." Your income potential depends upon your skill, areas of expertise, business acumen, the amount of time you can devote to writing, and more.

The first thing to understand is that freelancers often don't set their own rates. If you write for periodicals, you must generally accept the pay range offered by those markets. Some markets offer flat "per-piece" rates (ranging from $25 to $1,000 or more), while others pay by the word (anywhere from 1¢ to $1 or more). Many publications also offer a range of rates, depending on the author's experience and the complexity of the article. Needless to say, newer writers are generally paid at the lower end of the scale.

New writers tend to make one of two mistakes when looking at these figures. The first is to say, "Wow! I can sell an article for $1,000! I'll be rich!" If the first potential market that pops into your head is *Redbook* or *Cosmopolitan*, think again. The top-paying markets can afford top-of-the-line writers—writers with years of experience and a hefty sheaf of clips. While new writers *can* occasionally break into these markets, the odds are against you. Writing for *Redbook* isn't the way to launch your career, and it's a good way to get frustrated if that's where you're trying to start.

A second and equally damaging mistake, however, is to assume that as a new writer you can only write for low-paying markets. While lower-paying markets *are* more open to new (and inexperienced) writers, that doesn't mean you have to start out writing for a penny a word. In reality, the markets most open to new writers are those that pay anywhere from $25 to $500. This includes the majority of special-interest publications (see chapter 16). The key to cracking this type of market may lie more in your nonwriting credentials than in your actual writing skills.

To determine how much you can hope to earn, therefore, you'll need to look at the following questions:

- *What markets can you write for?* Begin by locating markets that match your interests and experience. For example, if you're an animal lover, look for pet publications. If you travel, look at travel publications. Don't waste time on publications that aren't within your area of expertise, no matter how much they pay. For example, if you know nothing about computers, don't expect to sell your first article to *PC World*! (you can get to those markets later).

- *How much do they pay?* Check the pay range of your target markets. If you find that you've chosen a field with only a handful of publications, brainstorm topics to expand your range (see chapter 6). This will give you an idea of the payment range you can expect. (I also recommend submitting your material to the *highest*-paying market on your list first, and working your way down to the lower-paying markets if and only if your submission is rejected by your first choice. Otherwise, if you submit to—and are accepted by—a lower-paying market *first*, you've lost any chance of selling that piece to a better market.)

- *How much time must you spend per article?* If it takes you ten hours to complete an article, you'll obviously be able to write (and sell) fewer articles per week or month than if it only takes five hours. This also tells you how much an article is really "worth." For example, it's obviously better to sell a ten-hour article for $100 than for $50. On the other hand, a ten-hour article that you sell for $100 is actually worth *less* than a two-hour article that you can sell for $50 (the first pays $10 an hour; the second pays $25).

✱ *How much time do you have?* If you can invest five hours a week in writing, and you estimate that it will take five hours to write a feature article, that translates into one article per week. However, you'll also need to allocate time to market research, queries, correspondence, and other administrative tasks, so in reality, you may be able to produce only one article every *other* week. Keep in mind, too, that *writing* an article per week isn't the same thing as actually *selling* an article per week.

It's also important to remember that freelance income doesn't start arriving immediately. Launching a freelance career involves a start-up period during which you're conducting market research and sending out your first queries and submissions. If you write primarily for print magazines, you'll find that it takes six to eight weeks to get your first responses, and another month or so before you see your first check—while it can take six months or more to get your first published "clip." Newspapers and online publications tend to work more quickly; newspapers tend to publish material within a few weeks of submission (at most), while some online publications may publish a piece within days, giving you virtually "instant" clips. Typically, however, you'll start to see a steady inflow of assignments (and payments) within about six months.

With so many variables involved, there are no hard-and-fast figures on how much a freelancer can expect to earn at a particular career stage. It's not unrealistic, however, to hope for revenues of between $5,000 and $10,000 in one's first year of part-time freelancing, and a steady increase thereafter.

What Does It Take to Become a Freelancer?

As I said earlier, one of the great things about this career is its lack of "prerequisites." You don't need a particular degree or educational background. You needn't have majored in English or journalism (in fact, this can hinder rather than help, as academic writing is very different from "consumer" writing). You don't need to be young (or old); you can launch a career as a freelancer at twenty or fifty or seventy.

What you do need is the following:

Writing Ability

Most people embark on a freelance career because they know they have good writing skills, and would like to turn those skills into a source of income. Others, however, wonder if they "have what it takes."[1]

If you fall into the latter category, the best way to find out whether you're a "good" writer is to start submitting your work for publication. Keep in mind that you *will* be rejected—and that this will often have nothing to do with your ability (see chapter 5). What you're looking for is a pattern. If your first twenty to thirty submissions are rejected with nothing more than a form letter, there's a good chance your writing needs work (or that you're targeting the wrong markets, or querying with inappropriate ideas). If, however, you're getting rejections with feedback, that's an indication that you're on the right track. Editors don't waste time commenting on "hopeless" writers. And, of course, acceptance is the best news of all!

If you *are* getting a stream of rejections, you may want to seek additional feedback. One approach is to join an online or real-world writing or critique group. Another is to take a writing course, again either online or through an adult education program. Again, look for patterns in the feedback you receive: Do you consistently hear that you have problems with organization, spelling, or grammatical errors?

The key to being a "good" writer is to accept the fact that you can always become a "better" writer. One has to be almost schizophrenic in this business; one has to silence that little voice that says, "I'm not good enough," and at the same time be honest enough to say, "I may need to improve."

Business Sense

While *writing* is often considered a creative process, *freelance writing* is a business. Your goal as a freelancer is not simply self-expression; it is the development of materials that you can sell to publications. This means being able to make business decisions about what (and how) to write. Instead of just saying, "I'd like to write about dogs," for example, one must ask, "What can I write about dogs that would interest an audience of experienced dog owners?"

The business side of freelancing includes regular market research. It also means handling a fair amount of what I like to call "administrivium"—negotiating contracts, billing clients, keeping accurate income and expense records, maintaining reasonably coherent files, and so forth. This book will also give you tips on how to manage these essential tasks.

Professionalism

If you can *appear* professional, editors will assume that you *are* a professional—no matter how little experience you have. This means learning how to send a query, format a manuscript, handle e-mail correspondence, meet deadlines, negotiate contracts, etc. It also means being able to manage one's emotions and to behave courteously and professionally at all times—even when dealing with editors who *don't*. Nothing will ruin a freelance career faster than a reputation for responding unprofessionally to rejection—e.g., by complaining, begging an editor to reconsider, or sending flaming e-mails.

Motivation

Thousands of people *desire* to write, but never actually do. To become a freelancer, your desire to write must be stronger than your desire to do any number of other things. Becoming a freelancer means taking steps to change your life, and these steps aren't always comfortable. It can mean changing your habits to squeeze in a few extra hours to write. It can mean giving up things that you enjoy, such as time spent reading or watching television, or even (to a certain extent) time spent with your family and friends.

Freelancing also requires the courage to sit down and face the keyboard and start translating your dream of writing into reality. I don't know of any successful writer who considers writing an *easy* job. Freelance writing means tackling challenges—projects that take you out of your comfort zone and cause you to push your abilities to their limits. There are days when you won't even consider writing to be *fun*—when you'd rather do just about anything, including dig ditches, than face the keyboard. (Don't worry: We all have those days, no matter how many years we've been writing.)

Motivation may also mean sticking to your decision even when no one around you supports it. While many freelancers are blessed with supportive families, others aren't so lucky. If, for example, your decision to freelance means leaving a paying job, you may find that family members resent that loss of income. Your family may also resent having to take on extra chores so that you'll have more time for writing (though it won't kill anyone to have to do their own laundry). Perhaps hardest of all, however, is when family and friends simply can't seem to understand *why* you want to write. When your mother keeps asking you when you're going to get a "real job," or your friends insist on calling you at home during the day because they know you're not actually "working," just smile and keep typing.

Perseverance

At times, freelancing can seem like a long, uphill struggle. Your file of rejection letters will *always* be larger than your file of acceptances. You will experience setbacks and discouragements. You will experience moments when you wonder if you'll ever sell anything (or ever sell anything *again*), or whether you were dreaming when you thought you could become a "writer." A successful freelancer isn't one who never has those problems or those doubts; a successful freelancer is one who perseveres in spite of them.

Discipline

One of the drawbacks of freelancing is that you don't have anyone "forcing" you to be productive. You don't have a boss standing over your shoulder, nagging you to get back to work, or telling you what to write and when. Often, the only deadlines you have are those you set for yourself. To be a successful freelancer, you need to be a self-starter—and you need to be able to finish what you start.

Many articles recommend that you write for a certain number of hours every day. Often, however, this isn't practical. I recommend that you strive for a *weekly* minimum, and get in that writing time whenever you can. Also, don't stress over *when* you write (e.g., "two hours before breakfast"). Discipline doesn't lie in formulas; it lies in forcing oneself to ignore all the excuses we have for *not* writing.

And now for the standard caveat: If you're dreaming of instant fame and fortune as a writer, then I'd advise you to seek another career. Freelance writing is not a quick path to riches or glory. Those who embark on this path with visions of overnight success rarely stay long, and their names are quickly forgotten.

That doesn't mean that you *can't* become famous, and even wealthy, as a writer. Those who have achieved this kind of success, however, didn't do so because they were looking for it. Instead, they set out to follow the dream of doing what they loved for its own sake. If you love to write, there are few things more satisfying than being able to do what you love for a living—and as one writer once said, if you do what you love, the money will follow.

NOTE

1. Note that some sources of feedback are less reliable indicators of actual writing ability than others. Positive comments from friends and family are nice, but not necessarily a guarantee that your work is ready for the market. Similarly, don't rely on "good grades" in an English course (or even a writing course), as the academic world often has different criteria than the publishing world.

CHAPTER 2

Getting Started

A career in freelance writing requires very little "startup investment." It does, however, require a few basic tools—equipment, resources, supplies. Here are some of the things you'll need to set up your "writing office"—even if that office is just a corner of the kitchen.

These tools and resources fall into two categories: the absolute necessities and the optional extras. The necessities are items that you'll need to acquire before you can go very far in your writing work—even if this means laying out some cash before you earn any income. The "extras" are important, but can usually wait until you see a profit.

The Necessities

A Workspace of Your Own

The very first thing you need to establish is a *place* to write. While some writers have launched their careers from a corner of the kitchen table, it helps immensely to have a space—even a very small space—that you can call your own. Most writers feel that this space also requires a door that can be closed against interruptions, distractions, and family members. (Another advantage of an enclosed workspace is that it's more likely to qualify for the home-office tax deduction.)

At the very least, you'll need the following:

* A desktop (even if it's a table) for your computer
* Good lighting for your computer and reading areas
* A flat surface to spread out notes, books, and other materials
* A place to file research notes, articles, correspondence, etc.
* A place to store your writing supplies
* A handy shelf for your most useful reference books
* A chair that provides good back support

You don't have to go to the office supply store and buy a mahogany desk (though I recommend shelling out for a good chair). Plenty of folks make do with a couple of boards laid across two filing cabinets and a bookcase made of boards and bricks. The key is to make that space *yours*—and to make sure that your family respects that space.

A Computer of Your Own

Not only will the majority of your potential markets expect you to be able to submit material electronically (either on disk or via e-mail), but they will also expect to be able to communicate with you by e-mail, and expect you to be able to review their guidelines on the Web. If you're serious about freelancing as a business, having your own computer is essential.

Notice that I said "your *own* computer." Many households have a "home computer"—but often, that computer is shared by all family members. If that's the case in your home, you'll find that your "writing time" generally takes second place to homework, games, checking stocks, downloading MP3 files, and general surfing. It's difficult enough to find time to write without having to compete for computer time as well.

If you don't have your own computer, this should be your first, and most important, business investment. It doesn't have to be expensive: For about $700 you can get a basic model that includes a printer, modem, screen, and all the software you'll need to start writing. You can also get good deals on used computers; many computer outlets sell "reconditioned" computers, and you can also find used hardware and software on Half.com (*www.half.ebay.com*).

Make sure that your computer is equipped with Microsoft Word, as this is the program most commonly used by publishers. Word documents can be produced by both PCs (Windows) and Macintosh, so you can use whichever "platform" you're most comfortable with. (Most recent Macs can also produce PC disks, so you don't have to worry about publications with "incompatible" systems.)

If you don't have space for a full-size computer, consider buying a laptop. Laptops now have just as much power and memory as a desktop model, with the added advantage of portability. If you do choose a laptop, however, I recommend getting a separate keyboard and mouse; for long writing sessions, you'll find a full-size keyboard much more comfortable (and far more ergonomic) than a laptop keyboard. I also recommend getting a full-size screen when you can afford it; a flat screen, for example, takes up very little desk space.

Most computer systems come "bundled" with an inkjet printer. Some of these are good; some are mediocre. Test-drive your printer; is the printout clear and easy to read? Leave a page lying out for a few days; does the ink fade? How long do pages take to print? If the printer that came with your system is of poor quality, consider investing in another; you can get a high-quality inkjet printer for less than $150.

Another option is a combination printer/copier. These range from $300 to $500, and provide fast, laser-quality printing plus the advantage of a home copier. (Mac users can buy special software to connect to PC printers.)

Some writers feel that they can't justify the expense of a computer until they're actually earning money from their writing. Businesses require certain startup expenses, however, and a computer of your own is the best startup investment that you can make. (It's also tax deductible, which is more than you can say for the computer being used for the kids' homework!)

An Internet Connection

There are two basic types of Internet connection: dial-up and high-speed. Most computers now come equipped with a built-in dial-up modem, which accesses your Internet service provider through your phone line. A dial-up connection contacts the service provider through a phone number, which may be local or "national" (i.e., toll-free). Dial-up accounts are offered by national services such as AOL, Earthlink, and Juno, and also by local Internet Service Providers (ISPs).

If you want *unlimited* Internet service—the ability to surf as long as you like without incurring extra fees—then you'll find the best rates through local ISPs. Most local ISPs offer unlimited service for around $9.95 per month. This usually includes an e-mail account (and sometimes more than one) and 5 to 10 megabytes of personal Web space. The disadvantage is that most ISPs offer *only* local dial-up service, so that if you needed to connect while traveling, you'd have to pay long-distance charges. (It is possible, however, to find independent ISPs that serve more than one region.)

Services such as AOL and Earthlink have the advantage of being national, which means that you can access them from anywhere in the United States. You can also keep the same e-mail address if you move. However, these services offer several tiers of pricing options; AOL's "light-use" plan, for example, offers very limited Internet access (only five hours per month) for the same price that most independent ISPs charge for unlimited access ($9.95). AOL charges from $19.95 to $23.90 for unlimited access, while Earthlink charges $21.95. Juno offers "free" access if you're willing to put up with lots of advertising (including pop-up ads) on your screen, or a paid service for $9.95 that offers "less advertising and fewer pop-up ads."

High-speed connections are provided by cable (usually offered by your local TV cable company) or DSL (which works through the phone line). The advantage of these types of connections is, needless to say, the high speed. If you do a large amount of research online, you'll find that a high-speed connection saves you time and frustration; you won't have to sit around twiddling your thumbs while waiting for a large or graphic-intensive site to "load." This option is also helpful if you like to network or chat, or if you have a large daily e-mail load (e.g., fifty messages a day or more).

The disadvantage, of course, is cost. DSL and cable generally cost around $49.95 per month (in some cases you can get a lower "introductory" rate of around $21.95 per month). You will also need to rent or purchase a special modem. You can usually rent a cable modem from your provider for around $15 per month, or buy one at a computer or office supply store for around $100.

The other disadvantage is that these services are not available in all areas. You can usually obtain a cable connection anywhere you can get cable television, as the Internet connection uses the same lines. Cable companies run regular promotions offering free installation, particularly to existing TV cable customers. DSL is considerably harder to get: You must live within a certain distance of a DSL "hub." You can check with your local DSL provider online to determine whether DSL is available on your street.

Finally, a high-speed connection won't do you any good when you're traveling. If you need to use the Internet on the road, you'll still need some sort of dial-up connection.

An E-mail Account

In addition to choosing the best way to get online, you also need to make decisions about the best type of e-mail account. In most cases, your service provider will give you at least one e-mail account, and often more than one. However, this is not your only option, and may not be your best option. For example, if you wish to use a personal domain name, you won't be able to create an e-mail account associated with that domain (e.g., "jane@mydomain.com") through an ISP such as AOL or Earthlink, or through your cable or DSL provider. Most independent ISPs, however, offer domain hosting and domain-related e-mail accounts for a small extra fee.

Many people opt for a free, Web-based e-mail account, such as Yahoo! or Hotmail. The primary advantage of such a service is that you can access your e-mail through the Web browser of any computer, anywhere. This makes Web-mail particularly useful for people who travel a lot. However, since free programs support themselves through advertising, this means that you not only have to view ads whenever you view your e-mail, but that advertising messages may be appended to *your* outgoing e-mail as well.

Free Web-mail programs also tend to impose tight limits on the amount of e-mail that can be stored in your inbox, so if you don't check your e-mail daily messages may begin to bounce. Some programs also impose limits on the length of messages you can receive, or convert long messages into attachments. It also requires an extra step to transfer your e-mail to your computer. Many Web-mail providers offer increased storage, reduced (or no) advertising, and other services, for a fee.

A Phone

Just as you need a computer of your own, you also need a phone of your own. This should be part of your basic workspace. It's usually easiest to conduct telephone interviews at your computer, so that you can jot down notes or look up information while you're talking. Your business phone needn't be fancy; you can pick up a cheap one for $10 or less.

You may also want to install a second phone line for business use, particularly if it's going to be difficult to ensure uninterrupted phone time while you're working. The cost of a second line, including installation, is deductible as a business expense (you can't deduct the cost of your first, "personal line," though you can deduct the cost of all business calls). A less expensive alternative is to subscribe to a second number on your primary line, with a "distinctive ring" that enables you to distinguish between personal and business calls. A fax machine can also be set up to respond to a "distinctive ring," so that you can have your phone and fax on the same line.

Having a second line, or second number, enables you to ensure that your business calls are always answered professionally—or by a separate answering machine when you're not available.

The "Writer's Market"

There is still no substitute for this comprehensive annual guide to markets. Published every fall, *Writer's Market* lists nearly three thousand magazine markets, plus book publishers, writing contests, and markets for other products such as greeting cards, screenplays, and more. Listings include contact information, payment rates, rights, and what each publication wants to receive from writers.

Writer's Market now comes in a basic edition (book only) and an "online edition" (book plus access to an online market database, which is located at *www.writersmarket.com*). One can also subscribe to the online database *without* buying the print book (which can be useful if you live outside of the United States and can't easily order the book itself). I recommend getting the print book if you can, however, regardless of whether you intend to use the online database; when researching new markets, there's nothing quite like being able to page through the book itself, marking interesting-looking publications.

Basic Writing Supplies

You'll need the following:

- Several reams of good-quality, 20-lb. white bond paper.[1]
- A box of 9 × 12 mailing envelopes.
- A box of #10 (business size) envelopes.
- Extra computer disks (both for back-up and for submissions).
- Postage in various denominations. (Invest in an inexpensive postage scale that lists current postal rates up to one pound, and buy postage that corresponds to those rates.)
- Your own supply of pens, pencils, felt pens/markers, erasers, paper clips, rubber bands, rulers, post-it notes, etc.
- File folders (and labels), as well as hanging folders if your file cabinet uses them. (For the economy-minded, there's nothing wrong with scavenging used file folders from your office!)
- Notepads, both large and small. Large notepads are great for jotting down interviews or research notes; small ones are good to keep by your computer (and everywhere else) to jot down ideas, reminders, etc.

A Professional Letterhead

You can design a letterhead at no cost on your computer, and save it as a file to use whenever writing a letter, or have it printed at a local print shop. Include your name, address, phone, fax, and e-mail. Avoid "cute" logos like pens or parchments, and don't use a "title" (like "author" or "freelance writer")—these are signs of an amateur. I recommend using a linen or parchment stock in a neutral color such as ivory or gray for letters (but not for manuscripts); this helps set them apart from the sea of white paper that clutters the average editor's desk.

Here's an example of a simple letterhead design:

Moira Allen
1234 Mystreet · Mytown, VA 20151
(123) 555-1234 · (123) 555-1235 (fax)
moira@writing-world.com

I use Zapf Chancery for the name and Palatino for the address. This example is reduced to fit the page size of this book; for an 8½ × 11 sheet of paper, I use a 24-point font for the name and a 12-point font for the address.

Optional Extras

A Fax Machine

Many editors expect to be able to fax contracts or galley proofs of your article to you. Being able to receive and send a contract by fax can shave a couple of weeks off the time it takes to get paid. A fax is also a good way to send an editor last-minute changes or materials. Don't fax queries or manuscripts, unless a publication specifically states that this is acceptable. I recommend a plain-paper fax, as the printout is easier to store and the ink doesn't fade.

A Copier

You'll find that you're constantly running to the local print shop to copy contracts, clips, correspondence, and a host of other materials. Having your own copy machine saves valuable time, and will eventually pay for itself. You can also buy an inexpensive copier that doubles as a laser printer (or a more expensive model that also acts as a fax machine).

Computer Peripherals

In addition to the essentials of a computer and printer, I recommend the following equipment:

- ❖ *A read/write CD-ROM drive.* CDs are the most efficient way to back up your files, particularly when you have a lot of them. They are more durable than diskettes or zip disks. There's nothing worse than believing that you've backed up an important manuscript only to have your computer declare that your backup diskette is "unreadable."
- ❖ *A label-maker.* There's no good way to print single labels or envelopes on a printer, and it's a pain to haul out the typewriter. This handy tool, however, lets you print mailing labels with the touch of a button; just paste the address from a letter into the label-maker window.
- ❖ *A scanner.* If you plan to sell photos—especially to online publications — this is an easy way to convert them to electronic files. A scanner is less expensive (around $100) than a high-quality digital camera, and lets you convert older photos to electronic files as well.

A "Writer's Bookshelf"

In addition to *Writer's Market*, you'll want a good dictionary that defines obscure words as well as everyday words. (A dictionary should define the words you *don't* know!) You'll also want a thesaurus (Roget's is good, as is

Webster's). If you plan to write technical, medical, or scientific articles, it's wise to invest in the appropriate dictionaries for those, too. Over time, you'll also probably collect some basic references on writing, as well as books that relate to your particular areas of interest or expertise. Here are some worth-while books for writers:

- *The Writer's Digest Guide to Manuscript Formats*
- *The Writer's Guide to Queries, Pitches, and Proposals*, by Moira Allen
- *Writing.com: Creative Internet Strategies to Advance Your Writing Career*, Second Edition, by Moira Allen
- *Every Writer's Guide to Copyright & Publishing Law*, Second Edition, by Ellen Kozak
- *How to Write a Book Proposal*, by Michael Larsen
- *The Portable Writer's Conference*, edited by Stephen Mettee
- *The Self-Publishing Manual*, by Dan Poynter
- *The Complete Guide to Self-Publishing*, Second Edition, by Tom and Marilyn Ross

A Separate Bank Account

It's a good idea to keep your business income and expenses separate by setting up a separate bank account. Banks charge whopping fees for "business" accounts—but as long as you're receiving checks in your own name, you don't need one. If you write under a pseudonym or business name and will receive checks under that name, you may need to set up a "doing business as," or get a business license (check with your bank for details). You can, however, write under a pseudonym and still get paid under your real name.

Spend a few days setting up your writing space. Take the time to get it just right. Make sure it is comfortable: You're not going to become enthusiastic about writing if each session puts you in desperate need of a chiropractor.[2] Make it esthetically as well as ergonomically pleasing: Put an attractive picture on the wall, a potted plant on the desk. (Mine is fake; they live longer.) If you can afford to go beyond the merely functional, pick out a desk that appeals to you visually—a desk that says, "This is the desk of a writer!" Take time to determine the best arrangement for your equipment; make sure everything is within easy reach—that you don't have to climb over the printer to reach your files, for example.

Then, leave it alone. Rearranging one's workspace and reorganizing one's files are two of the most common forms of procrastination. It *feels* like you're working, but you're not. Resist the temptation to keep tinkering with your space, and sit down and start *writing*. After all, the best tools in the world aren't going to help you if you don't use them!

NOTES

1. U.S. and Canadian writers will use 8½ × 11 paper; writers in most other countries will use A4 paper.

2. I do recommend using a chiropractor, however. Because of the amount of time spent at the keyboard, writers are prone to neck and back troubles.

CHAPTER 3

Making Time to Write

A re you wondering when you'll find enough time to start writing? If so, I have good news and bad news. The good news is, you'll never have more time than you do right now. The bad news is . . . well, that *is* the bad news.

Time is never "found." Time can only be "made." If you decide to wait until your kids are in school, or in college, or you have enough money to quit your day job, or retirement, you could wait forever. The only way to make those writing dreams come true is to start looking at the time you have *now*, and find ways to make that time work for you instead of against you.

Treat Time as an Investment

Some say, "Time is money." A more accurate statement might be, "Time is *like* money." We have only so much, and must make decisions about how and where to spend it.

Writing, like any new career, requires a startup investment of time. Many new writers, however, feel uncomfortable with that initial investment. Those long, unpaid hours at the computer or keyboard often feel "wasted" or "self-indulgent." Worse, many writers have family members who share this view.

This startup time is essential, however. It takes time to build your skills, sell that first article, and develop a client base. If you were to sit down today and send out your first set of queries, it might be two to four months before you receive a response, six months before you make a sale, and eight months before you actually see your first check. But if you don't invest time in that initial launch period, you'll never see that check at all.

Examine Your "Time Budget"

"Making time to write" doesn't mean finding "free" time; it means reallocating time from other projects and activities. Before you can do that, you must discover exactly where you're "spending" your time.

A good method is to purchase an appointment book that breaks the day into fifteen-minute segments. For two weeks, record where every block of your time goes—including eating, sleeping, brushing your teeth, etc. Be honest: If you lingered for an hour over breakfast reading articles about Leonardo DiCaprio, write it down (at least record it as "celebrity research"). If you're not sure how much time you actually spend on an activity, buy a timer that works as a stopwatch, and use it to track those activities. (You can find excellent timers at kitchen supply stores.)

The results of your log may surprise you. Do you ever have those days when you feel as if you never sit down from dawn to dusk, yet can't say, for the life of you, what you accomplished? This log will help you discover where that time went. You may be surprised by how long certain tasks take, and how many "unnoticed" tasks nibble away at your day. You may also find that you're spending a great deal of time on tasks that you don't care about nearly as much as you care about writing.

Examine Your Priorities

No matter what you're doing now—working, raising a family, going to school—you already have a "full" schedule. Your first reaction to the thought of scheduling writing time into that schedule is probably, "How? Where?"

Making time to write means making tradeoffs. You may have to give up some activities in order to reallocate that time. A good exercise at this point is to look at your log and categorize the various activities you pursue. Possible categories include:

- *Unavoidable tasks.* Your day job would be included here!
- *Necessary tasks.* Obviously you're not going to give up cooking dinner, washing clothes, getting dressed, eating lunch, etc. However, some of these tasks can be reassessed, rescheduled, or combined with other tasks (for example, instead of going out for lunch, consider spending that hour at your desk reviewing sample magazines or *Writer's Market*).
- *Tasks you enjoy.* Don't give up everything you enjoy; that's a sure way to burn out. If you feel that you would truly lose something of value by giving up a particular activity, put it in this category.
- *Tasks you perform because you think you "should."* Volunteer activities often fall into this category: You may not enjoy them, but you feel obligated to continue with them. Certain types of housework also fall into this category. (Is it absolutely necessary to press the sheets?)
- *Tasks someone else could perform.* We often handle tasks for others (such as hanging up a spouse's shirts) that they could just as easily handle themselves. Sometimes, delegating such tasks not only frees time for you, but helps others become more responsible and independent.

❖ *Tasks that take an inordinate amount of time.* Did it really take three hours to do laundry, or buy groceries, or wash the car? Why? In many cases, we lose time through distractions or "make work" for ourselves without realizing what we are doing.

❖ *Tasks that are purely recreational.* Reading, television, and computer games all fall into this category. So, in some cases, does "surfing the Internet" and handling e-mail. Don't imagine that you have to give up all recreational activities to become a writer; however, if these are occupying a large number of hours, you may wish to reexamine your priorities.

Eliminate Time-Wasters

We all have them. Some are conscious; some, however, creep into our lives in the guise of habits, procrastination devices, and assumptions about what we "should" and "shouldn't" do. Here are some of the most common:

❖ *Television.* Tape shows during the weekend (when you could be writing) and watch them during the week (when you may be too tired to write). Ask yourself if you're watching certain shows because you enjoy them, or simply out of habit. Let the rest of the family watch their favorites without you. If you eliminate two one-hour shows per week, that's two hours you've gained for writing. (Also, try combining TV with other tasks, like ironing or exercise.) The same applies to videos. Some folks rent three a night—one for him, one for her, one for the kids. Try alternating the "his and hers" videos instead, and let the kids watch theirs without you.

❖ *Junk mail.* No law says that you have to *open* junk mail. Develop the habit of tossing anything you don't want—ads, catalogs, etc.—straight into a trash bag or recycling bin. Spend time only on mail that matters.

❖ *Magazines.* Do you have a stack of magazines you never read? Publications you only skim? Consider canceling them (and saving some money in the bargain). Similarly, do you need a daily paper, or could you live with the weekend edition? (If it takes you a week to read the Sunday paper, consider canceling that too!)

❖ *Errands.* Errands take more time than you think, because they include travel time and "home" time (e.g., putting away groceries). They also drain your energy. Try to combine as many errands as possible into a single trip; run errands that must take you to different parts of town on different days. Keep lists so that you don't forget something and have to run out again. If you do forget something and can live without it, save it until your next trip (or send someone else!) Try to schedule a specific day of the week for errands so that you can plan around it.

- *Telemarketers.* Your mother taught you that it was rude to hang up on people—but she wasn't raised in the age of telemarketing. The best solution is to let your answering machine pick up; if you're in the midst of a project, turn off the ringer. Invest in a caller ID machine to help screen calls, or a "telezapper" that helps "zap" automated dialing machines. If you feel that you *must* pick up, tell the caller firmly that you're not interested and ask to be placed on their "do not call" list.
- *Household chores.* Sometimes, vacuuming can look more appealing than a looming deadline. When it comes to chores, I've learned to ask, "Will this still get done if I don't do it now?" I know that sooner or later, I *will* empty the dryer or the dishwasher—but if I leave my desk to empty it *now,* I may not recapture that fifteen or twenty minutes I could have spent writing. Another option (really!) is to hire household help to handle things like washing floors and vacuuming. Finally, make sure your family members are doing their fair share of the work; do you really want to explain to an editor that your article is late because you had to pick up your kid's socks?

Teach Others to Respect Your Time

Many of us have learned to drop everything when someone requests our attention. It could be a spouse, a child, a coworker, or that friend who calls every day to talk about her problems.

If you don't guard your time, no one else will. It is not enough to simply ask others to respect your "writing time." You must reinforce that request by refusing to drop what you're doing whenever someone interrupts you. Otherwise, people *will* interrupt—not out of malice or lack of consideration, but because you have given them no reason not to.

Many "writer moms" (and dads) enforce the "if it's not on fire or bleeding, don't bother me" rule. This is sometimes easier to do if you have a door that you can close, but that's not always essential. What is essential is convincing others that you mean what you say: When you say, "I am writing and cannot be disturbed," don't stop writing unless the house is on fire.

Protecting your time means cultivating the art of saying "no," "later," and "I have to go now." At first, this may seem the most difficult task of all, but eventually you will realize that your new attitude hasn't caused the rest of the world to view you as an ogre—and you're actually getting some quality writing done!

If you're looking for time to write, don't wait until tomorrow or next week, or until the kids have grown up and moved out of the house. Start today. You already have all the time you need.

CHAPTER 4

Setting Goals

*O*ne of the greatest challenges writers face is the lack of "structure" in our job. There's no one to tell us what to do, when to do it, how to do it—or even whether we've done it well. One way to overcome that challenge is to learn how to set goals.

While you may yearn to become a six-figure novelist who appears regularly on Oprah, that's not a goal. It's a dream—and the only way you'll achieve that dream is by setting *well-defined* goals.

Defining Effective Writing Goals

To be effective, goals should meet three criteria: They should be *measurable*, *attainable*, and *meaningful*.

Measurable

Many writers start with "qualitative" goals: I want to be a "good" writer, or a "better" writer, or a "successful" writer, or a writer who produces "worthwhile" material. But how do you define *good*, or *successful*, or *worthwhile*? Because these terms are so difficult to measure, such goals seem to continually slip from our grasp.

Goals are useless if you can't determine whether they've been met. (After all, it's always possible to become a "better" writer.) Thus, quantifiable goals—goals that can be measured by some form of output or results—are more effective. For example, you might set a goal of writing a certain number of pages per day, or sending out a certain number of queries per week. If you dream of becoming "rich" (or at least "self-supporting"), define a specific income goal—and a time in which you hope to reach it.

Attainable

The gulf between where we are and where we'd like to be often seems too great to span. Goals can help by breaking the journey into short, attainable steps. If your dream is to become a best-selling novelist, but you've never set pen to paper, consider setting an attainable goal such as attending a writing course, taking a class online, or simply studying a book on novel writing. A second goal might be to write your first story, the outline of your novel, or your first chapter. A third might be to seek feedback, perhaps by joining a critique group or by sending your story to an editor. Each goal marks a step toward your long-term dream, and each is attainable in its own right.

To set attainable goals, you must be honest with yourself about what you are able to achieve at the present stage in your writing career. If you have never earned a penny from writing, for example, it would be unrealistic to ~~not~~ set the goal of becoming "self-supporting" in a year. Similarly, if you've never ~~so'.~~ written anything longer than a holiday newsletter, it would be unrealistic to expect yourself to complete a 600-page novel in six months.

Attainability also means recognizing what is physically possible in the world of writing. I once spoke with someone who was frustrated at having "failed" to become self-supporting by writing science fiction short stories—despite the fact that markets for such work average around 5¢ per word or less. To earn even $25,000 per year (excluding taxes), one would have to write and *sell* 500,000 words per year (an average of two 5,000-word stories per week).

Meaningful

In writing, it's easy to be sidetracked by goals that appear worthwhile, but that don't lead in the direction you want to go. This can often be the result of having competing goals. For example, you may dream of becoming a novelist, but face the very real need to put food on the table. Consequently, it's easy to postpone that novel (which won't earn you a dime until it's finished) for more immediately lucrative projects. In a situation like this, remember that competing goals don't have to be an either/or proposition: You could resolve this problem by devoting 25 percent of your writing time to your novel, and the other 75 percent to articles.

Another common sidetrack is the pursuit of someone else's goals or recommendations for "success." Writing magazines are full of sure-fire secrets and formulas, but often fail to mention that these strategies don't work for everyone. For example, if you've set the goal of "getting up every morning to write before work," that may be fine—unless you happen to be a night person, in which case you'll either hate those hours of writing, or hate yourself for being unable to achieve the goal you've set. Similarly, if you've been told that a good writer always keeps a journal, but yours bores you to tears, you may come to the mistaken conclusion that you aren't a "real" writer, or waste a lot of time in a pursuit that has no meaning for you. At the same time, be careful about passing up opportunities just because they don't seem immediately fulfilling. Taking a writing class, for example, may not seem exciting, but it could help you work toward your long-term goals.

Short-Term versus Long-Term Goals

A wise writing strategy includes a mix of short-term goals ("Today I'll locate five craft markets") and long-term goals ("This year I'll begin writing that novel").

A good way to determine your long-term goals is to ask yourself where you want to be in six months, one year, five years, or ten years. By answering those questions, you define your vision and chart your course—and you'll be better able to determine whether a writing project will contribute to your goal or distract from it.

Long-term goals often build upon one another. For example, your goal for your first year of freelance writing might be to build as many clips as possible. Once you've established a portfolio, you might devote your second year to targeting more prestigious, better-paying markets. You might decide to move from being a "generalist" to a "specialist"—establishing yourself as an expert in a certain field. Conversely, you might decide to broaden your writing horizons by moving from tightly focused subjects to more diverse topics.

While long-term goals help you determine where you're going, short-term goals help you decide how to get there. If your one-year goal is to "sell ten magazine articles," your short-term goals might include conducting market research, writing queries, or submitting a certain number of articles per month.

Short-term goals are usually measured by "output." Output goals are those in which you have complete control over the results: mail ten queries per week, or write three articles or stories per month. Typical output goals include:

* Number of hours spent writing per day (or week)
* Number of pages produced per day (or week)
* Number of queries submitted per week or month
* Number of projects (articles, stories, or chapters) written per month or year

Note that these output goals have short timeframes. A short-term goal doesn't become a long-term goal simply by expanding the quota (e.g., moving from "10 queries a week" to "520 queries a year"). Instead, long-term goals are best measured by results. While you can control your output, you cannot always control the results. Even though you meet your weekly quota of queries, you can't control the editorial decisions and market factors that determine whether those queries will be accepted.

Review Your Progress

To determine whether you're "on schedule," ahead of schedule, or falling behind, it's important to review your progress regularly. Have you met your output goals, have you exceeded them, or did you set them unrealistically high? If you've met those goals, are you any closer to your long-term "result" goal—or does it seem as distant as ever?

Such assessments can help you determine whether you need to change your long-term goals, or the short-term strategies you're using to meet them. If, for example, your one-year goal was to "get something, anything, published," and you've accomplished that goal in the first month, it's time to set a new long-term goal. If, on the other hand, you've sent out ten queries per week for six months without a single positive response, it may be time to reevaluate your short-term goals: Perhaps you need to target different markets, reexamine the ideas you're pitching, or learn how to write a more effective query. In other words, if six months of "output" haven't brought you closer to your long-term "results" goal, don't waste another six doing the same thing!

Goals are not chains, meant to lock you into some sort of writer's bondage. As your interests, dreams, and skills change, your goals can (and should) change as well. A goal that had meaning a year ago may not seem so important now, while another goal you might not have dared aspire to suddenly seems attainable. Remember that goals are not your destiny. They are simply effective tools you can use to *reach* that destiny.

CHAPTER 5

Coping with Rejection

R ejection slips are the writer's gremlin, the nagging suggestion that we don't measure up. What can we do about them? How can we live with them? How do we make them stop?

Unfortunately, rejection is part of being a writer. Not just a beginning writer, either; experienced writers get them as well. (Maybe Stephen King doesn't, but the rest of us do.) One of the most important steps you can take as a writer is to learn how to cope with rejection—how to understand what it means to your career, and how to move on.

The first step in handling rejection is learning how to separate yourself from your work. You may pour your heart and soul into your writing, but you must also establish "boundaries" between yourself and your creation. Your writing may be like a child to you, but like any child, it must go out into the world to succeed or fail on its own merits. If you can't develop such boundaries, you'll go nuts—and stop writing altogether. Success will become impossible if you cannot bear the pain of failure.

But Why?

You've probably heard that editors who reject your work aren't rejecting *you*, and that's true. However, they may also not even be rejecting your work. Lack of quality is only one reason for rejection. There are many others. Pieces are often rejected for one of the following reasons:

❖ A *similar piece is already on file.* "Similar" can mean anything relating to the same topic. For example, if you submit an article on Antigua to a travel magazine, and the magazine has another article on Antigua on hand (even if it's vastly different from yours), it won't accept another.

❖ A *similar piece has been assigned.* Great minds *do* think alike—and you'd be amazed how often two or more writers will query on a similar topic.

✦ *A similar piece was published within the last two or three years.* Many publications won't repeat a topic for that long.

It's also possible to write an excellent article that still doesn't quite mesh with an editor's tastes in terms of style, tone, approach, angle, viewpoint, or even length. Again, this doesn't mean that your article was poor; it means that it came close but not quite close enough.

Another reason for rejection is sheer volume. If an editor can accept five articles per month out of a pile of five hundred, it isn't only the "bad" articles that are going to be rejected; perfectly good articles will be rejected as well. Your article may be perfect in every way, yet be sent back simply because it was number six in the stack from which the editor could accept only five.

"Good" Rejection Slips

Is there such a thing as a "good" rejection slip? Absolutely. Any rejection slip that offers information is good—because it helps you understand the reason for the rejection. Some magazines offer a "checklist" letter, listing common reasons for rejection and "checking" the one that applies to you. Finding out that someone else had already been assigned to the topic is a lot better than assuming the editor thought your article stank.

Even better than checklists, however, are rejections that include a personal note. Even a scribble shows that the editor thought enough of your piece to respond personally. Treasure those scribbles; they mean you're making a positive impression.

Still higher on the list of "positive" rejections is the "please try again" note. When an editor asks you to come back with another submission, believe it: No editor will say this unless she means it. This is often the result of a submission that "just misses" acceptance for one of the reasons listed above. Quite often, the editor truly wishes she could purchase your piece, but can't—and doesn't want to lose the opportunity to grab you as a contributor. Whenever you're asked to try again, *try again!*

Self-Honesty

While there may be dozens of reasons why an editor rejected your piece that have nothing to do with quality, a writer must also be willing to ask honestly whether, in fact, quality *was* the issue. When we write, we often become so involved in a piece that an accurate assessment of quality becomes difficult. Often our work isn't as good as we thought it was—or wasn't what our target market required.

Good writing is a skill, not a gift, and skills are refined over time. Sure, there are occasional "prodigies" who craft the perfect bestseller the first time they pick up a pen—just as there are "prodigy" musicians who play perfectly the first time they pick up the violin. For the rest of us, perfection is achieved by plodding and by endless practice, which may, for a time, make everyone around us "cover their ears and wince."

The reality of writing is that when you start, you think you're pretty good. After a year, if you've been writing steadily, you're likely to look back on those first efforts and wonder what on earth you saw in them. After you've been writing for five years, you may look at those first-year masterpieces and wonder why you didn't burn them on the spot. This process never ends: As you continue to improve, you'll feel this way twenty years from now. To some, this scenario sounds depressing—but what would be even more depressing is the idea that you *can't* get better!

What you write today is the best you can do—today. Tomorrow, quite probably, you'll do better. But only if you don't stop writing today.

It Sank. Get Over It.

Someone created a T-shirt with a picture of the *Titanic* on the front, and, on the back, the words: "It sank. Get over it." The same can be said of rejection.

"Getting used to" rejection doesn't mean that rejection loses its sting. It doesn't. Nor is this a bad thing. I suspect that the day rejection ceases to hurt is the day one has lost one's passion for writing. Pain isn't a bad thing. Pain simply means we care.

At the same time, there are things you can do to ease the sting. The next time your material comes back with one of those awful slips, try one of these:

❖ *Have a rejection party.* "Celebrate" your rejection with a pizza, a dish of ice cream, a trip to the movies. You have a right to celebrate: You have to be a writer to be rejected.
❖ *Start a rejection slip file.* Besides being useful for taxes (it proves to the IRS that you're conducting a business), it can come in handy down the line, when you're famous. Then you'll be able to say, with a smug flourish, "Well, I was rejected forty-eight times before my story/novel/article was accepted by Megabucks Publishing. . . ."
❖ *Send your material to the next publisher on your list.*
❖ *Write something else.* Better yet, start writing something else the minute your last piece is finished and out the door. Rejection stings less when your mind is occupied with a newer, and therefore more interesting, project.

Remember, there is something worse than rejection, and that's never writing (or submitting) anything to be rejected in the first place.

PART II

STARTING YOUR ARTICLE

CHAPTER 6

Finding Ideas

One of the most common complaints of new writers is, "I don't have anything to write about." This isn't true. Everyone has *lots* of things to write about; the trick is to figure out how to convert one's experiences into marketable article topics.

But first, you need to know what *makes* a marketable article topic! And that means knowing what editors want.

What Do Editors Want?

To answer this question, take a look at the contents of any magazine. You will find that *most* of the articles involve some type of "how-to" information. A health magazine, for example, will offer information on how to eat right, lose weight, overcome fatigue, stay fit, recognize the symptoms of serious illness, and so forth. A pet magazine will discuss how to take better care of your pet. A crafts magazine will give you project tips and designs, or suggest equipment.

The next category is "pure information" that doesn't necessarily help a reader accomplish anything. Profiles and historical features usually fall into this category. Some magazines (such as *Discover* and *Smithsonian)* focus entirely on information. While a few "information-only" publications (like *National Geographic*) have a large audience, most such publications (such as *Military History Quarterly* or *Archaeology)* have a much narrower market.

You'll also discover that most publications run very few "personal-experience" articles, often no more than one per issue. Some don't run any. Those that do tend to focus on *exceptional* experiences: for example, a family's battle to save a sick child. Magazines that publish personal essays or opinion pieces are even more rare (e.g., *Reader's Digest* or *Guideposts)*, and considerably harder to crack. While some publications include a "reader essay page" in the front or back, these receive hundreds of submissions each month, which means high odds against breaking in.

The answer to "what editors want," therefore, is simple. First, editors want articles that will help readers improve some aspect of their lives. Second, editors want articles with interesting information. Unless a publication focuses on information, however, you'll find that the ratio of "how-to" pieces to "information" pieces is often as high as ten to one.

To break into the periodical market, you need to become "reader-focused" rather than "author-focused." As you begin to mine your experiences and expertise for article topics, you'll find that you have many opportunities to share information and help readers improve their lives.

Digging for Ideas

The first step in coming up with article topics is determining where to look for ideas. Here are some places to start:

- Your personal life—home, family, personal history, life experiences
- Your interests and hobbies
- Your workplace, expertise, or professional background
- Your education
- Your memories—nostalgia or, conversely, trauma
- Your activities—vacations, family events, community activities, etc.
- Your observations—the people, places, and things around you
- Your interests—things that intrigue you, even if you don't know much about them (yet)

Ideas also come from the *process* of developing ideas:

- From brainstorming a topic
- From reviewing magazines and looking at articles
- From researching market sources
- From researching a topic (your research for one article can lead to "spin-off" articles for other markets)

Here's the million-dollar question: *Do I have to write about what I know?* Writing about what you know has several advantages:

- It saves work.
- It gives you an "instant credential" (your experience).
- It's easier to research.
- It's more comfortable.

It also has disadvantages, however:

✦ It's easy to overlook what you know because it's so familiar.

✦ Too-familiar subjects may seem boring and not excite you as a writer.

✦ It's easy to get stuck and fail to expand your knowledge base or market potential.

One way to move beyond "what you know" is to write about what interests you. You know what you'd like to learn more about, what you find absolutely fascinating. An alternative to writing about what you know, therefore, is to write about what you *don't* know—but wish you did!

No matter what you write, you're going to end up doing research. So why not research subjects that are of interest to you? You don't have to know a lot about them to start with. You simply need to believe that, because this topic fascinates you, there's a good chance that it might fascinate someone else.

Brainstorming Ideas

As you begin to develop ideas, imagine that your mind is working like a telephoto lens. Sometimes you want to "zoom out" to get the "big picture"—to see the perspective, the surroundings. At other times you need to "zoom in" to sharpen your focus, to concentrate on the details. This process goes back and forth as you work your way from "idea" to "article topic."

A good way to start is with a wide-angle focus. Take another look at the list of "idea sources" I provided earlier. Jot down the areas you would like to explore for article ideas. For example, let's try "personal life."

If I were "brainstorming," I'd write this topic at the top of a piece of paper or computer file. (By the way, sometimes ideas flow better when you use old-fashioned approaches. If you find you're not getting anywhere by staring at the computer screen, take a pad of paper and a pencil to another room and work there. Sometimes the computer brings out our "inner editor" and we need to "shut that off" by taking a more physical approach to writing.)

Anyway, you've put "personal life" at the top of your "idea" page. Now, shut down that inner voice that is whispering, "No one wants to know about my personal life!" This is true, actually, but that's not what we're here for. We're here to find out what aspects of your personal life might lead to articles that people *will* want to read. So let's jot down a few things about "personal life."

✦ *Family.* Do you have a spouse? Children? In-laws? Parents? Grandparents? Siblings? Extended family? Family members that don't speak to each other? Family members in other countries, or of other cultures? Are you adopted? Is anyone in your family adopted? What about topics like marriage, divorce, childbirth, or death?

❖ *Holidays.* Jot down a list of the holidays you celebrate. Does your family have special ways of celebrating particular holidays? Does it avoid certain holidays? Does your family celebrate holidays that are less familiar to the general public? Are holidays joyful or stressful? What are some of the activities you share with your children during a particular holiday? (This category might include "birthdays" as well.)

❖ *Pets.* Do you have a family pet? How about past pets? Pets of your childhood? How do you take care of it? What problems do you experience with your pets? What activities do you pursue with your pets? What challenges have you faced and overcome? What tragedies have you endured? How do your pets interact with your children?

❖ *And so on . . .*

This is part of the "zooming out" process. Notice that we started with a single idea—"personal life"—and expanded that idea into at least three subtopics (family, holidays, pets). We then expanded each of *those* topics into several more specific areas. If you try this exercise with all eight of the subject areas proposed at the beginning, you could find yourself with dozens of potential topics.

This is also a good exercise to do with a partner—a spouse, significant other, or writing buddy—who can help you come up with ideas you might otherwise miss. Someone who knows you is likely to think of things that you might overlook simply because they're too "familiar."

Focus and Expand

So far, none of the subjects listed above are sufficiently focused to serve as article topics. The next step, therefore, is to zoom in even more closely and then to expand once again.

On another sheet of paper or file, select *one* of the topics that you have generated. For example, you might select "holiday activities" as an area to explore further. However, this is still too general. Zoom in further: What holiday? What activities?

The immediate temptation is to tackle Christmas because it offers so many topics. On the other hand, it's also the holiday that gets the most "ink," which means you're competing with a lot of other writers. So let's focus on a holiday that gets a little less press: Easter. It's time to brainstorm again, jotting down everything you associate with Easter. Here's my list:

❖ Eggs
❖ Bunnies

✤ Easter baskets
✤ Easter egg hunts
✤ Onion-skin Easter eggs
✤ Rabbits—good as pets?
✤ Chicks—same question
✤ Easter history/folklore
✤ Easter in other countries—Greek Easter candles
✤ Easter trees . . .

Now we're getting somewhere. Some of these topics are still a bit vague (what about "Easter eggs," exactly?), but others are ripe for the plucking. Let's see what articles we might be able to generate from this list.

✤ *Easter baskets.* Is there someone in your town who makes fancy Easter baskets? (Check the classifieds for a "gift basket" store.) That might make a profile for a local paper.

✤ *Onion-skin Easter eggs.* If you don't know how to make these, don't worry. Sooner or later, I'll get around to writing *my* holiday article on this family tradition.

✤ *Rabbits/chicks: Good as pets?* Your local paper might be interested in an article on why one shouldn't give bunnies or chicks to the kids. Interview a representative of your local humane society, and check online to find statistics on how many bunnies are sold in pet shops at this time of year.

✤ *Easter history/folklore.* This is a perennial favorite. I know, because it was one of the very first articles I ever sold to a newspaper—and I am still selling that exact same article nearly twenty years after I first wrote it. No reason why you can't do a bit of research and sell something on this topic too!

✤ *Easter in other countries.* My husband and I visited Greece on our honeymoon, and I remember seeing families returning to the islands after shopping on the mainland, all carrying elaborately decorated Easter candles. This might be an interesting feature for a travel magazine or travel section of a newspaper.

✤ *Easter trees.* These are very popular in Germany, and are just beginning to catch on in the United States. This could be a nice, crafty "how-to" article on how to make your own—something you could sell to a local paper, or to a crafts or home-decorating magazine. Or you could slant this as a children's activity—how kids can make an Easter tree—and aim for a family publication, such as *Family Fun.*

I've just identified five articles that I might be able to write, with very little effort, from this one subject. Easter, however, is itself a subtopic of a larger category—holiday activities. Imagine how many more article ideas you could generate if you looked at other holidays! You can follow other branches—holiday foods, holiday safety, holiday reminiscences, nontraditional holidays—and develop dozens of possibilities.

Keep in mind, too, that you're likely to find areas in which your categories overlap. If you have children, it's going to be easy to put together topics that combine "holidays" and "children"—crafts, safety tips, inspirational stories, etc. Or you might combine "holidays" and "grandparents" for a nostalgic look back at holidays in your past. And so on . . .

Don't Eliminate the Negative

Chances are that the first topics to strike you as good article ideas are positive. Maybe some of the more negative things that came out on your list made you shudder and move on quickly. But don't overlook the value of "negative experiences" in this exercise. Let's say, for example, that you hate Christmas because that's when the entire "clan" gets together, and everyone picks up the old fights where they left off the previous year. By the time the holiday is over, you're so stressed that you wish Christmas could be banned forever.

Not a very happy picture, right? Besides, who wants to hear about your troubles? No one, perhaps—but stop and think for a moment. Do you suppose you're the only family with this problem? Might there not be hundreds of families who go through something similar every year, and hate it just as much as you do? Can you write something that speaks to those families?

Here's where "writing what you know" meets "writing what you don't know." What you know is that you hate Christmas because it involves a huge, stressful family gathering. What you don't know is how to change that. If you could find out, you could share that information with other families, and write an article that might make a profound difference in many lives!

One approach might be to write a story that portrays your family in such a way that others see *their* families in your experience, and, at least, find a way to laugh about it even if they can't change it. Or, you could look for someone who *does* know how to "change" this family dynamic—a professional counselor, for example. Try running an online search on "holiday stress" and "family gathering" and see what comes up. (Find out more about conducting research online in chapter 9.) Chances are you'll find not only online information but names of experts you can interview for more tips.

Once you begin brainstorming ideas and mixing and matching idea categories, you'll stop worrying about "what to write." Instead, you'll start wondering whether you'll ever have time to write up all the great article ideas you've developed!

CHAPTER 7

Categories, Subjects, Topics, and Slants

f you went through the exercises in the previous chapter, you should have a selection of ideas for articles. Some of those ideas are nearly ready to go. Some of them aren't. The goal of this chapter is to help you bring at least one of those ideas to the starting gate by choosing the right market, the right audience, and the right slant for that audience.

I talked about "zooming in" and "zooming out" as one way to help you develop ideas. Another way to look at article development is to view it as a process of refinement. You start with the raw ore—a lump of material, such as knowledge or a loose collection of ideas ("my family")—and refine that ore through a succession of stages until you have "pure metal" that you can work into an article.

To begin this process, you need to be able to recognize the difference between a *category* of ideas, a *subject*, a *topic*, and a *slant*. Each of these is a stage in the refinement process, bringing you closer and closer to an article.

Category

This is where most writers start. A category is not an idea for an article; it may not even be a subject. Often it's a catch-all bin full of ideas, subjects, etc., that interest a writer. For example, if I were to say, "I want to write historical articles," I'm speaking of a category. I haven't defined a subject—I haven't even defined a period or type of history. However, I *have* defined the area in which I'd like to proceed, both in developing article topics and in locating markets. The same applies if I said I wanted to write about "health" or "pets" or "families" or "cooking."

Choosing a category is an important step. It tells you where to start your refinement process. It tells you, for example, that you should start researching markets that fit into this category. If your category is "pets," how many pet magazines or related markets (such as online pet stores) are there? What do they want? Do they accept freelance material? Gathering the answers can help you move on to the next step.

Subject

This is the next level. Once you have a category of interest, pick a subject out of that category. If your category is "holidays," your subject might be "Christmas." From my category of "history," I might choose a subject such as "Mary Queen of Scots." However, these are still not article topics. You can't simply write an article about Christmas because the obvious question an editor is going to ask is, "Well, what about it?" Similarly, many lengthy books have been written about Mary Queen of Scots; if I want to write an article about her, I must choose something more specific.

Topic

This is where the process starts to get interesting, because this is where you begin to develop the seed of your actual article. Let's suppose that I know lots and lots about Mary (I don't), and I've decided to focus on her years of imprisonment under Queen Elizabeth. That's the beginning of my topic. But what am I going to say? I could still spin this off into four or five (or more) articles. That's where it's helpful to have done some market research to find out what type of article might actually *sell*.

So, off I go to a Barnes & Noble to see what kinds of magazines might accept an article on Mary. Obviously *Redbook* is out. However, I pick up copies of *BBC History Magazine, Renaissance, Realm, British Heritage,* and *Scottish Life.* I flip through my treasures and discover that *BBC History Magazine* is written primarily by experts, and generally focuses on topics being covered by BBC. *Renaissance* (which is produced by the Society for Creative Anachronisms) is nice, and might be a place for a general historical piece. *Realm* focuses more on travel, and I can't figure out how to contact them. *Scottish Life* focuses more on modern life than on history. *British Heritage,* however, focuses on visiting places with an interesting historical background. I decide to focus on that market.

By studying the publication, I know that it focuses as much on *location* as it does on *history*, so a general article about Mary's imprisonment probably wouldn't sell here. But a guide to the various *castles* where Mary was imprisoned sounds ideal. It also would provide great photo opportunities. So now I've refined my topic to something specific and workable: "The castles where Mary was imprisoned."

Slant

I have a topic, but what am I going to say about it? I can't just say, "Mary was imprisoned in X castle, which is located *here*, and looks like *this*." I need to look at that magazine again, and determine which slant is going to attract the editor. Since *British Heritage* focuses on places people might like to visit, my slant is going to be: "How you can visit the castles that imprisoned a Queen." In my article, I'm going to take the reader on a guided tour of the castles where Mary was imprisoned. Where are they? What are they like? Can you still visit Mary's accommodations? I'll provide a bit of history of each castle, details about Mary's stay, and what you'll find if you visit today. The article will have a nice sidebar on how to get there, any pertinent tour details, hours, etc. If I've read my market correctly, this is exactly the sort of thing (a mixture of travel and history) that should get this editor's attention.

(You know, I'm starting to like this article idea. Obviously, however, it requires a trip to England. Be right back. . . .)

The point is: You can't sell an article on the basis of a category ("history") or a subject. You *may* be able to sell an article on the basis of a topic, but it's difficult. Your best chance of selling an article is to research markets as part of your "refinement" process, choose one that you like, and *slant* your article directly toward that market.

Here are some tips on how to develop a workable slant.

❖ *Step out of your shoes and into the reader's shoes.* When you begin generating ideas, you're looking at areas of your life and experience and interests that might provide good material. To translate that information into potential articles, however, you have to step out of your "writer" shoes and into "reader" shoes. Start asking, "*Why* would a reader want to know about this? *What* would a reader want to know about this? *How* can this material be useful or helpful to the reader?"

❖ *Think "how-to" whenever possible.* The vast majority of what is published in magazines and other periodicals (not counting "news" in newspapers) focuses on a "how-to" component. The number of magazines that focus exclusively on "information" (history, news, etc.) is actually small. Most publications are looking for articles with "take-away" value —something the reader can apply in his or her life.

❖ *Think in terms of a* phrase *when developing your slant.* Try to avoid slants that are simply subjects ("haunted castles" or "Christmas decorations"). Express your slant in an active phrase: "Tour the haunted castles of Scotland," or "Decorate your home Victorian style." Your slant may even become the title of your article: "How You Can Decorate Your Home . . ."; "Best Places to Visit in . . ."; etc.

✤ *Forget about "I" (the writer) and focus on "you" (the reader).* To be an effective writer, it's vital to move past "I" and focus on "you, the reader": how this can help *you*; why *you* should visit this location; how *you* can get the most out of a trip to _____"; ten ways that *you* can overcome this problem; why *you'll* love this product; etc. Putting "you, the reader" into your slant is the most important step you can take toward winning over editors.

Once you have a slant, you have something else that is vital to the next step: your *core concept*. You have the central idea, theme, point (or whatever you choose to call it) that your article is *about*. You should be able to sum up your slant and core concept in a single sentence: "My article is about how you can visit the castles of Mary Queen of Scots' imprisonment." Everything else must relate to this core concept, and that's what we're going to look at in the next chapter.

CHAPTER 8

The Outline Demystified

I don't know any writer who likes the prospect of creating an outline. That's probably because we all remember being taught that horrible "1, 2, 3–A, B, C" format in high school. (Hands up, everyone who used to get around those exercises by writing a paper first, and then creating the outline after the paper was done?) Relax—I'm not going to "teach" that kind of outline.

An outline is simply a way to construct a road map of where you want to go with your article. Another way to look at an outline is to think of it as a filing cabinet. When you research your article, you're going to gather a lot of information. How will you know what to put in and what to leave out? By creating an "outline" that places "headers" on the files in your cabinet, you'll know whether the information you've gathered fits into the "files" you have, or whether it doesn't. If you don't have a "file" for this information, chances are that the information doesn't belong in your article.

For example, when I decided to go full-time as a freelancer in 1996, one of the first articles I pitched was a piece on cancer in cats. I chose to write the article because my own cat had recently died of cancer. When I got the assignment, I roughed out the areas I planned to cover:

✤ Types of cancer
✤ Breed-specific cancers
✤ How to detect cancer
✤ My experience with a cat with cancer
✤ Preventing cancer
✤ Treatments
✤ Hope for the future
✤ Hi-tech treatments
✤ Diagnostic techniques

A quick look at this list showed me that some ideas were actually sub-categories of others. "Breed-specific cancers" fit under "types of cancer," while "diagnostic techniques" fit under "how to detect." "Hope for the future" fit under "treatments." One category stood out as *not* fitting with the rest: "my own experience." I ended up with four "file folders" to work with:

- ❖ Types of Cancer
- ❖ Detecting Cancer
- ❖ Treating Cancer
- ❖ Preventing Cancer

This, by the way, is an outline. It can be as simple as that. Besides serving as a framework for my article, it provided a framework for my research: I knew what types of questions I had to ask, based on the information I wanted to include. I researched the article on the Web and interviewed experts, asking questions based on my four topic areas and "filing" that information in the appropriate place. If information came in that didn't fit into one of these four areas, I knew that it probably didn't belong in my article.

I also had a slant, or *core concept*: "What you need to know about cancer in cats." (Note again how a slant can make a great title: "Is your cat at risk of cancer?" or "How you can reduce your cat's risk of cancer.") Having that core concept or slant is essential. It tells you what is vital to your article—what is at the center of your idea—and what isn't.

Five Ways to Approach the Outline

I'm no fan of "1, 2, 3–A,B,C" outlines. This approach tends to get one bogged down in the mechanics. (Is this a subset of number 2? Should I move this section *here?*) There are easier ways to put your ideas and information in order.

1. Ask Yourself What Questions a Reader Would Ask

What would a reader want to know about this subject? Make a list of those questions. For example, a reader interested in cancer in cats might want to know:

- ❖ How common is cancer in cats?
- ❖ What kinds of cancer affect cats?
- ❖ What cats are at greatest risk?
- ❖ How can I tell if my cat has cancer?
- ❖ What can I do if my cat has cancer?
- ❖ What kinds of treatments are available to me?

❖ What are their success rates?
❖ What are the risks to my cat?
❖ How long will my cat live if it has cancer?
❖ Can I prevent my cat from getting cancer?
❖ Where do I go to get more help?

Sometimes, simply jotting down a list of questions is all you need to define the basic areas your article will cover, and even the order in which you might wish to cover them.

2. Think in "Subheads"

Most published articles are divided into sections with subheads. This is a good way to organize your information (and putting in your own subheads always pleases an editor). The four "file folders" that I developed for my feline-cancer piece would also serve very nicely as subheads:

❖ Is Your Cat at Risk?
❖ Protecting Your Cat from Cancer
❖ Detecting the Signs of Cancer
❖ Choosing a Treatment Plan

Subheads help you organize your information logically. You'll also be able to determine whether your article is "in balance." If you have 250 words under one subhead and 1,000 under another, chances are you need to reorganize the article.

3. List Events or Concepts Chronologically

What happened first? What happened next? What happened after that? What happened last? This approach works well for an article that focuses on events that occurred over time (e.g., a historical piece, or a personal profile). For example, women's magazines often publish stories about how a family coped with a child's illness. A chronological outline of such an article might look like this:

❖ Family notices something isn't right with the child.
❖ Family goes to traditional doctor.
❖ Family gets reassurances, goes home.
❖ Child gets worse.
❖ Family seeks more help; gets more reassurances.
❖ Child gets worse.
❖ Family gets desperate; seeks more information.

- ❖ Family finds special doctor/support group/online information.
- ❖ Family locates specialist/special treatment/new cure.
- ❖ Family is warned of risks of treatment.
- ❖ Family goes ahead with treatment.
- ❖ Child gets better.

4. List Points in Logical Order

Many how-to articles have an obvious logical order: Do this first, do this next, do this next, and do this last. Your outline here may consist simply of a list of things to do, and the order in which the reader should do them. This works well for a how-to article, for example.

A travel article might also have a logical order, based on the order in which one would visit a location. If, for example, you'd start at Point *A* and travel to Point *X*, a logical way to present your information is in the order in which the traveler following your route would encounter it. This works even for a single location: Trace the route a traveler would take if walking through a site, such as a castle or museum.

5. Make a List

List all the pieces of information that you'd like to include in the article. Then, go over that list and assign numbers to each item based on its importance or priority. For example, if you're writing a piece on ways to improve communication between spouses, jot down a list of all the suggestions you want to cover. Which tips are most important? Which are less important? Which could be omitted without any real harm to your article? You may find, when you're done, that you have a selection of *key* points, and perhaps a few "leftovers" that aren't as useful. In some cases, your list may become the actual structure of your finished article ("Five Ways to Improve Communication with Your Spouse"); in others, it may become the "hidden" structure that underlies your piece, even though you aren't numbering the points in the final article.

Working within a Word Budget

A final consideration to keep in mind as you outline an article is your word budget. Every magazine has length requirements for feature articles. Such articles typically range from 1,000 to 3,000 words, with the most common length being 2,000.

One of the most common amateur mistakes is to propose an article that seeks to address more topics than can be covered effectively within the required word count. Editors are quick to spot this error—and equally quick to reject such queries.

For example, I recently reviewed a query letter from a woman who wanted to write about a controversial treatment for breast cancer. So far, so good. However, in 2,000 words or less, the writer wanted to cover traditional cancer treatments, alternative treatments, a profile and history of a woman who chose such a treatment, interviews with her doctor and other patients, and a discussion of why women aren't told about alternative treatments.

As an editor, I'd reject this query because it is unfocused and impossible to cover in 2,000 words. In addition, since the woman had only begun treatment, the writer would have been unable to offer a conclusion—i.e., did it work?

Resist the temptation to throw everything you have, including the kitchen sink, into your article! Remember, *if it doesn't relate to your core concept, it doesn't belong in your article.*

This can be tough. You do all that research and have all that great information, and it's *hard* to throw some of it out. But don't despair. Chances are, you can use your extra information to write a completely different article for another publication. There is also the option of including sidebars to your main article, which I'll cover in the next chapter.

Think about your word budget as you outline. Keep in mind that the more subtopics you include in your article, the fewer words you'll be able to allocate to each topic. If you have four major subtopics, you can devote approximately 500 words to each of them. If you have ten, you can give each no more than 200 words. (Keep in mind that you'll also need an introduction, a conclusion, and some allowance for "transitions.")

This brings up the difference between an "in-depth" article and an "overview." If you have only a few subtopics (three to five), you can write an "in-depth" article. If you have a lengthy list of subtopics, then you'll probably end up writing an overview. An article titled "Ten Tips on Beating Holiday Stress" is almost certainly going to be an overview: It will give you ten ideas, but not a lot of in-depth information on any one of them. An article titled "Put an End to Holiday Stress," which involves an interview with a therapist and four or five basic suggestions, is likely to be more in-depth.

Should you focus on an in-depth piece or an overview? This gets back to your market research. What type of piece does the market you're targeting prefer? Choose the type of article that seems most likely to appeal to the editor, and audience, of your chosen market. (*Family Circle,* for example, loves lists: 100 ways to clean your house with basic products; 50 inexpensive "dates" to share with your spouse; 30 things to do on a rainy day.) Just be aware that the more subtopics you have, the less information you can provide about any of them.

CHAPTER 9

Conducting Research on the Web[1]

*N*ow that you've selected an idea, developed it into a topic, and perhaps even outlined your article, the next step is to fill in the gaps. While you may have chosen a topic that draws upon your own experience and expertise, chances are that you're also going to have to do some research before you can actually write your article.

In the "old days," this could be a writer's most time-consuming task. Thanks to the Internet, however, research that once might have taken days (or weeks) to complete can often be handled in a few hours or less. No longer do you have to drive to the library, comb through catalogs to find a likely reference, search for the reference only to find that it's been checked out (or missing since 1992), ask for another book through interlibrary loan that will take weeks to arrive, and so forth. While libraries are still rich sources of information, a lot of the searching we once did in the stacks can now be accomplished with the touch of a button.

Defining Effective Search Terms

Internet search engines enable you to research general subject areas (e.g., everything you wanted to know about seventeenth-century costumes), or look up the answers to specific questions ("What is the planetary mass of Jupiter?").

The key is to define an effective search term (or set of terms). Your goal is to choose terms that will bring up the most relevant sites, while excluding those that are irrelevant.

To accomplish this, your terms should be as specific as possible. Often, a good method is to specify two, three, or more precise words that you want to find within the same document. For example, if you wanted to research "cat care," simply searching on "cats" would bring up a host of inappropriate sites. However, by entering terms such as "cats" and "care," you'll get more focused results. An even better approach is to ask yourself what type of phrase an article on "caring for cats" would be most likely to contain (e.g., "how to care for your cat," or "how to take care of your cat").

Another approach is to determine what terminology an expert would use. If you're researching "cancer in cats," for example, using a combination of terms like "cats" and "cancer" will certainly produce good results. However, searching on "feline oncology" may be even more productive, as this is the terminology that would be used by veterinarians.

To search for more than one word in the same document, you'll need to know how your search engine works. Most major search engines, including Google and Alta Vista, now assume that if you enter multiple search terms, a site should include *all* of those terms. It is no longer necessary to specify "and" in a multiple-term search. To search on a specific phrase, enter it in quotation marks ("how to care for your cat"). You can also exclude terms that you don't want, by specifying "not" (in Alta Vista) or "–" (in Google). For example, if you wanted to find information on limericks, you might choose to search on "limericks not Ireland" to exclude sites that discuss the town rather than the poetry.

Keep in mind that search engines are specific. They can't "guess" or provide information that is "close." They can only find *exactly* what you enter. Needless to say, spelling is important! (Google will prompt you to re-enter a search term if a word appears to be misspelled.) Most engines rank the results based on how many times your search term appears in a document, or how close to the beginning of the document it appears (along with a number of other variables). That doesn't mean, however, that you should look only at the first few results provided. You may find that the perfect site is number thirty on the list, or even number fifty. (If you scan three pages of results without finding a likely site, however, you probably need to refine your search.)

Another thing to keep in mind is that different countries use different spellings. If you're using American spellings, your search may exclude non-U.S. sites that could offer valuable information. If a word has both an American and a British spelling, try both (e.g., "catalog" versus "catalogue"). Similarly, if you're searching for information about a specific date, remember that while the U.S. format would be "May 4, 2001," the European format would be "4 May 2001."

Moving Beyond Search Engines

Search engines are not the only way to find information online. They're just a great place to start. Here are some other information sources.

❖ *Newspapers.* If you're researching a story that relates to a particular area, or local events, or an area's history, you might find it useful to check the newspaper archives for that area. Some newspapers put only current issues online, but others are building extensive archives. (You'll find a selection of newspaper sites at *www.writing-world.com/links/magazines .shtml.*)

❖ *"Gateway" sites.* If you want to find the best references on a topic, go find someone who has made that topic their specialty. That site is likely to have the best links to the best references—far better than what you'll turn up on a search. Start your search with a search engine; if you're lucky, this will take you to one or two really good sites on the topic, from which you can explore the links those hosts have selected as "the best."

❖ *Webrings.* You can find a lot of information through Webrings. When you find a useful site, scroll to the bottom of the page, and see if it is part of a Webring that seems relevant to your research topic. Some Webrings have a "list" link that lets you view all of the members of that ring. Others allow you to view from five to twenty links at a time.

❖ *Databases.* Information in databases may not turn up on an ordinary search, because many database pages can't be "spidered" by Web-search robots. Thus, there's a huge amount of information online that can only be found if you know where to find the databases. What you *can* do is use a search engine to *find* databases. Just type in a search term that you'd like to find information on, plus the term "database." Databases are also a good place to find images and original manuscripts that have been scanned and stored as PDF files or graphic files.

Is It Accurate?

There's a flip side to the joys of searching out data—the question of whether what you find is accurate!

Unfortunately, the Internet offers just as much misinformation as information. One classic example is an article that appeared in the *Boston Globe* in July 2000, touching on the grim fates of the fifty-six men who signed the Declaration of Independence. This article was based on an e-mail that has been making the rounds since about 1995—an e-mail that was also passed along as "fact" by Ann Landers. As *American Journalism Review* columnist Carl Cannon pointed out, this e-mail (and the *Globe* article) was, in fact, almost entirely false.

According to the oft-quoted account, five signers of the Declaration were captured by the British and tortured to death as traitors, while nine fought and died in the Revolutionary War. In reality, no signers of the Declaration were tortured by the British, while two were merely injured in the war (none died). One signer who supposedly "died in poverty" actually became governor of Pennsylvania.

The Internet is also a hotbed of urban legends, hoaxes, and scares. You've probably gotten an inbox full of "virus threats" characterized by the tell-tale phrase, "Please pass this on to everyone you know." Perhaps you've heard that the government is about to start charging everyone for using e-mail, to help subsidize the Post Office (it isn't). Even accurate information (such as the news that certain cold medicines were to be withdrawn from the market) gets circulated long after its "time," until it becomes misinformation simply because it is out of date.

How can you determine whether the information you find is accurate? It's impossible to be 100 percent sure, but by asking the following questions about everything you read, you'll improve your chances of getting "the right stuff."

❖ Does the author, site, or information appear to exist primarily to support a particular point of view? Why is this information online in the first place? Does the material contain an obvious bias toward a particular point of view, agenda, or belief? If so, chances are that the material will at least be slanted toward that bias—even if it is, itself, factual—and there's also a very good chance that information that does *not* support the author's views will be omitted.

❖ Does the site seem "overly emotional"? It's often easy to spot "emotional" sites—they're full of boldface phrases and LOTS OF CAPS. They often look as if the author is "shouting" at you. If a site uses phrases like "Don't believe what those Commie bastards in government are trying to pull off!!!", I'm inclined to believe that the author has an axe to grind, and that accuracy may not be his highest priority.

❖ Is the author trying to sell something? I'm always wary of sites that purport to offer "valuable medical information" that "doctors won't tell you," but just happens to be available in the author's book, or that supports a line of products, such as supplements or exercise equipment. That doesn't mean that an author who is trying to sell a book is necessarily providing misinformation—but if the information seems primarily offered as a sales pitch, beware!

❖ Who is the author? Does the author have any credentials? The Internet is a place where absolutely anyone can post anything. Keep in mind, however, that a *lack* of credentials does not necessarily mean that the information will be inaccurate; the Internet is also a place where thousands of ordinary folks post highly accurate information based on their personal research. If the author doesn't have credentials, look for references (e.g., a bibliography) that can help confirm the information provided.

❖ Is the site up to date? On Netscape, you can check on how recently a site has been updated by going to the "View Page Info" command on your browser. This will bring up a window that gives some basic information on the site, including the date of the last update. Another way to determine if a site is current is to test a few of its links. If you find that most of the links are "dead," you can assume that the author has not updated the information recently.

✤ Does the information agree with other sites on the same topic? When I see ten sites that list Shackleton's death on January 5, and only one that lists it on January 4, I'm inclined to believe in the voice of the majority. By reviewing several sites on a topic, you'll get an idea for what the "accepted facts" are, and be able to spot a site that seems out of line.

Here are some other ways to protect yourself—and your writing—from inaccuracies:

✤ Never assume that information in an unsolicited e-mail (e.g., something that is passed on to you by a friend, or through a discussion list) is factual unless you have checked it thoroughly or are familiar with the original source. E-mail has been the most prolific source of legends, myths (like the "signers of the Declaration" story), virus hoaxes, urban legends, and outdated information. E-mail gets forwarded forever, and it seems to appeal to the gullible, who pass on stories like, "I passed out in a hotel room and woke up without a kidney." Hoaxes also include warm-and-fuzzy stories, such as tales of sick children needing prayers or greeting cards. *Never* cite information that comes from an unsolicited e-mail without verifying its accuracy.

✤ Check the hoax pages for stories that are too good (or too bad) to be true. (For example, Osama bin Laden does *not* own Snapple!) You'll find information on common hoaxes and "urban legends" at the Urban Legends Reference Pages (*www.snopes2.com*), and information on computer virus hoaxes at the Computer Virus Hoax Page (*www.vmyths.com*).

✤ Don't rely on a domain suffix to "validate" information. Don't assume that a ".com" suffix indicates a "commercial" site; anyone can use this suffix, and some of the best information on the Web is available through .com addresses. Conversely, don't assume that a ".edu" site must be accurate; this does not necessarily indicate that the site is *sponsored* by a university, only that it is hosted on a university server.

✤ Use common sense! Often, your own instincts will be the best guide. If something looks fishy, don't trust it just because it's "online"—or even because it seems to be backed by some impressive credentials.

Using Published Sources

While it's appropriate (and often necessary) to conduct research online and in other published sources when writing an article, how you *use* that research in your article is another issue. Editors aren't fond of articles that are filled with quotes drawn from other published materials (such articles tend to look too much like college research papers). Editors much prefer "live quotes" that you've gathered from interviews.

If you use quotes from published sources, it's important to be sure that you aren't crossing the subtle line between "research" and "plagiarism." It isn't always easy to determine where this line is; a certain amount of quoting, for example, is usually considered "fair use" under copyright law. Here are some "do's and don'ts" to consider when quoting published sources.

- Use the information to *support* your article, not to actually *write* that article. I once reviewed a piece on pet training that was based entirely on quotes drawn from various authors' published books. If the quotes had been removed, there would have been no article, which indicated that the writer really didn't have an original article of her own.
- Use quotes sparingly. The question of whether something is "fair use" often depends on the amount of material being quoted. You aren't likely to get into trouble if you quote a few lines or even a paragraph from a published work, but be cautious of using anything more extensive.
- Ask yourself whether the author of the material you're quoting would have a problem with the amount of his or her work that you're including in your own. (Another way to approach this is to ask yourself whether *you* would have a problem with someone quoting similar amounts of material from *your* work.)
- Make sure that your quotes don't contain the "essence" of the previously published work. If you quote an author to the extent that reading your article is like reading a condensed version of the author's own work, you have a problem.
- If possible, go to the authors you're quoting and get "live" quotes instead of using material from their published works.
- Attribute the information. You don't need to footnote your information; simply provide a reference within the text, such as "Dr. Gordon Chalmers of the American Institute for Research notes in his book, *Good Stuff by Chalmers*, that. . . ." Make sure that the reader will not draw the mistaken conclusion that a piece of information originates with *you* rather than with your *source*.
- Provide a list of references for the editor. Some publications insist that all facts be supported with references and documentation, so be sure you can show where your material came from.

The good news is that copyright infringement lawsuits are actually extremely rare: It's not likely that an author is going to take you to court for having used too many quotes from his or her published work. However, the question "Can I be sued?" should be of far less concern than the question

"Will this damage my reputation as a writer?" Editors who see an article chock full of quotes from published sources aren't going to take you to court; they're simply going to send you a rejection slip.

NOTE

1. Portions of this chapter appear in my book *Writing.com: Creative Internet Strategies to Advance Your Writing Career*, Second Edition, from Allworth Press (2003).

CHAPTER 10

Conducting Interviews

While you can get loads of wonderful information from the Internet (or from books or magazines), it's important to remember that an article is not a research paper. Forget about finding lots of information in previously published resources and spitting it back out in ten pages. While some publications accept material that is "pure research" (such as historical topics), most editors don't want articles that draw heavily on published sources. What they want are "live quotes."

Interviews frequently scare new writers. We feel that we don't have the "credentials" to ask for an interview—that we may even insult an expert by approaching him. I'll share a little secret: If you're not the outgoing, go-get-'em type, you may *never* enjoy doing interviews. (I've been doing this for more than twenty years, and I still don't like making that call!) But this can be your little secret (and mine). You can hate interviews and still present a professional "face" to your interviewee.

Making Contact

Your first step is to find appropriate experts to interview. If you're doing a profile, obviously your main interviewee is the subject of that profile, but you may also want to interview people who know that person (a boss, a spouse, a friend). If you're covering a particular topic, you'll want to interview people who are experts on that topic. For an article on feline cancer, for example, you need to interview someone who specializes in animal cancer treatments. Often, the easiest way to find experts is to search your topic online.

Many writers wonder whether to contact prospective interviewees before or after they have an assignment. Having a list of interviewees can certainly help you *get* an assignment; conversely, actually having an assignment is more likely to encourage interviewees to talk to you. I generally contact interviewees only after I have an assignment in hand. However, if I believe that my query will be strengthened by the promise of an interview by an important expert, I will contact that person in advance and ask if he or she would be willing to talk to me *if* I obtain the assignment. (So far, no one has ever said no!)

I don't recommend conducting interviews before you have an assignment. This could prove a waste of your time and theirs. (There are exceptions to this rule, of course. For example, if you're traveling and come across someone perfect for an interview, don't miss the opportunity!)

The next question is whether to interview by phone, e-mail, or in person. If you're profiling someone local, an in-person interview is usually best, as you'll be able to pick up more visual details—the person's appearance, environment, mannerisms, etc. Telephone interviews are the next most "personal" way to talk to someone, and are particularly useful if you expect to need to ask lots of questions and get clarification on the answers. They're also useful if you want to let the interviewee take more control of the interview, and more or less "follow his lead," rather than keeping the discussion to a predefined list of questions. (When setting up a telephone interview, be sure you know what time zone your interviewee is in, and that you know exactly what time the interview is supposed to occur in *both* time zones. There's nothing so embarrassing as discovering that the call you thought you were supposed to make at 9:00 A.M. your time is actually being received at 6:00 A.M. by your interviewee.)

E-mail interviews can also be very effective. They are less intrusive than telephone interviews, and can be more comfortable for you if you're nervous about actually talking to someone in person. Just be sure that they are equally comfortable for the interviewee. Some people like the option of writing down their responses; an e-mail interview gives them more time to consider the questions, come back to them, and so forth. Others, however, don't like writing, and may give much less useful responses "on paper" than they would by phone or in person. (I'll discuss e-mail interviews in more detail below.)

Once you find a potential interviewee and decide how you'd like to conduct the interview, the next step is to ask for the interview. Remember, *the interviewee doesn't need to know you're nervous.* You may be shaking in your boots, but he'll never know. If you're going to interview someone by phone or in person, the first contact should usually be made by telephone. Simply call the person and explain who you are and what you are writing about. For example:

> "Hi, my name is Moira Allen, and I'm working on an article for *Cats* magazine about cancer in cats. Would you be willing to talk to me about some of the treatments your clinic provides for feline cancer patients?"

If you don't have an assignment yet, just say, "I'm working on an article about. . . ." Nine times out of ten, they'll never ask what publication it's for. If they do, just say, "I'll be pitching this to . . ." and fill in the magazine name.

If the person says yes to the idea of doing an interview, ask when would be a good time. Frequently, the person is likely to say, "This would be a good time," so *be prepared to do the interview on the spot*. Have your interview questions ready and make sure you've called when *you* have time to do the interview. It's embarrassing to have to tell your interviewee, "Oh, gee, sorry, I don't have time to talk to you right now; can we schedule an appointment?" If the person *does* want to do the interview at another time, he or she may want to know how long the interview will take, so you should have a time estimate (e.g., half an hour). Generally, *you* should call the person for the interview (it should be on your nickel). The exception is when a person can't guarantee being available at a certain time, and would prefer to control the timing of the interview by calling you. (Businesses, for example, will often prefer to call you, and will often arrange the call through a secretary.)

If you aren't comfortable simply cold-calling a person, or can't find a phone number, try to make contact by e-mail. The same approach works just fine (leaving out the "Hi" part). Close your e-mail with something like, "Could I call you next week to discuss this?" Include your phone number; some people will be happy to call you back.

Before the Interview

By taking the right steps to set up your interview, you can ensure that you will make a good impression, get the information you want, and (perhaps) gain a contact you can use for future articles.

❖ *Prepare your questions in advance.* By having a list of questions handy, you'll be able to answer an interviewee who asks, "What do you want to talk about?" Create "open-ended" questions rather than questions that can be answered "yes" or "no." For example, if you're interviewing a children's author, don't ask, "Do you enjoy writing children's books?" (If the author just says "yes," you have to come up with another question, such as "Why?") Instead, ask something like, "What do you enjoy most about writing children's books?" or, "What is the most fulfilling part of writing children's books?" These questions will elicit a more in-depth answer.

❖ *Ask for a specific amount of time.* Do you want half an hour? An hour? This will help your interviewee schedule the appointment (and is especially important if you're scheduling through a secretary).

❖ *Be honest about your purpose.* If you don't have a firm assignment, don't pretend that you do. (You can, however, explain that you're "pitching" the article to a specific market.) Don't claim credentials that you don't have.

Unless you're trying to interview a celebrity, you'll find that most people are willing to talk to "ordinary" writers.

✣ *Let the interviewee schedule the interview.* Often, you'll be asked what time is convenient. Instead of setting a time yourself, suggest a range of times, such as "any afternoon next week," or "any time on Wednesday or Thursday." This gives the interviewee flexibility to work you into the schedule. Try not to leave interviews to the last minute; while many interviewees try to be helpful with respect to deadlines, you never know when someone will be out of town, too busy, or otherwise unavailable.

✣ *Ask the interviewee how he or she would prefer to be interviewed.* Many people now prefer e-mail interviews, as this allows them to respond on their own time, and gives them the leisure to provide more in-depth answers. However, if you feel that you may need to follow up on questions, or have more control over the interview, you may prefer to push for a telephone interview. (Another option is to send your initial questions by e-mail, and then follow up on any additional questions or clarifications by phone.)

✣ *Be prepared to e-mail your questions to the interviewee in advance.* Business executives often prefer this, as it enables them to prepare for the specific types of information you're looking for. This won't always work if you're conducting a sensitive, personal, or controversial interview, but it does work if you're just gathering basic facts.

During the Interview

Keep your interviewee happy with the interview process by remaining courteous and professional—no matter what! As long as you remain polite, your interviewee is unlikely to be offended, even if your questions are sensitive or controversial.

✣ *Be prepared.* Again, having a list of questions prepared in advance can help you guide the interview in the direction you want it to go in. It can also help you double-check to make sure you've gotten all the information you need. Note that you may not actually ask every one of your questions; often, an interviewee's response to one question will give you the answers to other questions.

✣ *Remember that the interview is about the interviewee,* not *about you.* You're there to gather information, not to judge the person or the material. It doesn't matter how you feel about the person, whether you agree or disagree with his or her perspective, or whether you like what you hear. Keep in mind that if you remain calm and nonjudgmental, you're likely to get far more material than if you react negatively to the interviewee's responses.

❖ *Interact with the interviewee.* Don't just fire off questions and jot down the answers. Respond. Make "uh-huh" and "I see" and "Oh, really?" noises. Let the interviewee know you're listening and genuinely interested in the information. Volunteer an occasional comment that shows you understand what you are being told.

❖ *Let the interviewee set the tone.* Don't assume familiarity; let the interviewee determine whether the discussion proceeds formally or informally. Don't volunteer personal information or "chat" unless the interviewee has indicated that this seems appropriate.

❖ *Pay attention to nonverbal parts of the interview.* If you're writing a profile and interview someone in person, jot down details about the person's surroundings, appearance, tone of voice, etc.—anything that will give the reader a clearer picture. Did the person's clothing clash with the "personality" you expected? (e.g., a rich CEO wearing torn cutoffs). What did you notice about the person's environment? Was it filled with mementos, or barren and austere? Did it seem to reflect the interviewee's interests and personality, or clash with them? What did you notice about the person's body language and facial expressions—did the person seem comfortable or tense? Pay attention to questions that make your interviewee tense; they could lead to important information. (Don't be afraid to ask "tough" questions when appropriate.) Does the person's facial expression or body language match the words? For example, if someone says, "I have a wonderful marriage," but sits back with crossed arms and a frown, you might have doubts as to the truth of that statement. Gerald Nierenberg's *How to Read a Person Like a Book* is an excellent guide to body language.

❖ *Keep the interview "on track."* Interviewees will often go off on tangents. In some cases, a tangent can bring up more interesting information, but if you only have a short period of time for the interview, and the tangent isn't giving you the information you need, you'll need to bring the conversation back on track. One way to do this is to use the interviewee's earlier responses to redirect the interview, e.g., "Getting back to what you were saying earlier about . . ."

❖ *Don't be afraid of silences.* Silences are wonderful tools. They make people uncomfortable, and thus, people tend to try to *fill* them. If you're not getting a response to a question, or if the response seemed too short or insufficient, just wait a moment without saying anything—often this will cause the person to say more. Don't rush to fill silences yourself!

❖ *Always thank the interviewee when the interview is over.* I usually conclude with a promise to let the interviewee know when the article is scheduled for publication and to send a tearsheet when it is published.

A common question is whether to tape interviews or transcribe them by hand. I prefer both. I hate transcribing taped notes, so I try to write everything down, but a recording provides a good backup if I can't read my hand-writing, or if the interviewer talks so fast (or gives so much information) that I can't get it all down. It's also a good way to support your article later, in case an interviewee claims you've misquoted him. (Always save your tapes for a couple of years!)

When I interview by phone, I usually type responses directly into the computer. Some answering machines will enable you to make a recording of a conversation; if you do so, however, be sure to inform the interviewee that you're taping the call. (In most states, it's illegal to tape a telephone conversation without permission.)

After the Interview

An interview isn't necessarily over just because you've hung up the phone. You may need to come back for more information or clarification. You may also want to call upon that person's expertise for other articles. The following courtesies can help keep you in the interviewee's good will.

❧ *Send a thank-you note by e-mail or snail-mail.* Let the interviewee know when and where the article will be published, or provide that information once you have it.

❧ *Ask your editor to send complimentary copies of the issue to each interviewee.* Be sure to include a list of interviewees (with their addresses) when you send in your article. If an editor balks, ask for extra copies to be sent to you, so you can send them yourself.

❧ *When the article is published, send a copy with another thank-you letter.* I like to contact interviewees once an article comes out to make sure they received a complimentary copy from the editor. If they didn't, send them a copy yourself; it will be appreciated.

Many interviewees will try to pressure you into letting them "review" (and in some cases, "approve") an article before it goes to the editor. The consensus among authors and editors on this point is to say *no*. Never promise to let an interviewee see your article before it goes to press. Never give an interviewee any "approval power" over your article. If an interviewee puts any pressure on you to do this, simply say you're sorry, but your editor won't permit it.

One reason many interviewees want to see an interview before it is published is because they've had bad experiences with writers who want to put their own, biased spin or slant on an interview. In such a case, be understanding but firm. (If you have done previous interviews that show your balanced and professional reporting style, share those with the interviewee; this may put his mind at ease about your approach.)

The only exception to this rule is when you're interviewing someone about a highly technical subject and want to be absolutely sure you've gotten all the information right. In such a case, the only interest the interviewee is likely to have in reviewing the article is the same as yours: accuracy. If I have any doubts about how I've transcribed and presented the interview information, I may pass it back to the interviewee for a check—but *not* for "pre-approval."

E-mail Interviews

E-mail can be an effective and convenient way to conduct an interview, and is often appreciated by busy experts who don't have time for a face-to-face or telephone interview. It enables you to compose questions carefully rather than "on the fly," and gives your interviewee time to respond carefully as well. (Another plus is that the interviewee gets to do all the typing!) E-mail also offers a good way to follow up on a traditional interview, when seeking clarification or additional information.

E-mail interviews are less effective when you're trying to develop a profile that includes not only the individual's words but also your observations of the person's appearance, actions, skills, emotions, tone of voice, etc. They are also less effective if you don't know enough about a subject to develop useful questions, or when you're more likely to get information from the natural flow of questions and answers than from a predefined script. In an e-mail interview, you can't change direction if a more promising tangent emerges from the conversation; you can't nudge the interviewee back on track if the conversation strays or ask follow-up questions if your first questions don't elicit enough information; and you can't ask for immediate explanations or clarification.

The following strategies can help you develop and refine an e-mail interview:

❖ Determine your goals before writing your questions. Decide exactly what you need to know; then develop questions that will best elicit that information.
❖ Ask open-ended questions rather than questions that can be answered "yes" or "no."
❖ Explain why you're asking a particular question, so the interviewee knows what type of response you're looking for.
❖ Let the interviewee know what audience you're writing for, so the interviewee will know how detailed or technical the information should be.
❖ Keep your questions as clear, uncomplicated, and short as possible.
❖ Keep your list of questions short. Ten is good; twenty is likely to tax an interviewee's patience.

❖ List your questions numerically, and leave space between each question for the interviewee to insert the answer.

❖ Include a final "open" question—e.g., "Is there anything else you'd like to say on this subject that hasn't been covered above?"

❖ Let the interviewee know when you need the answers. Remember that the interviewee is doing you a favor, and is under no obligation to meet your deadline.

❖ Don't be afraid to ask for clarification, or to follow up on questions or answers that beg for additional information. And always thank your interviewee!

E-mail Surveys

Another way to gather information via e-mail is to conduct a survey. E-mail enables you to send a list of questions to hundreds of potential respondents at no cost.

At the same time, caution is in order. Some respondents may regard a survey as a form of spam. Your e-mail should state the nature and purpose of the survey as quickly, succinctly, and courteously as possible. Assure respondents of privacy, and guarantee that you won't cite anyone by name or organization without permission. If you're soliciting comments as well as statistics, ask respondents to indicate whether or not they may be quoted, and how they should be cited.

Like interview questions, survey questions should be short, clear, and well-organized. Unlike interview questions, however, survey questions should encourage "yes" and "no" answers, or answers to a multiple-choice selection. Respondents are more likely to answer a short questionnaire than a long one.

An easy format is to follow each question with the answer options (e.g., "yes" or "no") on separate lines. Place a set of parentheses in front of each option, with space for a response. Here's an example from an e-mail survey I sent to a number of magazine editors:

1. Do you accept e-mail queries?
☐ Yes
☐ No

2. How do you prefer to receive manuscripts?
☐ Hardcopy (printed)
☐ On diskette
☐ By e-mail, in the body of the message
☐ As an e-mail attachment

This enables the respondent to simply insert an "x" in the appropriate space and mail the form back as a reply. If you're offering a multiple-choice question that could have more than one answer, indicate whether you want the respondent to "check only one" or "check all that apply."

To ensure your respondents' privacy, place all your survey addresses in the "BCC" (blind copy) field of your header. Leave the "To" field blank. If you have a large number of addressees, send the survey in several batches rather than all at once.

When you mail your survey, several may bounce back immediately as undeliverable. Keep track of these bounces so you know exactly how many surveys actually reached their destination. This will enable you to calculate the correct percentage of responses. For example, if you send out one hundred surveys, get ten back as undeliverable, and receive fifty responses, you have a 55 percent response rate.

The bulk of your responses will typically arrive in a flood within the first two or three days of your mailing. After that, the flood will taper to a trickle. At some point, you'll have to decide when it's time to cut off the survey and tally the results, even if you're still getting an occasional response. Set up a filter in your e-mail program to route responses to a separate mailbox until you're ready to tally them.

Once you've completed the survey, make a list of the respondents and send them a thank-you note for participating. If respondents are interested in the results of your survey, let them know when and where the article will appear.

Using Interview Material

Once the interview is finished, write up your notes as soon as possible, while it is still fresh in your mind. Try to be as clear and accurate as possible.

You'll often find you have too much information to actually fit in your article, but that's fine. Some of what you've gathered might spin off into another article, or you might find that a personal experience makes a great sidebar. Interview material is like raw ore; your task now is to refine it, and find the "precious metal" hidden inside. (By the way, by granting an interview, the interviewee is considered to have granted you the "right" to use those responses, not only in the original article but also in other articles you might choose to write.)

The one absolute rule of using interviews is this: *Never twist a person's words to imply something other than what the person meant.* Do not use quotes out of context, or partial quotes, as a way to make it seem someone said something they did not.

Other issues are less clear. For example, there are two schools of thought on "cleaning up" quotes. Let's say you have interviewed someone who does not express himself clearly or in an educated way. Maybe his quote sounds something like "Well, uh, y'know, really, that's tough, but I'd have to say, I think, probably, I'd want to see the guy fry, y'know?" Some writers and editors suggest using the entire quote. Others who would use only the last eight words (or even cut the final "y'know"). The "use it like it is no matter what" school says that if a quote is grammatically incorrect, you still use it just "as is"; other writers feel this can cause unnecessary embarrassment for the interviewee, and that minor corrections to grammar are acceptable as long as they don't change the meaning (and tone) of the quote.

This can get a bit sticky when you're doing e-mail interviews. When you interview someone on the phone, you don't know whether the person knows how to spell, and you don't care, because you're writing it down yourself and are therefore responsible for the spelling. But what if a person has sent you an e-mail interview full of misspellings? Should you use it verbatim (or riddle it with "sics" to indicate that he, and not you, was the source of the misspellings)? My view is that, unless you have a *profound* reason to keep those errors, it's better to clean them up. Not everyone has a perfect grasp of spelling, and I believe an interviewee should not be made to look stupid— especially when that person has done me the favor of giving me the information I asked for.

I compared interview material to ore, and that's exactly what it is. You don't want to dump everything the person said into your article. Instead, you want to mine it for quotes that add *spice* to the article (assuming it is not a straight Q&A piece). That doesn't mean you can't use more of the person's material; however, you'll find your article usually works best if you paraphrase most of the interview and add direct quotes that bring home the point you're trying to make.

Here's the text of an e-mail interview I conducted with author Kate Elliott:

> The *American Heritage Dictionary* defines culture as "the totality of socially transmitted behavior patterns, arts, beliefs, institutions, and all other products of human work and thought characteristic of a community or population." According to the OED, the word "'culture' is related to 'cultivate'" in the sense of tending crops.
>
> Words grow from specific roots for a reason. Definitions of "cultivate" include "To improve or prepare (land), as by plowing or fertilizing, for raising crops . . . To grow or tend . . . To promote the growth of . . . To nurture . . . To form and refine." (*American Heritage Dictionary*)
>
> I think that these definitions and that relationship between culture and cultivation can give writers clues as to how to approach writing, and creating, a "believable" culture in a fantasy or science fiction novel.

For that purpose, one can draw out the metaphor of tillage, however labored it might become in time: When the writer creates a culture in the science fiction/fantasy field, she starts with untilled ground, a kind of blank slate. That ground has to be prepared, tended, formed, and refined. A culture, likewise, must show arts, beliefs, institutions (to whatever extent), technologies, and roles. In the role of "cultivator," the writer can, in addition, not merely impose her own notions onto that developing culture but see what comes of giving it a little room to evolve naturally in the course of planning and writing the novel.

Here's what I wrote in the final article:

Elliott likes to draw an analogy between "culture" and "cultivate," two words that spring from the same root. "When a writer creates a culture, she starts with untilled ground, a kind of blank slate. The ground has to be prepared, tended, formed, refined. Likewise, a culture must show arts, beliefs, institutions, technologies, and roles. In the role of 'cultivator,' a writer doesn't simply impose her own notions onto that developing culture, but gives it a little room to evolve naturally in the course of planning and writing the novel."

Finally, remember that an interview is *not* about the *interviewer*. I've read too many interviews in which the writer keeps intruding upon the interview—with thoughts, reactions, interpretations, personal observations, etc. For example, I've seen interviewers write things like, "I really felt a connection with what Mary was saying about her marriage, because of my own bad experiences. . . ." If the article is about *Mary*, what is the interviewer doing in this picture?

This can be not only intrusive (the reader sees more of the *interviewer* than the *interviewee*), but unethical if the interviewer attempts to "interpret" the interviewee's comments for the audience—especially if the interviewer is trying to cast the interviewee in a bad light. If you feel that an interviewee is a horrible person, let that person's words *speak for themselves*, and let readers draw their own conclusions.

CHAPTER 11

Starting Your First Draft

*F*ew things are more intimidating than the blank page (or screen) when you have a deadline. You may have known exactly what you wanted to say when you wrote your query, but now, perhaps, you have a stack of research notes and no idea how to get started. Or, perhaps you're stuck on the first sentence. This doesn't just happen to "new" writers; it happens to us all. Here are some ways to get that article going.

Step One: Identify Your Subject

The first step is to ask yourself whether you know exactly what your article is supposed to be about. Now that you've done your research, your brain may be stuffed with all sorts of information, and you're having trouble "sorting it out." It's time to go back to the basics.

Make sure you can state the central concept (or "thesis") of your article *in a single sentence*. Make sure, as well, that this sentence has no more than one "and" in it. For example:

> TITLE: Your Child's First Hike
> *Market:* Family-oriented travel or hiking publication
> *Good Topic Sentence:* "How to introduce your child to hiking safely and enjoyably."
> *Bad Topic Sentence:* "How to introduce your child to hiking, and what to pack, and where to go, and a look at my own experiences taking the kids on hikes, plus a look back at my first hike when I was a child. . . ."

> TITLE: Discover the New Olympic Sport of Skeleton!
> *Market:* Winter sports publications
> *Good Topic Sentence:* "What 'skeleton' is and how to get involved."
> *Bad Topic Sentence:* "What 'skeleton' is, how to get involved, profiles of some

notable skeleton athletes, a history of skeleton and the Olympics, and places where you can learn how to do it, plus some of the risks. . . ."

The purpose of a topic sentence is not only to help you focus on the central point of your article, but also to *limit* you. Everything in your article should relate to that topic sentence. If it doesn't, then it doesn't belong in the article, no matter how interesting it may be. A tightly focused topic sentence will keep you on track; a rambling topic sentence will get you lost.

Another way to define your topic sentence is to turn it into the first question the reader would ask about the subject. For example:

- How can I introduce my child to the sport of hiking?
- What is "skeleton," and how can I get started in this sport?

By turning your thesis into a question, you know exactly what your article has to "answer." Here are some other sample questions that would make good "core concepts" for articles:

- Should I refinance my home?
- How can I learn to crochet?
- How do you cook chestnuts?
- How can I communicate more effectively with my spouse?
- What do I need to know about "natural" vitamins?
- Where can I stay in New York for less than $100 a night?
- What are some romantic things I can do for less than $20?
- How can I keep the kids entertained on a rainy day?
- What would be an ideal gift for my mother-in-law?

Not every article idea can be expressed as a question, but you might be surprised by how easy it is to turn *most* ideas into questions. From there, the process becomes much simpler: Your goal is to *answer* the question.

Step Two: Identify Your Subtopics

Once you've defined your topic statement, identify subtopics that support the original thesis. For example, your article on a child's first hike might cover:

- How to make a trip enjoyable.
- How to make a trip safe.

An article on whether to refinance one's home might include:

❖ Circumstances in which refinancing is a good idea.
❖ Circumstances in which refinancing is a bad idea.
❖ How to get more information.

Each of these subtopics may lead to more logical subtopics.

❖ Child's hiking trip ⇒ Safety ⇒ Risks: Common trail hazards, including sunburn, dehydration, toxic plants, insect bites, animals/snakes, injuries such as cuts, bruises, sprains.
❖ Child's hiking trip ⇒ Safety ⇒ Precautions: Warning your child about hazards, things to pack in case of hazards, how to protect against sunburn, etc.
❖ Child's hiking trip ⇒ Safety ⇒ Remedies: What to do if any of the hazards are encountered (e.g., how to treat poison ivy, snake bite, etc.).

If you have too many subtopics, remember that you can always pull one out and use it as a sidebar. The key is to make sure that everything you're trying to cover in the article *directly* relates to your core topic. If it doesn't, save it for another piece.

Step Three: Identify Your Audience

Besides establishing the question your article will be answering, you also need to know who will be *asking* that question. If, for example, your article is covering "how to plan for retirement," you need to know who will be reading the piece. The questions asked by a twenty-year-old single woman would be very different from those asked by a forty-year-old man with children about to enter college, or a recently divorced woman, or someone who is self-employed.

Going back to our "child-hiking" article, you would want to know whether you're writing for experienced hikers, or a more general magazine, whose readers may *not* be that experienced. You'll have to explain many more basic concepts to the latter audience, while the more experienced audience might be more interested in high-tech equipment suitable for kids, or the best hiking trails for kids in a particular region.

Step Four: Identify Your Limits

Be sure you know how long your article is supposed to be. (I discussed "word budgets" in chapter 8.) You have only so many words to allocate to each "point" in your article. The more points you want to make, the fewer words you can budget to each point. The fewer points you need to cover, the more "in-depth" your coverage can be on every point.

While there is no hard-and-fast rule about how many words you should devote to a single subtopic, I feel that for an in-depth article, you need a budget of at least 300 to 500 words. A 2,000-word article would give you room for four major subtopics.

If you need to cover a larger number of subtopics, your article will become more of an "overview." Overviews often work well as "list" articles. For example, you might write an in-depth piece on "how to keep your children entertained on a rainy day," *or*, a list titled "Ten Ways to Keep Your Kids Entertained on a Rainy Day."

Step Five: Identify Your Structure

Next determine the best order in which to present your information. You may also have defined this order in your outline. Here are some typical ways to structure your article:

- *Logical order.* What comes first, what comes next, what comes after that? What is the first question a reader would ask, the second, the third, and so on?
- *Chronological order.* What happened first? What happened next? What happened after that?
- *Instructional order.* What should the reader do first? What does he do next? What is step one, step two, step three?
- *List order.* Lists work well for articles like "Ten Ways to Entertain Your Children on a Road Trip," or "Twenty Ways to Clean Up Stains and Spills." Shorter lists work fine without numbers; longer lists often benefit from numbering. Your number can also become your title.

If all else fails, try what I call "sculpting." Just write down paragraphs, at random, based on your research information. Don't worry about putting them together in a logical sequence, or polishing them; the goal is to get something on the page. I call this "sculpting" because it reminds me of the process of throwing wads of clay into a pile that will eventually become a sculpture. The first step is to simply get all the clay in the right place. *Then* you can worry about shaping and smoothing.

Style and Presentation

Once you know what your article will include, you need to address *how* you want to write it. This section looks at some of the "tools" you can include in your basic article-writing toolkit.

ur own distinctive style over time. However, style is also
arket you're writing for. Your articles may have a great
variation, while still retaining your unique "voice." Some
issues to consider here are:

❖ *The level of the audience.* Knowing your audience's reading level, and its
level of knowledge/expertise on your subject, will have considerable
influence on how you approach your article. Does your audience expect
technical terminology, or simple writing with lots of explanations? Does
it expect the author to be a friendly, hand-holding guide, or a more
authoritative "expert"?

❖ *The appropriate "narrative voice."* Should you write your article in first person ("I/we"), second person ("you"), or third person ("he/she/they/one")?
Again, this depends on the publication. Some publications use *no* first-
person narratives; some prefer it. Some types of articles (such as how-to's)
rely on second person ("Do this, then do this."). Some prefer third ("One
can achieve this effect by . . .").

❖ *Personal versus impersonal.* Some publications prefer more personal, conversational articles; some prefer articles to be very impersonal, present-
ing information without a sense of the author being "present" in the
article. I prefer a balance: I like articles to be accessible and "user-
friendly," but I don't care for "chatty Kathy" pieces that ramble on about
what the writer thinks about everything he or she is discussing.

Presentation Elements

You don't have to write every piece as a straight narrative from beginning to
end. There are lots of ways to add variety to your writing, including:

❖ *Anecdotes.* Used sparingly, anecdotes can spice up a piece, providing personal examples to illustrate your information. Your entire article can be
based around an anecdotal example, or, you could open with an anecdote
that introduces your subject, and then close with a concluding anecdote
that shows how your introductory story "turned out."

❖ *Interviews/quotes.* These should also be used sparingly. Instead of quoting
everything a person says, paraphrase the bulk of the information you
obtain through interviews, and use direct quotes that highlight the content of your article.

❖ *Statistics.* Some people love numbers; some people don't. Statistics can be
a useful way to back up your point, but they can also cause some readers to nod off. Watch out for sentences like, "In 1984, 50 percent of the
2,000 hotels in the 55-mile radius of Metropolis experienced a 92 percent increase in their revenue, for a total of $72 million. . . ."

❖ *"Made-up" anecdotes.* Some publications like to illustrate a point with "artificial" anecdotes: "Because John backed up his computer data, his business didn't fail when his computer crashed. Unfortunately, Mary didn't. . . ." I've never been a fan of this approach, but some editors like it!

❖ *Personal experiences.* Even in a more factual "how-to" piece, you can use personal experiences to illustrate your topic. For example, if you were writing about caring for a pet with diabetes, you might use your own experience to help put the reader at ease (if you can do it, he can do it!), and provide a logical way to "walk through" the information. Keep in mind that in such articles, the experience is the "vehicle" for your information, not the *point* of your article.

Beginnings, Middles, and Ends

Every article needs a beginning—an introduction that "hooks" the reader and draws her into the article. Generally your introduction should be no longer than one paragraph. Use it to establish what the article is about and why it will be relevant or interesting to the reader. (You will often find that your query hook works well as an article hook, or vice versa.)

The "middle" of your article—or rather, everything that falls between your introduction and conclusion—should fulfill the promise made by that introduction. Don't promise anything you can't deliver! Also, make sure the tone of your article matches the tone of the rest of the article; don't open with a joke and move on into an article that is morbid and depressing.

Your conclusion should provide a sense of closure to the article. The reader should feel that everything that needed to be said has been said. Try to *mirror* your introduction in your conclusion. For example, if you open with an anecdote, close with an anecdote. If you open with a quote, close the quote. Bring the reader "full circle" with the conclusion of your piece.

One common approach to the "beginning-middle-end" structure is to set up your article as "problem-solution-call to action." Here, the introduction establishes a problem to be solved or question to be answered. It may explain *why* this issue is a problem, *why* the reader needs to know more, *why* the reader needs to take action. For example, a common type of health article is "symptoms you can't afford to ignore." The introduction explains that these symptoms can be signs of serious illness—establishing the *problem* that needs to be solved. The middle goes over the symptoms and what they could mean. The end is a "call to action": If *you* see these symptoms, go to a doctor!

Articles that cover a personal experience should conclude with "the end of the story." There's an obvious corollary: *Don't try to write an experiential article until you know the end of the story!* For example, if you've just gotten divorced, don't try to write an article about "surviving divorce" until you've actually gone through the process and are in a position to look back on it. (See chapter 12 for more information on writing personal experiences.)

Sidebars

Once you've finished your article, chances are that you'll have information left over that is perfect for a sidebar. Editors love sidebars. Some publications require them. For example, travel magazines generally require sidebars that explain basic "how to get there, where to stay" information. In other cases, sidebars add extra information or interest to a feature. (Note that you don't need to "format" a sidebar when submitting it; just add it to the end of your article with its own heading and word count.) Here are some basic types of sidebars:

❧ *Lists.* If you have a list of short pieces of information, consider pulling this out into a sidebar. For example, on that article about hiking and children, consider making a list of trail hazards, or first-aid supplies or equipment to take along. If it's for a regional publication, consider listing local trails that are good for children.

❧ *Personal experiences.* Sometimes a short personal account makes a good sidebar to a longer, more factual piece. When I edited *Dog Fancy,* I always liked to balance a technical medical article with a personal article about the same topic.

❧ *Factual information.* The reverse is also effective: Try balancing a personal article with a brief overview of factual information on the topic.

❧ *Quizzes.* Editors love quizzes. For example, I sold *The Writer* the quiz in chapter 31 as a sidebar to an article on how to survive as a full-time freelance writer.

❧ *Where to find it.* A sidebar on where to find more information, where to buy products mentioned in the article, where to find organizations related to the topic, etc., is always useful. Consider listing online resources as well.

Sidebars are (a) a great way to use extra information you can't fit into your article, (b) a sneaky way to get past a word limit, and (c) a good way to earn extra money, because editors often pay extra for sidebars.

Five Flaws That Can Lead to Rejection

Articles with excellent ideas and information can still be "marginalized" by structural flaws. The good news is that these flaws are usually easy to correct. Following are five flaws I often see in otherwise well-written manuscripts:

1. Rambling Introductions

If your introduction wanders on for three, four, or even five paragraphs, you have a problem. Such introductions often fall into one of these categories:

❖ The personal introduction, in which the writer introduces herself, her background, her credentials, or a personal experience that "sets the stage" for the article itself.

❖ The analogy, in which the writer compares what she is about to discuss to something else. For example, I've received many articles that compare writing to gardening ("learn to prune") or cooking ("choose the right ingredients").

❖ The "setting-the-stage" introduction, in which the writer takes several paragraphs to explain background information.

If 500 words of your 1,500-word article is "introduction," you're cheating the reader, and yourself. The reader loses because he gets only 1,000 words of information, and you lose because if the editor cuts the introduction, you'll only get paid for 1,000 words instead of for the 1,500 you actually wrote.

The solution: Limit your introduction to a single paragraph, or two at most. You don't need to spend a lot of time describing how you found out about a problem, or how you talked to five people to get your information, etc. Cut to the chase, and pack the body of your article with information too useful to cut!

2. Explaining "Why" but Not "How"

Another common flaw is the tendency to write about the importance of doing something without explaining *how* to do it. For example, a writer may explain why one needs to develop believable characters, but not how to actually do it.

The solution: Limit the "why" part of your article to the introduction (e.g., a paragraph on why believable characters are important). Use the rest of your article to show the reader exactly how to solve the problem you've established. Instead of giving the reader "ten reasons why characterization is important," offer "ten steps toward building stronger characters."

3. Asking the Wrong Questions

Even experienced writers can fail to ask (and answer) the questions a reader is most likely to ask about a subject. It's not enough to write about what you know: You also have to figure out what the reader *doesn't* know.

The solution: Put yourself in the reader's shoes. If necessary, find someone who knows less about the subject than you do, and ask that person what he or she would want to learn from your article. Common "reader" questions include:

- ✦ What is it?
- ✦ Why should I be interested?
- ✦ How can I get involved?
- ✦ What do I need to know/learn/buy/obtain to get started?
- ✦ What are some of the perils and pitfalls, if any?
- ✦ Where do I get more information?

An article that answers all of these questions, on any subject, is likely to please readers *and* editors.

4. Lack of Organization

Some articles appear to have been jotted down as ideas came to the author, without any reordering. Even if an article contains good information, most editors don't have time to reorganize it paragraph by paragraph. If a piece has to be rewritten to make sense or read well, it is likely to be rejected.

The solution: As I said above, identify the logical structure of your article, and (as I mentioned in the preceding chapter), "think in subheads." By establishing specific sections, you'll find it easier to determine where the information belongs.

5. No Conclusion

A surprising trend in articles crossing my desk is the lack of endings. All too often, when an author runs out of information, the article just stops.

Like that.

Endings are important: They bring closure, wrap up the loose ends, and help the reader make sense of what has gone before.

The solution: Always provide a conclusion to your material, even if it's just a couple of sentences. One way to conclude an article is to summarize what you've already said. Another is to refer back to the introduction: If you opened with an anecdote or analogy, consider closing with a related anecdote or analogy. If you asked a question in the introduction, recap the answer in the conclusion. Don't just leave the reader wondering whether the typesetter somehow lost the last paragraph of your article!

While these five flaws aren't the only reasons for rejection, they offer a useful checklist to keep in mind the next time your article comes back with a polite "No thank you." And by avoiding them in the first place, you'll greatly increase your chances of getting an acceptance letter the first time around!

CHAPTER 12

Personal-Experience Articles

When I was editor of a national pet magazine, my desk was swamped with "personal-experience" articles—accounts of some funny, moving, or tragic event in the author's life. The majority of those articles went straight to the rejection pile.

It wasn't because they were poorly written. Many were quite good, and every bit as funny or moving as they claimed to be. We simply could not use them, because they did not match our editorial focus.

Personal-experience articles often make up 75 percent or more of a typical magazine's unsolicited submissions. Yet they are the least likely to be accepted. The reason is that personal experience pieces are typically about the *writer*. What editors are looking for are articles about the *reader*.

That can create some tough odds. For example, if an editor could purchase ten articles per month out of one hundred submissions, a personal experience piece might have a one-in-seventy-five chance of acceptance, while a service article's chances could be as high as nine in twenty-five. (Of course, in reality editors receive far more than one hundred articles per month, and may purchase fewer than ten.)

You can beat those odds by offering an editor the best of both worlds: a personalized service piece. To do this, you must ask yourself how your experience relates to the reader. For example:

❖ Is this an experience the reader might wish to share, or enjoy?
❖ Is this an experience from which the reader can learn or benefit?
❖ Is this an experience the reader might wish to avoid?
❖ Is this an experience that will help the reader cope with difficulty?

Experiences to Share

Have you had an experience others might wish to share? Perhaps you've achieved a success or a goal, or simply had a good time. Would others want to do the same? If the answer is yes, you're in the ideal position to tell them how.

For example, perhaps you've just come back from a great vacation. Tell us about it! Most travel articles are personal-experience pieces at heart. But they are written in such a way as to become the reader's experience as well, either vicariously, or by enabling the reader to duplicate the experience.

If your vacation involved a fascinating destination, tell us how to get there, what to see, where to find the best food and lodgings, or what to expect from the culture or environment. Tailor your account to your audience: Will your readers want to know about the most challenging hiking trails, the best restaurants, or how to get a bargain in the shops or bazaars? Should your article focus on little-known details of an exotic culture, or the nuts and bolts of travel and hotel arrangements?

Focusing on the service aspects of your article broadens the market dramatically. That story of your "best camping trip ever" can discuss equipment and supplies for one magazine, the "ten best campgrounds" in a particular region for another, and how to get the kids unplugged from their Gameboys and into the great outdoors for a third. In short, you should be asking not only how the reader can benefit from your experience, but how many *different* types of readers might be able to benefit.

Keep in mind that your experience should be one a reader would like to share in the *future*, not one he or she has already shared. Readers aren't interested in articles about things they've already done. They are interested in new experiences, in things they might want to do—so show them how!

Experiences That Enrich

If any single focus dominates the article market, it is "how to improve your life." Self-improvement themes fill magazines of every description: how to improve your health, well-being, relationships, careers, skills, homes, hobbies. Nothing attracts a reader like the promise that an article will make life *better.*

To tap into this market, explore areas in your life that you have made better. Topics may range from the deeply personal (overcoming a fear, meeting a challenge) to the seemingly trivial (brightening your work area with potted plants). Any improvement that you've made in your own life could be an improvement someone else would like to emulate.

Suppose, for example, that you quit the corporate rat race to start your own business. Presumably, your goal was to improve your life (I've never read an article about someone joining the *corporate* world to improve his or her quality of life!). Your article could tell us not only why you did it, but how, including the advantages and disadvantages of the decision.

Has your decision led to more quality time with family members, more freedom to control your life and destiny, more opportunities to enjoy the "little things" like gardens and sunsets and the freedom to linger over the morning's coffee and bagel? On the downside, can you help the reader cope with the difficulties of developing good work habits, handling the lack of social interaction, and coping with no paycheck or benefits?

Self-improvement articles don't necessarily have to be based on life-changing experiences. In many cases, an area of your life that *hasn't* changed can also be the basis of an excellent article. For example, is your relationship with your spouse running smoothly, with few hassles or arguments? Are your children well-behaved, getting good grades, and staying off drugs?

If your life is going well, keep in mind that thousands of readers would love to know your secrets for a successful relationship or how to raise happy and well-adjusted children!

Experiences to Avoid

Sometimes, the experiences from which we learn the most are the negative ones. Writers, of course, don't simply learn from their mistakes; they write about them. (At least, they should!)

Experiences that you wish you could have avoided often make wonderful service articles. What would you have done differently, if you had known then what you know now? What would you do differently today? It may be too late for you to avoid a problem, but it's never too late to help another.

Unpleasant experiences don't necessarily lead to unpleasant articles. Someone once said that comedy equals tragedy plus time. Sometimes, the best time to write about your experience is when you're finally able to look back on it and laugh. The resulting article will not only be useful, but entertaining as well.

For example, what about that disastrous family hiking trip you took in the MegaBugga Woods? The trip during which your dog broke its leash and tangled with a skunk, you got the worst sunburn of your life, and your child became a hands-on expert at identifying poison ivy? By the time your sunburn faded, you knew you had an article! Throw in a sidebar on how to identify toxic plants, or the type of protective clothing to wear, or first-aid supplies to carry along, and you'll have an article that could find any number of markets.

Of course, not every unpleasant experience lends itself to such light-hearted treatment. Some are more serious, and should be handled with sensitivity and care. Yet even potentially devastating experiences can often be avoided with the proper precautions. If you've suffered through such an event, you will be providing a valuable service to others by putting those precautions on paper.

Experiences to Endure

Some painful or traumatic experiences cannot be avoided; they can only be endured. When someone faces a tragedy or loss, they often want to hear from someone else who has been through a similar experience—someone who understands, who knows how it feels, whose advice and comfort comes from the heart.

That's the big difference between a "coping" article written by an expert, and one written by an ordinary person who has been there, endured, and somehow managed to pull her life together again. Experts have good advice (which you may be able to incorporate into your article), but your experience "humanizes" that advice and makes it meaningful to the reader.

Writers will never run out of markets for articles on how to cope with grief, trauma, or loss, because people will never cease to experience these things. And because traumatic events affect different people in different ways (even within a single-family unit), an effective article can reach many different markets.

For example, suppose you're writing about losing a job. You might focus on how this experience affected you, and how you coped with feelings of anger, loss, helplessness, and frustration. You might write about how you found a new job. You might deal with issues of financial adjustments, or how to find support during your job hunt.

Your options don't end there, however. Unless you're single, with no one to support but your cat, the loss of your job will affect others as well. How did it affect your spouse? How did it affect your children? How could a reader help his or her own family members cope?

Any type of loss, large or small, raises issues and emotions that must be dealt with, either as an individual or as a family. By using your own experience as the basis for a service article, you send the message that resolution and recovery are possible.

First Experiences

Remember the first time you _____ (fill in the blank)? Remember the novelty of the experience? The emotions it evoked? The insights it revealed to you? These factors make "first-experience" articles very tempting to writers, who want to share those feelings and insights with others.

Unfortunately, magazines are flooded with "first-experience" pieces ("my first puppy," "my first baby") that are poorly conceived and even more poorly written. Many submission guidelines flatly state "no first experiences." You can still beat the odds, however, by finding ways to match your experience to the market.

❖ *Look for readers who haven't shared your experience.* If you want to write the story of your first dog, remember that every reader of a *dog* magazine has probably already had a similar experience. The discoveries that seemed new to you will most likely be old hat to these readers. Instead of thinking "dogs = dog magazine," look for an audience that *will* find your experience new and different. An article about the difference a new pet made in a single parent's relationship with her child, for example, might sell to a family or parenting magazine.

❖ *Look for an uncommon element.* A "my first dog" story will sell to a pet magazine if there's something unique about the dog, its owner, or their relationship. For example, I once accepted an article about a canine escape artist who chewed through a chain-link fence to get free. Readers appreciated the conflicts faced by this writer: Could she confine the dog without harming it, or would she have to give up this "problem pet"? Your resolution must be appropriate to the audience; had the author sent the dog to the pound, we wouldn't have bought the article.

❖ *Look for an unusual perspective.* A story about "my first trip to the supermarket" would be as exciting as Valium—unless, perhaps, the supermarket is in a foreign country and you can't speak the language, read the labels, or guess the prices. The "outsider looking in" approach can often be the key to a sale. But there's a catch: You must know enough about the "inside" to understand what makes your perspective unique and different. I once sold an article to a dog-show magazine on my reactions to what seemed, to me, the bizarre world of dog shows. To do so, however, I had to know enough about the sport to understand what would come across as humor, and what would come across as ignorance, or even stupidity.

❖ *Look for smaller "first experiences."* Instead of writing about your first dog, write about a specific event. How about the first time your dog became ill, or your first obedience class or dog show, or the first time you took your dog camping? Such stories can focus on areas where others may not have shared your experience, or where they may be able to learn from it.

Experience as Expertise

While some publications seek writers with "expert" credentials, others seek writers who have the kind of expertise that only comes through personal experience. While an expert can provide useful technical information on a topic, it is the writer like you—the one who has "lived it"—who can bring that information to life for the reader. Your experience brings you special credentials, including:

❖ *Understanding.* You may have a better understanding of the needs and interests of a reader than an "expert." You know what aspects of a topic need to be communicated to a reader like yourself, and how to get that information across. For example, while a veterinarian might write about the pathology of a particular pet disease, you can share what it means to be the owner of a pet who has that disease.

❖ *Communication.* Writers serve as translators between the technical experts and the audience. The veterinarian you interview might tell you about histolytes and platelets, but it's up to you to convert this information into terms the reader understands, and to frame it in a meaningful context.

❖ *Balance.* An article written by a leading authority on a particular subject may be brilliant, but one-sided. Writers, however, can examine controversies from all sides, following up leads and exploring various angles by interviewing experts with differing opinions or in different fields.

❖ *Tact.* Some experts simply aren't good at communicating with a "lay" audience, yet don't take kindly to having their work edited. However, writing clearly and working with editors to polish and refine your prose is part of a writer's job. If you take that job seriously, editors will find you a joy to work with and will come back to you again and again, letting *you* handle the difficulties of talking to experts!

❖ *Flexibility.* Experts, by definition, are specialists. An editor won't be able to ask an expert on dermatology for an article on obedience training. You, on the other hand, may be able to cover both subjects (and you'll be able to find experts to interview for the information you lack).

Using Experiences Wisely

Once you've decided *what* experiences to write about, you must decide *how*. While there are many ways to use experiences effectively, these four are perhaps the most common:

❖ *As a framework to support the factual information you wish to present.* Use your experience as a vehicle to "carry" the information you've gathered from expert sources, such as interviews or research. Show how that information affected, or is reflected in, your own experience. Use phrases like "we learned" or "we discovered," instead of "experts say."

❖ *As anecdotal material to illustrate the factual information.* Use the factual information as your framework, and highlight each point with an experiential example or illustration.

❖ *As an anecdotal lead and conclusion.* Some articles begin and end with an experiential anecdote (e.g., "When Mary's house burned down, she had no idea her troubles were just beginning . . ."). The body of the article, however, may be purely factual, with few personal details.

❖ *As a sidebar.* You may prefer to restrict your article to the facts, and use the personal experience as a sidebar to illustrate and enhance those facts.

Another approach is to use the factual material as a sidebar to the personal story. (This works particularly well when your facts can be presented as a list.)

Getting the "I" Out

A while back, I read an article about canoeing in the Alaskan wilderness. Here's an example (paraphrased) of the author's account:

> After a long day of paddling my canoe through the twisting waterways of the Someplaceorother Delta, I was glad to see the sandbar on which we would camp that night. The sun was setting, and the colors on the river reminded me of a blurred watercolor painting. I watched as a skein of geese descended toward some marsh I could not see, their wild cries reminding me just how far I had traveled from the land of cell phones and car alarms. As I steered my canoe to the shore, I marveled yet again at the magnificence of this wilderness. . . .

What's wrong with this picture? Nothing, if it's intended as a self-portrait. If it's intended as a portrait of a location, however, it fails miserably. Why? Because instead of seeing what the author sees, I am forced to watch the author "seeing" it; instead of being allowed to react to the images presented, I am forced to share the author's reactions. The author can't get out of the way.

First-person narration isn't necessarily a bad thing. In many articles, it is desirable and appropriate. In many others, however, it is out of place. One of the things an author needs to know is when to be part of the scene—and when to remain invisible, framing the picture without entering it.

When writing an interview, for example, watch out for references to "self" (I sat, I asked, I listened, I turned on my tape recorder, etc.). If you want to describe a location, don't write, "I settled myself in one of Mary's overstuffed chairs" when you could just as easily write that *Mary* settled herself in one of those chairs. Another way to remove yourself from the scene is to choose verbs that do not require an indirect object. For example, instead of saying "Mary proudly showed me her award," choose another verb: "Mary proudly displayed her award."

When writing about exotic destinations, you want to convince the reader that you actually climbed that mountain, slept in that hotel, eaten in that bistro. One way to sharpen your focus is to remove "interpretive" or "reactive" statements from your article. If you liked the food in a particular restaurant, don't say you *thought* it was good; just say it *was* good. If the hotel bed was lumpy, don't say it *felt* lumpy, just say it had lumps. Try to avoid telling the reader how you felt or reacted; instead, paint a vivid picture of the experience to evoke a reaction in the reader. Watch out, as well, for "me" phrases—"they told me, it seemed to me, he showed me," etc. Whenever possible, use verbs that can act alone. For example, instead of writing, "The locals told me that a ghost walks those halls at night," try, "Locals say . . ." or, "Locals claim . . ."

Because self-help and how-to articles often result from personal experience, it is tempting to include hefty doses of that experience in the article. Such an article really isn't about you, though; it's about the reader. Thus, the easiest way to "stay out of it" is to consciously shift from a "me" perspective to a "you" perspective. Whenever you find yourself writing in the first person, consider whether you could express the same information in another way, such as second person ("you can do this"), third person ("many people do this"), or directive ("do this!"). Each of these approaches shifts the viewpoint of the article away from the narrator and toward the reader.

Writing, by its nature, is an "invisible" occupation. Consequently, it can be tempting to try to stand for a moment in the spotlight of our own creations. The bottom line is simple, however: The less editors see of *you*, the more they'll want to see of your *work.*

Some Final Tips

Besides asking yourself how the experience relates to the reader, you must also ask yourself how *you* relate to the experience. For example:

❖ *You must be "over" the experience.* If you don't know how the story ends, you're not in a position to write about it. If an event is painful, you need sufficient time to have gained some "closure" before you're ready to write about it for others.

❖ *You must offer a solution.* Readers want to know how to change things, fix things, make things better. If you see no hope for improvement, write about something else.

❖ *You must offer the reader an attainable goal.* If your idea of the perfect vacation is to climb Mt. Everest, that's fine, but the experience may find a rather limited readership. Offer readers an experience they can attain, and offer specific steps to help them attain it.

❖ *You must offer evidence that your suggestions work.* If, for example, you're describing "Ten Ways to Get Your Novel Published," you must have published a novel!

Whatever approach you choose, it's the "been there, done that" element of your story that will bring your article to life. Editors hunger for articles that combine useful, factual information with the warm, human touch of experience. Turning your story of "what I did" into an article on "how you can do it" is one of the best ways to save your material from the slush pile.

PART III

FINDING THE RIGHT MARKETS

CHAPTER 13

Exploring the Markets

I have to smile at listings in the *Writer's Market* that advise would-be contributors to read "five or six back issues." Yeah, right! I don't know about you, but I can hardly keep up with my own subscriptions, let alone the sample copies I tend to order in abundance. At an average of $4 per back issue, the cost of ordering more than one issue of anything would be prohibitive.

At the same time, those publications make an important point: If you don't know anything about a publication, you'll find it difficult to target an appropriate article or query to its editor. How can you understand the needs and interests of the audience? How can you match the style or tone of the publication? How can you catch the editor's eye? How can you avoid submitting an article on a topic that was covered two months ago?

Fortunately, there are ways to explore the marketplace without breaking your bank account. Consider the following possibilities:

❖ *Start with magazines you know.* What magazines do you read on a regular basis? Chances are these publications reflect your interests and expertise. Look carefully at the craft, hobby, or special-interest publications on your list. Most likely, you buy these because you pursue that interest, and could develop an article for that market. A word of warning, however: If your subscriptions or purchases include only the top "general interest" or "women's" magazines, and you're a beginning writer, this advice does not apply.

❖ *Visit newsstands.* Bookstores like Borders and Barnes & Noble offer newsstands featuring magazines you won't find in your local grocery store. You will also find publications that aren't listed in *Writer's Market*. If you can find a "real" newsstand—a store devoted entirely to magazines—so much the better! (Many of these carry international magazines as well as domestic publications.) Newsstands are treasuries of new markets, and the issues usually cost less than special-ordered "back issues" (for which you may have to pay shipping as well as the cover price of the magazine itself).

❖ *Check* Writer's Market *for free back issues.* I usually rank the listings in *Writer's Market* by price: free, postage, less than $3, and more than $3. I send for the free copies first, then those that ask only for postage costs. Then I order those that cost less than $3, and finally, after careful consideration, I order the most interesting of the rest. When ordering a back issue, save yourself a SASE and ask for the writer's guidelines at the same time.

❖ *Ask for writer's guidelines of any publication that interests you.* Some guidelines are excellent, giving you far more information than a *Writer's Market* entry. Others, however, mention nothing about rates or rights or other vital information. Others are simply vague: "We want sharp, well-written articles that will appeal to our audience." (Well, *duh!*)

❖ *Research guidelines online.* Many magazines are now posting their guidelines on their Web sites. This makes life easier for everyone: You don't have to send a SASE and wait six weeks for a response, and they don't have to print hundreds of copies of their guidelines. When you locate a magazine's Web site, look for such options as "guidelines," "submissions," "tips for writers," "write for us," or "contact us." Also, explore some of the guideline databases online (you'll find a list of these at *www.writing-world.com/links/guidelines.shtml*). You can search databases not only for a specific magazine, but also for certain categories, such as subject area or payment rate.

❖ *Research back issues online.* Many publications post article archives on their Web sites. These archives are often the "best of the best," which will give you an idea of what excites the editor. Read a few articles carefully to get an idea of their tone, style, content, and depth of coverage. Are they written for a technical audience or for the layperson? Do they offer overviews of a subject, or in-depth reporting? Do the authors have special credentials, or can "anyone" write for this publication?

❖ *Look for back-issue indices.* Even if a magazine doesn't publish articles online, it may offer an index of back issues. This will give you an opportunity to determine what has already been published in the past year or two, so you don't waste time with an article that duplicates past effort. (Once a magazine has covered a particular topic, it will usually wait two or three years before considering that topic again, even if your article offers a different angle or focus.) Many magazines also publish an annual index that you can obtain with a SASE.

❖ *Look for new markets online.* Newsstands like Newsdirectory.com offer links to magazines not only in the United States but also throughout the world. You can search these listings topically or geographically, and you're certain to find publications you have never heard of. Also, explore each publication's Web site for additional magazines; for example, while *Writer's Market* lists two or three pet magazines belonging to "Fancy Publications," that particular company actually produces more than thirty monthly and annual publications.

❖ *Subscribe to a marketing newsletter.* Several excellent e-mail newsletters offer market information, including:

- *WritersWeekly—www.writersweekly.com*
- *Writing for Dollars—www.writingfordollars.com*
- *Writing World—www.writing-world.com*
- *WorldWide Freelance Writer—www.worldwidefreelance.com* (focuses on non-U.S. markets)
- *Gila Queen—http://GilaQueen.us*
- FreelanceWriting.com Magazine Guidelines Database—*www.free-lancewriting.com/guidelines/pages*
- *Freelancing for Money—http://freelancing4money.com* (a weekly newsletter available for a paid subscription)
- *WriteMarketsReport—www.writersweekly.com* (a monthly e-mail newsletter available for a paid subscription)

Whenever you see a listing for an interesting publication, follow up for more information: visit the Web site, write for guidelines, or request a sample copy.

Many of these resources also cover online markets; the rules for evaluating a market and breaking in are generally the same.

Finding Free (and Almost Free) Magazines

Here are some ways to locate sample copies without paying a penny:

❖ *Visit the library.* Most libraries have extensive magazine sections, and you can either browse back issues there or check them out and take them home. Many libraries can also order other publications for you through interlibrary loan, though this can take a while.

❖ *Check your library for a "magazine exchange" corner.* Many libraries allow patrons to drop off unwanted magazines, and on some days you can find lots of interesting titles. Check the dates, though: A pile of magazines from the 1980s is not going to help you determine what a publication is covering today. (Some libraries are also catching on to this resource; our local library charges 20¢ apiece for used magazines.)

❖ *Check the magazines at your doctor's office.* If you find something that interests you, ask the receptionist if you can "borrow" it, or bring along unwanted magazines of your own to exchange. (Some offices also offer free publications; I've found free regional parenting magazines at women's clinics.)

✦ *Keep your eyes open when visiting bookstores or specialty stores.* I sold an article to a country crafts/collectibles magazine I found in a craft boutique. I've also found interesting tabloids in the Barnes & Noble foyer.

✦ *Respond to "free issue" offers.* Many publications send out offers for a free issue. I recently received offers for a free issue of Britain's *Realm* magazine and *Scottish Life*, and needless to say, I said "yes" to both. If you don't want the subscription, just write "cancel" on the invoice. Many magazine sites have free trial offers on their Web sites. You can also find free trial offers through general magazine subscriptions and "free stuff" Web sites. These sites often offer free three-month trials. You'll have to provide your credit card; you then have ninety days to cancel the subscription before your card is charged. Here are some sites that offer ninety-day trials:

  • ABaseforMagazines.com—*www.abaseformagazines.com*
  • ArkRoyal.com—*www.100-free-magazines.com/list-all.html*
  • Free2Try—*www.free2try.com*
  • FreeSiteX—*www.freesitex.com/magazine.html*
  • FreeWell.com—*www.freewell.com/free/Free_Magazines*
  • MagsNow.com—*www.magsnow.com/?source=overture*

✦ *Sign up for free subscriptions through Half.com.* If you buy more than $15 in merchandise on the used-book site Half.com (*www.half.ebay.com*), you'll be presented with an offer for a free trial period for a variety of magazines.

✦ *Use airline mileage credits to pay for subscriptions.* If you accumulate only small amounts of frequent flyer miles (not enough to add up to free travel), find out if your program offers magazine subscriptions. It's a great way to use up a few hundred miles here and there.

✦ *Ask magazines if they provide a free sample copy.* Approach them as if you were a would-be subscriber, not a writer!

✦ *Exchange magazines with friends, relatives, and writing buddies.*

✦ *Ask for gift subscriptions to magazines that interest you.*

✦ *Ask to be added to a publication's "complimentary copy list" once you've begun to write for them (even if you've sold them just a single article).*

Finally, don't hesitate to order a sample copy of a publication that looks like a valuable market. There is no substitute for actually being able to see a publication before you write for it—so if you have to pay, do so. Remember that the cost of sample copies is a business expense, and can be deducted from your taxes.

Evaluating a Market: Is It Right for You?

Finding publications is only half the battle. Once you've found a publication, how can you determine whether it is a good market for you? What clues can you glean from a magazine about how to "break in"? When I review a new magazine, I am looking for answers to four sets of questions: demographic, technical, personal, and business.

Demographic Questions

"Demographics" simply means "audience": What type of person will be reading your article? The answers can be found not only in a magazine's editorial pages, but also in its advertisements and illustrations. For example, are all the photos of glamorous models, or does the magazine include "real" people as well? A close look at any publication should give you valuable clues about the following audience characteristics:

❖ *Gender.* Is the magazine aimed at men or women, or both (e.g., a fitness magazine with tips for both sexes)? Or would it appeal to a certain type of person regardless of gender (e.g., *Smithsonian* or *National Geographic*)?

❖ *Age.* Most magazines target specific age brackets, such as "youth," "twenty-something," "adult" (twenty to forty), or "senior." Sometimes that target audience is obvious from the magazine's title or content (e.g., *Seventeen*); sometimes it can be determined from the advertising (e.g., *Reader's Digest*). Don't try to pitch an article on "planning for early retirement" to a magazine that targets twenty-something executives!

❖ *Ethnicity.* Except for publications that actively target a specific ethnic group, most "general interest" magazines still focus on the interests of white readers. Some, however, are actively trying to break that pattern by seeking more diverse, multicultural material (particularly around the holidays).

❖ *Economic bracket.* How much is a reader prepared to spend? This can make a big difference when writing about, say, collecting exotic antiques or taking a dream vacation. Advertising is a good way to determine the audience's economic bracket. I recently reviewed two "country lifestyle" magazines that looked similar on the surface; one, however, contained ads for expensive antique reproductions, while the other contained ads for collectible frog figurines.

❖ *Religion.* In some markets, religion is unimportant; in others, it is. Religion may be implied rather than overtly stated. For example, while *Reader's Digest* is not a "religious" publication, it clearly assumes that most of its readers prefer material with a conservative Christian slant. Other publications may assume just the opposite, and reject material that even hints of a "traditional religious" viewpoint. Within the religious marketplace itself, one must also be aware of the differences between (and even within) denominations.

✤ *Geography.* Does a magazine focus on city pleasures or country delights? Does it focus on "active" recreational activities available in the region, or on more intellectual pursuits? Even a magazine that is distributed nationwide may have a larger readership in certain parts of the country, and will be most interested in articles that will appeal to readers from that region.

✤ *Lifestyle.* "Lifestyle" issues (including interests, activities, and values) cut across all other demographic groups. Two magazines that target "young women," for example, may have very different audiences: Does a woman's magazine assume its readers spend most of their time in the office, the kitchen, or the bedroom? Values are also important: You won't find an article on "how to cheat without getting caught" in *Woman's Day*, and you don't find many pieces on "fidelity" in *Cosmopolitan*.

These demographics can give you a picture of your target audience. But is that all you need to know? Just because a magazine targets young, upwardly mobile professional women doesn't mean you necessarily want to write for it. You may also wish to consider:

Technical Issues

The technical aspects of a magazine include:

✤ *Physical presentation.* What is the quality of the publication? Is it printed on glossy paper or newsprint? Are articles laid out effectively, or are they pasted up by hand (and not too carefully)? Are the photos clear, or do they look like someone's Polaroids? A magazine that is poorly produced usually has a low budget—and that means it probably doesn't pay well.

✤ *Writing style.* Magazines that appear to address similar audiences may, in fact, have very different editorial styles. Read one or two articles carefully. Do you like the way they are written? Can you imagine writing in a similar style? If the style seems jarring to you, or violates your personal sense of taste, you may not be able to write for that magazine, simply because your style is at odds with the tastes of the editor.

✤ *Depth.* How much research, investigation, or analysis is involved in a magazine's content? Don't bite off more than you can chew: If you don't have the connections to get the right interviews, or the experience to provide the level of analysis required, or the budget to visit five different locations to "get the story," don't sweat it. That doesn't mean you'll never penetrate that market; it simply means you may not be able to break in today. Meanwhile, there are hundreds of other publications that can offer the experience and clips you need.

Personal Issues

When I evaluate a magazine, I want to know not only what it says to a reader, but what it says to me. For example:

✤ *Does the magazine interest me?* Often, when I try to study a magazine, I find my eyes glazing. I find myself skipping and scanning rather than actually reading. The material doesn't "hook" me, and I may reach the end of the magazine without finishing a single article. Can I write for a publication whose editorial focus doesn't keep my attention? Probably not. The editor's tastes and mine clearly do not mesh, and I doubt I could change my own style to match the editor's preferences.

✤ *Does the magazine share my values?* A writer is also an individual, with his or her own set of "demographics"—values, ethics, background, etc. The question of ethics is no different in the business of writing than in any other business: Are you willing to compromise what you believe in just to earn a paycheck? If the answer is "no," don't struggle to write for markets you don't agree with, or to produce articles that violate your own values or viewpoint.

✤ *How will my material be presented?* If a magazine suffers from poor presentation—bad editing, poor design, or inappropriate illustrations—your work may look worse when it comes out than when you sent it in. No one stops to ask whether the bad grammar was the result of poor editing; most people will assume it was the fault of the writer. And while no one will blame you for a bad paste-up job, it certainly won't present your work in the best light. If my review of a magazine indicates that "clips" from this publication would do me more harm than good, I'll try elsewhere.

✤ *Would I be proud to be featured in this publication?* I recently examined a woman's magazine that looked like a potential market for a health article I wanted to write. A look at the magazine, however, gave me second thoughts. Most of the advertisements seemed to be for sexual aids (and most of the articles focused on this topic as well). While I might have sold the article, did I really want to show off "clips" of my work displayed next to a four-color, half-page ad for vibrators? If a magazine makes you uncomfortable, angry, or disgusted, move on. (You'll feel happier about where your checks are coming from.)

Obviously, many of these decisions are highly individual—which is why I clustered them under "personal." Your decisions might be different from mine, and neither of us would be "right" or "wrong." The point is that as writers, we are individuals, and our tastes and values are as important as those of the markets we are trying to penetrate. If those tastes and values don't mesh, we could waste a lot of time trying to break into markets that will never be right for us—and "success" may not taste so sweet. By learning to evaluate markets across a broad spectrum of issues, however, you'll find those that not only you can work with but also thrive with, and to which you'll become a valued contributor.

Business Issues

There is no excuse for a writer to get the acceptance stage and only then ask, "Oh, by the way, what do you pay?" If you haven't already obtained this information, you're hardly in a position to start negotiating your way out of a bad contract. Plus, you've probably invested a lot of energy and emotion into getting that article out the door and accepted—and if you suddenly discover that the publication pays poorly or demands all rights, it's hard to "pull out" once you've so nearly achieved your goal. It's also unprofessional. Before you approach a market, therefore, find out the following:

❖ *What does the magazine pay?* Most magazines post a range of payment rates in their guidelines. Some pay flat rates (e.g., $200 per feature); others pay by the word (e.g., 5–10¢), others pay by the printed column or page.

Some magazines that pay by the word will pay for the actual number of words you submit, regardless of editing. Others pay only for the number of words they actually *publish.* Thus, if you submitted a 1,500-word article, but the editor trims 500 words, you'd only be paid for 1,000 words. Find out which basis of payment is being used. If you're asked to submit an invoice, you should generally submit it for the number of words in your original article. If you're given a contract, it should indicate the actual payment, not just a per-word figure.

Magazines that pay by the printed column or page generally can't give you a precise payment rate until the article is typeset and laid out. Generally, such magazines pay "on publication," since they can't calculate a payment until the magazine is ready to go to press. However, an editor will generally be able to give you an estimate based on the length of your article.

Magazines that pay a flat rate generally have a range of rates, depending on the difficulty of the article (e.g., the amount of research required), the expertise of the writer, and how much work the editor has to do to whip the article into shape.

Keep in mind that almost all quoted rates are (a) ranges and (b) represent the *lowest* range that a publication is willing to pay. Many publications offer higher rates to regular contributors, and to "better" contributors (i.e., folks who do lots of research and whose work needs little or no editing). I generally don't recommend asking about "higher pay" on your *first* submission to a publication, but if you expect to be working for that publication on an ongoing basis, or if the editor comes back to you with new assignments, *start asking how to get a higher rate.* Even if you don't get one, it never hurts to ask.

✿ *Does the magazine pay extra for sidebars or illustrations?* Editors often try to get away with paying a flat rate for text and photos. However, if you don't provide photos, the editor will have to pay another photographer extra, so there is no reason why *you* shouldn't receive that compensation. If you're submitting photos, find out what a magazine pays for artwork alone (e.g., $25 per black-and-white photo). Find out how much it pays for articles (e.g., 10¢ per word. Then, discuss getting paid for *each* item rather than a "package deal." Offer the editor a "deal," if you wish ($15 per photo instead of $25, for example) but try not to let the editor pay you the same amount for "text and photos" as he would for text alone. (Keep in mind too that cover photos generally pay very handsomely; if you're a good enough photographer to get a cover, you should be paid for it.)

Some publications won't pay extra for sidebars, but others will. Generally, sidebars "pay" if you're being paid by the word. They're a good way to sneak in extra material over and above your "assigned" word count. Thus, if you're writing a 2,000-word article that pays 10¢ per word, add on a 500-word sidebar and see if you can't boost the payment up another $50!

✿ *When does the publication pay?* There are two basic payment schedules: "on acceptance" and "on publication." A publication that pays "on acceptance" will pay you once the article has been received, approved, accepted, and contracted for, regardless of when it is actually published. A publication that pays "on publication" will pay you only after the material has been published—and not necessarily *soon* after!

Most markets that pay "on acceptance" will pay you only after you have signed a contract. Here's where it can get a bit sticky: Some editors can be *very* slow to actually send that contract! One of my regular markets, for example, takes as long as a month to send out a contract—and another month to pay after the contract has been signed and returned. Thus, "pays on acceptance" in this case means "pays sixty days after acceptance."

✿ *What rights does the publication require?* This question can be even more important than the question of payment, because it determines what you can do with your material in the future. Print publications tend to be far more demanding of rights than electronic publications. The reason is simple: A print publication can easily (and inexpensively) launch a Web site, and might have a future need for electronic rights. An electronic publication, however, cannot easily launch a *print* publication—so it is not likely to need your print rights. Thus, while most e-pubs *don't* ask for any form of print rights, most print publications *do* ask for some (or all) electronic rights. (See chapter 21 for more information on rights.)

Don't make the mistake of thinking these issues don't matter when you're starting out, or that you "don't care" what a publication pays or what rights it asks for, as long as you can get your name in print. It *does* matter, and you'd be surprised at how often you want to resell an article you thought you'd only use once. Professionalism is something you need to practice from the very beginning, because the only person who can protect you in the marketplace is *yourself.*

Should You Write for Free?

Many writers believe that one's career must begin with nonpaying markets, and that this is the best way to build clips (and experience). If, however, you have a choice between offering your material to a paying or a nonpaying market, there is no logical reason to choose the latter. The nonpaying market will always be there if you fail to sell the piece, but it need not be your first choice, or even your second or third.

Does this mean you should never write for free? Not at all! There are many excellent reasons to do so; "being new" just isn't one of them. Here are some better reasons:

- *For fun.* Sometimes you may want to write something for the sheer enjoyment of it. (After all, someone must be writing all those variations on "how to bathe your cat" circulating on the Internet!)
- *To support a cause.* Instead of contributing money to organizations or issues you believe in, you may choose to donate your writing skills. Your "payment" is often simply the knowledge that you're increasing awareness of an important issue.
- *To help a favorite organization.* You may enjoy contributing to your company, community, or church newsletter. Be careful, however: Once such organizations realize that you can write, you may be flooded with requests for more freebies.
- *To enhance your career.* Many unpaid markets can be career-builders—including your own Web site. Writing FAQs for your site (or others), contributing articles to professional newsletters, or writing for professional journals can be good ways to build your reputation.
- *To help and inform others.* At a certain point in their careers, many writ-

ers feel an urge to "give back" some of what they have learned. You may decide to write about "what you know" in order to help others in your field, or to repay the mentoring you received at one time.

Just as there are good reasons to write for free, there are also bad ones:

✦ *To see your name in print.* Don't assume that the only way to get a byline is to give your work away. If you send your work to a paying market, you might get a double thrill: Seeing your name in print, *and* seeing it on a paycheck.

✦ *To find out if you're "good enough" to get published.* Nonpaying markets are not a good place to test your abilities. Many such markets are stuck with whatever they can get, which means they often don't have the luxury of "rejecting" mediocre writing.

✦ *To polish your skills.* Nonpaying markets don't appreciate being dumping grounds for bad writing. If you want to polish your work, do so through a class or critique group.

✦ *Loyalty.* It can be difficult to abandon an editor who accepted your work when no one else would. However, recipients of such loyalty can sometimes misuse it. Don't let such a relationship interfere with your ability to move on.

Writing for free is an option, never a necessity. The bottom line is that if your writing isn't good (and you know it), your energies are best spent seeking ways to improve it. If your writing *is* good, and you believe in it, don't sell yourself short by failing to sell yourself at all!

CHAPTER 14

Writing for Special-Interest Publications

*N*o matter what your favorite activity or hobby, chances are that a magazine covers it. Special-interest publications make up the largest segment of the consumer-magazine marketplace. These magazines are always hungry for new writers, including beginners without a portfolio of clips. One reason is that many such publications don't pay high rates; another is the need for fresh voices and perspectives.

"But I'm Not an Expert"

You don't have to be an expert in your favorite hobby or sport to write for such magazines. Experts often don't have time to write articles about their hobbies, which is why many articles are written by enthusiasts. If you care about your subject, that enthusiasm will show in your writing, and will also engage the enthusiasm of others. As an enthusiast:

❖ You know what interests you about a hobby or activity, so you'll be able to develop topics that interest readers like you.
❖ You know the types of questions someone like yourself would ask.
❖ You know what it's like to start with the basics, and are thus qualified to help other beginners.
❖ You know the "language" of your specialty, whether it's the lingo of fly-fishing or the jargon of the dog-show circuit.
❖ You have a desire to learn more about the subject, and can share your knowledge with others.
❖ You have experience in the subject area.

These qualities appeal to an editor as much as a sheaf of clips. Non-writing credentials should be an important part of your pitch to a special-interest publication: "I've been quilting for ten years," or, "I've owned

Norwegian elkhounds for most of my life." Even a pitch like, "I've always been fascinated by . . ." can get an editor's attention.

Understanding the Markets

Writer's Market offers a host of special-interest categories, from "animals" to "travel." Each of these offers an equally large number of subtopics (under sports, for example, you'll find subcategories ranging from archery to wrestling). It's not enough just to find a magazine that covers your subject, however. Your research also needs to determine three additional things:

❖ The magazine's degree of specialization. A magazine titled *Pet World*, for example, is aimed at a very different audience from one titled *Turtle Monthly*.

❖ The expertise of the audience. Does the magazine target beginners, experts, or both? If a magazine is designed for experienced gardeners, for example, you won't break in with "My First Vegetable Patch."

❖ The mindset of the audience. Two magazines on the same subject may take very different approaches. For example, a dog magazine aimed at breeders won't want an article on adopting mixed-breed puppies, while one for pet owners won't be interested in an article on breeding and whelping.

Magazine "Must-Haves"

"But what can I possibly say about pets/fly-fishing/paper airplanes?" The answer lies in determining a magazine's basic article mix: the "must-have" categories that appear in every issue. To determine this, you'll need to review the contents of several back issues (or search for an index of back issues online). You'll find that most special-interest publications publish a mix of articles that fit into the following topic areas:

❖ *How-To Articles.* Most special-interest publications are by nature "how-to" magazines: how to repair a car, plant a garden, raise a puppy, catch a fish, knit a sweater. Within that general subject context, how-to articles focus on specific issues: how to do something new or unusual, solve a common problem, develop a skill, or increase one's enjoyment. Don't pitch an article on "how to raise a puppy," for example; pitch a new, effective way to housetrain your puppy or teach it basic obedience commands at home.

❖ *Health and Safety.* Many special interest areas (especially sports and recreation) involve health and safety issues, such as how to avoid hazards, how to handle emergencies, or how to improve one's health by participating in an activity. Pet magazines always need this type of article (including nutrition and first-aid pieces). You don't have to be a doctor or a vet to write these pieces; many markets prefer such articles from the perspective of a typical "participant."

- *Equipment.* What are the tools of your trade? Consider an article on how to choose the right equipment, how to determine the tools needed for a specific project, how to take care of your equipment, how to build equipment (e.g., how to build a doghouse), or how to use equipment safely. (This information can often be built into a how-to piece.)

- *Seasonal.* Some activities are seasonal by nature; others have seasonal concerns. If you love gardening, for example, think about the off-seasons: "How to add fall color to your garden," or "how to winterize your fruit trees." Pet magazines look for articles on summer travel and winter safety; consider, for example, seasonal-related health issues (such as flea control). Remember that seasonal articles should be submitted four to six months in advance.

- *Destination.* With a little imagination, you can incorporate a "destination" slant into many types of articles. For a fishing publication, you might cover the "Top Ten Trout Streams of Northern Idaho." For a dog magazine, you might cover "The Ten Most Dog-Friendly Parks in the U.S." For a quilt magazine, consider covering an event like "Pennsylvania's Annual Amish Quilt Spectacular."

- *Historical Background.* Though these are low on some publications' lists, a well-written background piece can still be a good way to break in. One way to make this type of article work is to combine it with "how-to" tips: For example, a look at the "history of English pewter" could include tips on collecting or care.

- *Personal Profiles.* Some magazines love these; others don't. Personal profiles usually highlight someone whose work has achieved recognition, who has made a significant contribution to the field, or who is doing something unique or unusual. For example, a woodcarving magazine might be interested in someone whose work has just been featured in the Smithsonian, or an immigrant who has "carved out" a new life with a rare "old-country" skill. Some magazines prefer to combine "who" with "how," such as an embroidery publication that ran an article on a lace maker who used traditional techniques, along with information on how the reader could apply those skills.

- *Current Issues and Controversies.* If your interest area is affected by controversy or legislation, a magazine may be interested in such coverage. A pet magazine, for example, may be interested in anti-breed legislation or other laws restricting pets. Be sure the issue has more than regional appeal, however; does it establish a precedent that could affect enthusiasts nationwide? Also, be aware that controversies may be time sensitive; will this issue still be "hot" by the time it sees print six months from now?

❖ *Personal Experiences.* These are generally lowest on a magazine's "must-have" list. Most publications publish, at most, one per issue—yet most are flooded with such articles. While it's not impossible to sell such a piece, you must be sure your experience is truly unique and avoids the "been there, done that" factor. "My First Puppy," for example, will be of no interest to readers who have already had several "new puppy" experiences. (Chapter 12 discusses writing personal-experience articles.)

To improve your chances of a sale, look for categories that overlap. For example, consider a "how-to" article that includes a discussion of the equipment needed for the project, or a seasonal article that covers health hazards. Editors are always happy to find an article that fills two "must-have" slots at once.

Take a look at your favorite activity, sport, hobby, or love. Ask yourself what you could say about that topic that would fit into one of the categories listed above. Be creative, and don't limit yourself to the things you already know. Instead, consider what questions you might ask, what you'd like to learn more about. If you have questions, chances are that a magazine's readers will have those questions as well—and by answering them, you could turn your curiosity into a sale.

Should You Specialize or Generalize?

Q: In planning to write magazine articles, should I stick to a specific topic to start, or pursue several at once? I have several areas of knowledge and interest (dogs, nutrition, natural health, Christianity, theatre), and I'm not sure where to begin. Each area seems to require such in-depth expertise that I'm afraid if I don't specialize, I will not be deep enough in each "industry" to do it justice. But I don't want to limit myself or my writing opportunities to one area.

A: Writing for special-interest magazines doesn't mean one must necessarily write *only* in that specialty. There are benefits to sticking to one's areas of expertise—and there are benefits to expanding beyond a specific area. Each option has advantages and disadvantages. Understanding them can help you make the best choice for your writing career.

Specialization

Specialization makes life easier: It allows you to focus on developing your writing skills without having to learn new subjects at the same time. Specialization can help you build a reputation as an "expert" in a particular field. It also helps you build on previous work as you "climb" from lower-paying markets to better, more prestigious publications. As long as you remain within your specialty, your clips will always be relevant, and editors may be familiar with your reputation even before you begin to work for them. (Keep in mind, however, that in some fields publications won't accept work from writers who write for their "competitors.")

For specialization to benefit you, you must choose a field that allows for such upward mobility—i.e., a field that has a large selection of markets. The first question you need to ask, therefore, is, "What is the market for my field?"

If the writer who asked this question chose to specialize in "dogs," for example, she would find her opportunities somewhat limited. There are only three high-paying dog publications (meaning they pay $300 or more for feature articles): *Dog Fancy, Dog World,* and *The American Kennel Club Gazette. Dog Fancy* and *Dog World* are both owned by Fancy Publications; *Dog Fancy* focuses on dogs as pets, while *Dog World* has traditionally focused more on breeding and exhibiting, as does *The AKC Gazette.* Other publications include *The Bark* and *Dog and Kennel;* moving down the ladder, one will find several smaller, more specialized markets, such as *Gun Dog* or *Mushing.* Each publication has specific requirements, and most won't accept reprints from other publications. The market for dog articles outside these publications is even more limited.

On the other hand, the market for "nutrition and natural health" is considerably larger. Besides a number of high-paying health and nutrition magazines, the market includes general-interest publications that regularly feature articles on some aspect of health or nutrition. A writer focusing on this area of expertise might be able to place articles in general women's magazines, parenting publications, fitness magazines, and even more specialized publications, such as sports and recreation magazines. This particular writer could also combine her interest in health with her interest in Christianity, and sell health and nutrition pieces to Christian family magazines. (She might even sell a piece on natural health care for dogs!)

The question, therefore, is not so much whether to specialize, but whether the area in which you wish to specialize offers a wide selection of market opportunities, or only a handful of relevant publications. If you choose the right topic, your area of expertise can help you open many doors; if you choose too narrow a topic, however, you're likely to find yourself "stuck."

Generalization

The benefits of generalization are simple: The more subjects you can write about, the more marketing opportunities you'll find. If you're serious about making a living as a freelance writer, generalization can help ensure that you never run out of markets to write for.

Generalization can be a good approach if you don't want your name associated exclusively with one type of writing. Perhaps you enjoy writing about dogs—but you don't want to be known as a "pet writer," because you fear this label will hinder your ability to convince editors that you can write about other topics. You may also want to build a more diverse portfolio of clips that will reflect your ability to handle a wide range of topics.

Generalization requires good writing and research skills. When you generalize, you won't always be able to rely on your own expertise; instead, you'll have to learn how to ask the right questions about subjects you know very little about. Since you're not an "expert," you'll need to find good interview sources. Most of all, you need a willingness to take chances, to say "yes" to assignments that may take you out of your comfort zone.

While this can mean more work, it also means that once editors can rely on you to turn in a well-researched article on any topic, your range of assignments is likely to increase. Nor do you have to worry about the limitations of your "niche": The market is wide open. You may write for a dog magazine today, a health magazine tomorrow, and a Christian publication next week.

Generalization also has its downside, however. When you generalize, you lose the advantages associated with being recognized as an "expert" on a particular subject. Some publications prefer writers with subject-specific credentials, whether those credentials are experiential or in the form of a list of publishing credits in the field.

There is no "one-size-fits-all" answer to the specialize/generalize question. Either decision will open some doors and close others (or at least make them more difficult to enter). In this area, as in many others, the answer is, "It depends." Never let anyone tell you that you "should" choose one road or the other. You must make this decision for yourself, based on your interests, your goals, and most of all, on what will bring you happiness and fulfillment as a writer.

CHAPTER 15

Writing for Newspapers

by Sue Fagalde Lick

Newspapers are often overlooked as a market for freelance writing. Any writer who is serious about writing, selling, and communicating with readers, however, needs to consider newspapers as a possible market. Here's why:

- Most people read at least one newspaper regularly. In her book, *Freelancing for Newspapers*, Jill Dick notes that there are two thousand daily newspapers and seventy-five hundred weeklies in the United States, and that an estimated eight out of ten American adults read a newspaper every day. That doesn't begin to address non-U.S. newspapers and the special-interest newspapers.

- Newspapers come out more often, and there are more of them, so they require more editorial copy. On daily and weekly general-interest papers, staff writers cover most of the news and many of the main features. The Associated Press and other wire services provide national and world news. But there are many stories staff and wire services don't cover. That's where freelancers come in. Smaller newspapers generally have smaller staffs. How do they survive? Freelance writers!

- Special-interest papers are everywhere. Go out for coffee, and you'll probably see a rack with entertainment newspapers and papers put out by special-interest groups: gays, Hispanics, coffee aficionados, and others. Go to the library, and you'll find even more papers. Visit an antiques store, and you'll find newspapers on antiques. You may receive a church newspaper. Most religions have local, regional, or national publications. And don't overlook newspapers aimed at particular industries, such as *High Technology Careers* and *Computer Systems News*.

How Do Magazine and Newspaper Writing Differ?

Many of the tasks involved in writing for newspapers and magazines are the same. But there are differences.

Mission

The mission of many general-interest newspapers is to be the place where readers look for news and features about their area. Remember the slogan "location, location, location?" For newspapers, it's "local, local, local." If there's no local angle, they don't want it, no matter how fascinating or well-written it might be.

Other papers center on a particular group or interest. The newspaper put out by the Catholic Archdiocese of Chicago may run some wire stories about Catholics outside of Chicago, but it won't run anything about Methodists. I used to work for a Hispanic newspaper called *El Observador*. The editors made it very clear that if the subject did not have a connection to the Hispanic community, it would not get in.

News Peg

Timeliness is often a factor in getting an article published. Editors may ask, "Why write this story now?" A feature on an artist is more likely to sell if it can be tied to an upcoming gallery show. A school program may be deemed worthy of a feature if it's new, being considered for budget cuts, or has just won an award. Stories that can be tied to holidays or anniversaries of major events have a greater chance of getting published. Stories on chocolate sell for Valentine's Day; religious stories abound as Easter approaches; skiing sells in January.

Timing

While most magazines are put together at least two months in advance, news and sports sections of the newspaper are written, edited, and laid out less than twenty-four hours before publication. Feature sections are generally planned a little farther ahead. This may be a week or, in the case of holidays or other special events, a month or two. For weekly newspapers, get your queries in at least two weeks ahead; for monthlies, allow at least two months.

Pay

Many newspapers pay less than magazines; I have seen local papers that pay less than a penny a word. Five to ten cents a word is more common for community weeklies. This won't make you rich, but can help if you need experience and clips. The big dailies generally pay at least $100 for columns and opinion pieces, more for feature articles. The *Chicago Tribune* pays up to $500 for travel pieces. The *Christian Science Monitor* starts at $200 an article.

Writing Style

Most of us have heard of the "inverted pyramid," the traditional style for newspaper stories. In essence, you start with the most important information and work your way down to the least important, so that if the story is too long, the editor can cut it off from the bottom.

If you wind up writing news stories, you will still need to employ the inverted pyramid. However, most freelancers write features (non-news stories) in which the style is similar to that of magazine articles.

Words versus Inches

Some editors will ask for a number of inches rather than words. You can ask them how many words or characters that includes, or you can figure it out for yourself. With a ruler, measure an inch of type. Count how many lines there are per inch (most commonly six), then determine the average number of words per line and multiply that by the number of lines. Do this for several column inches to come up with an approximate number of words per inch. (Some editors use the number of characters to determine column inches. Some computer programs will give you the character count as well as the word count.)

Finding Freelance Opportunities

Now the fun begins. Gather up all the newspapers you can. Set aside the ones that don't interest you, because you don't want to write for a publication you don't want to read (trust me). Now start reading. Go for the big paper first. If you don't subscribe, buy one at a newsstand or go to the library. You should go there anyway; you'll find newspapers you didn't know existed.

You're looking for two things: sections with articles written by freelancers, and subjects that seem to fit the paper's mission but aren't being covered. For example, if your daily newspaper rarely touches on your neighborhood, maybe they need a freelance correspondent. If nobody seems to be covering your city council or school board—or your local churches, artists, or sports teams—there's an opening for you.

For most dailies, the feature sections are the most likely freelance outlets. These include sections on food, home and garden, travel, entertainment, arts and books, religion, and business. There is also generally a "living" or "community" or "our town" section. There may be a special Sunday magazine or feature section. Big papers covering large areas may have weekly sections focusing on particular neighborhoods. Read these sections especially carefully. Look at the bylines at the end of stories. Are the writers identified as staff writers or are they listed as "special writers," or some other category that lets you know they're not part of the staff? Those are freelancers.

Look in the paper for names of the editors. Each section usually has a separate editor. You can often find them on the editorial page. Sometimes newspapers run lists of editors in the front or local section. If you can't find the name in the paper, don't give up. Many papers have Web pages now. One way to find a newspaper online is to search for its title through a search engine; another is to use one of the many newspaper list sites (see *www.writing-world.com/links/magazines.shtml*). Worst case, make a phone call and ask for the name of the editor. Make sure you also ask how to spell it.

The same method goes for specialty newspapers. Read the paper, look at the masthead, look at the bylines, look for blurbs in the paper asking for submissions. Or, call the newspaper. Ask if they use freelancers and whom you should address material to. The worst they can say is no.

Types of Newspaper Articles

* Personality profiles are standard in newspapers as well as in magazines. You interview someone of interest to the local community or special-interest group because of what he does or his history. A profile may include research from other sources, including interviews of friends, family, and co-workers.

* Human-interest stories. Jill Dick writes: "Study the 'ordinary' stories told by 'ordinary' folk and you'll soon realize . . . that there is a huge depth of warm-hearted humanity that doesn't make the front pages and is often obscured by the constant daily dirge of evil, death, and destruction man everywhere wreaks on his fellow man. Thousands of 'good' stories are just waiting to be told—and when they are, they touch many hearts."

* Business features are big in local papers, partially because they help sell advertising, but they also let the community know what's available. Look for a news peg, such as a business just opening, selling a new product, moving to a new location, or planning to close. Maybe your favorite lunch place is about to start serving dinner. Time for a story.

* Reviews come in many forms. The bigger newspapers may run reviews of books, plays, concerts, restaurants, movies, or computer software. See who writes these stories. If you don't see reviews of the thing you're interested in, query and see if they'll let you do it. It helps to have some sample reviews ready. Try one just for fun.

* Roundup pieces are popular with many editors. I have written every-

thing from where to get a good hamburger to a survey of services offered by local funeral parlors. Travel sections may run "best cruises" or "best playgrounds to take the kids." The food section might do a roundup of local wineries or culinary schools or places to eat pancakes. In the spring, papers look at wedding-related topics, such as the most romantic places to get married or the best places to hold a reception. These are not terribly creative to write, but they are lucrative, and editors love them.

❖ How-to articles help a reader solve a problem, whether it's how to build a birdhouse, how to clean the scuzz off the bathroom floor, or how to buy a digital camera. You don't always need to be an expert on the subject. You just need to interview someone who is.

❖ Opinion pieces allow you to sound off on a subject. These usually go on what is called the op-ed page, meaning it's the page opposite the one with the staff editorials. Dailies sometimes run a whole opinion section on Sundays. These are rarely just one writer's opinion with nothing to back it up. Such pieces require some research or knowledge, a bit like the essays you wrote in high school or college.

❖ Personal-experience articles appear in many feature sections, especially travel stories. Here, using the first person, you tell of something that happened to you, using sights, sounds, smells, colors, moods, and physical description to help the reader experience what you have experienced. A news peg would help you get it published. Your experience as a temporary Santa Claus would be perfect at Christmas.

❖ Investigative articles delve into a subject, ferreting out information that has not been made public before. Often they unmask government wrongdoing, expose a health issue, or look into a crime or disaster. These require a lot of work, using multiple sources to go below the surface, and tell a complete story. Usually staff writers do the investigative pieces, but it is possible in some markets for freelancers to contribute. Pacific News Service, a syndicate that specializes in investigative journalism, comes to mind.

❖ News stories are covered by staff and wire services on large newspapers, but community newspapers may hire stringers to cover city council, school board, special events, and other news. The term "stringer" comes from the old custom of using a string to measure the number of inches a writer should get paid for. In many cases, you'll have less than twenty-four hours to attend the event and write the story. It's a rush, but it is exciting to be there when news is happening and present it to the readers right away.

Do You Need Pictures?

Editors also look for "art"—the newspaper name for photos, drawings, maps, charts, or any other entity that can dress up the page. Without art, your story may wind up below a less-interesting story that has pictures. Larger newspapers usually use their own photographers exclusively, but if you're an artist or a good photographer and can provide your own art, you have a huge advantage when writing for small- and medium-size publications. Not only will editors be more inclined to buy your stories, but you will get paid extra for every photo or drawing.

Newspapers originally used only black and white, but many now use color (particularly since photos may also be used online). More and more papers are also switching to digital photography, using photos that go directly into the computer system. However, some papers still use film and darkrooms, so check first before sending photos.

Querying a Newspaper

Magazine and newspaper queries are virtually identical, so check chapter 17 for details on how to write a query. The real difference lies in how (and when) editors *respond*. Newspapers are notorious for the nonresponse. This also applies to e-mail queries.

The delay at newspapers stems from the extreme workload most editors have. If your manuscript arrives while editors are on deadline, they probably won't see it for a few days. By then, it might be completely buried in an avalanche of letters, faxes, and e-mails. This means you need to be gently proactive. Wait two weeks, then contact the editor.

Follow up with a short note, telephone, or e-mail the editor. (Do not drop in at the office. Chances are the editor will be busy or not even there, and he will definitely resent the intrusion.) A mailed note runs the risk of getting buried along with your query. A telephone call is direct and often works best. In fact, it could open up a dialogue that leads to other things. However, do not expect the editor to remember your piece or know where it is. Chances are he'll have to make a note and get back to you.

Before you call, find out when the best times are to talk to the editor. Usually that's shortly after the paper comes out. For a daily morning newspaper, editors start work in the afternoons, finishing late at night. The best time to call is early in the afternoon before the deadline crunch hits. For an afternoon paper, reverse the process. For a weekly paper, or for weekly sections of a daily paper, call the editor after the paper goes to press. Sometimes this is the day before publication, sometimes it's several days before. Check the paper for deadlines—if not for copy, then for advertising. Assume that's when the editor will not want to talk to you.

However you approach it, be polite. Don't whine and don't be critical. Try to be as helpful as possible. "I mailed you a story idea about warts on June 3, and I was wondering if you had decided yet." If the editor says no, don't throw a hissy fit and don't push. Say, "Thank you very much for your time." You might calmly ask what you might have done to make the idea more likely to be used, but don't press too hard.

If you still want to write for that newspaper, come up with another idea and get it out there. You might even mention it while you're calling about the first idea. Chances are the editor will ask for something in writing, but it wouldn't hurt to say, "Would you be interested in a story on . . . the new bakery that makes donuts without holes?"

Simultaneous Submissions

While it's never a good idea to send the same stories to *competing* newspapers (newspapers that serve the same market area), you can often sell the same story to *noncompeting* papers. For example, newspapers published in Florida and New York may have completely different readers and contents. Papers that are owned by the same newspaper chain, such as Gannett or Knight-Ridder, often share stories. This can be a boon for the writer if his or her story is chosen not only by the local daily or weekly but also by its counterparts in the same company.

You're safe offering the same story to noncompeting newspapers as long it fits their mission in some way. Travel articles are particular adaptable to multiple sales because they're not tied as tightly to the local area. Columns, how-to's, roundup pieces, and features of national or international interest can be submitted to multiple publications. It is also possible to reslant the same idea, taking the same basic facts and connecting them with a local person, place, or organization. If the newspapers are in completely different markets, I wouldn't mention your multiple queries, unless you have actually sold the article. Then you may need to give credit to the paper where it appears first.

Ideally you want to sell only first serial rights or one-time rights (see chapter 21 for more information). That means you can resell the article again and again. Some publications will buy the rights to a story for a specified time (e.g., six months or a year). Some papers will insist on buying all rights. Then you need to decide whether or not the pay and exposure are worth it. Sometimes they are. Often on smaller papers, the editor doesn't have a firm policy about rights and will let you keep them just for the asking. Know what you're selling. Get it in writing. If the editor doesn't send you a contract, send the editor a letter or e-mail describing the assignment and your understanding as to the rights you're licensing. Also find out if the paper is going to publish your story online as well as in print. Ask how long it will be there, and whether you will be paid extra for this.

Writing the Article

We've all heard the saying "Just the facts, ma'am," but if all we provided were facts, our stories would be so dry no one would want to read them. Like fishermen, we need to hook the readers and keep them reading.

Consider your audience when writing your article. Are they young, old, or a mixture of all ages? Are they college educated or not educated at all? Do they live in the city or the country? Are they rich, poor, or somewhere in between? Are they likely to know anything about your topic, or must everything be explained?

Keep in mind that you're writing for the masses—for your family, your friends, for doctors, lawyers, construction workers, and the teenager who bags your groceries. We don't need to "write down," but we do need to make sure no one is left behind. That means we cannot assume they know things most people would not know.

Writing the Lead

Start with a headline, probably the same one you used for your query. This is your theme and your story should never stray too far from it. Then move into your "lead paragraph." In a news story, the duty of the lead is to tell us in a nutshell what happened. An easy way to develop this paragraph is to think of what you would tell your spouse or your best friend if you had to quickly summarize what this is all about. You rush in excited about what you just found out and you say: "A boat just ran aground at Lost Creek. That's the third one this month. Luckily nobody was hurt this time" (true story that happened practically outside my door); or "Wow, did you know that whales eat 500 tons of food a day?"

In a news lead, it is important to spill the most important facts immediately, moving down the story to the more minor elements. For a feature story, you have more leeway. You definitely need to get to the point soon, preferably by the third paragraph, but you can start in many ways, such as:

❖ A *startling statistic:* "Last year, 10,000 junior high school boys brought knives to school despite increased security and the installation of metal detectors." (I made that up.)
❖ A *scene:* "Jake Barnes leaned against a bale of hay, tore off a wad of chewing tobacco with his teeth, and stared out at the sun setting over the cow pasture, ignoring the government officials standing by the road talking about running a freeway right through his ranch. 'Ah, I heard all that before,' Jake said."
❖ A *quote:* "Up until I adopted Charlie, I didn't think I ever wanted kids. One look at his big blue eyes changed everything."
❖ An *anecdote:* "Peter will never forget the day he caught his first fish. . . ."

After the Lead

The lead should draw the reader in. It should also set you on the path for the rest of your article. Your second or third paragraph grounds the reader by explaining what's going on. "Now that I have your attention, here's what I want to talk about." The statistics on kids and weapons would probably lead to a paragraph introducing the main topic of your article: how school security programs have failed. The ranch scene might move into a paragraph about how this time it was really happening and the new freeway would disrupt a whole way of life for Jake and others like him. The adoption quote could move into a story on unusual adoptions. The fishing story could move into a feature on Peter's work as a commercial fisherman or his crusade to save his favorite fishing spot.

With any luck, from here, the story should flow from one point to another, until you have covered each topic in your outline. In a feature, you will want to complete the circle by harking back to the quote, the scene, the statistic, that your article opened with.

You may want to close with information on how to contact the person you're profiling, places to find more information, where to make reservations, etc. Check the newspaper to see how they format this information and plug in the names, phone numbers, e-mail addresses, or Web sites.

Quote Correctly

Newspaper articles use lots of quotes from people or printed sources. Number one rule: Write it the way they say it. It's okay to correct minor grammar errors, but in general you need to transmit exactly what your source said. If quotes are too jumbled or awkward, paraphrase them, giving the source credit for the thought if not the exact words. Don't take things out of context just to make your story work better. Our job is to write the truth, even when it's clumsy.

With written material, you need to give credit to the source. Newspaper articles don't come with footnotes, so incorporate the attribution into your prose, as in, "Roger Wilco wrote on December 12 in the *New York Times . . .*" or, "Webster's *New Collegiate Dictionary* says. . . ." Try not to use a lot of quotes from written material (and if you must, paraphrase as much as possible rather than quoting directly.) Getting someone to actually say it is much more convincing.

Beware of making statements without attribution. If you say the sun rises in the east and sets in the west, no one will challenge you. If you say man is going to land on Jupiter by 2010, you'd better have a source to back it up. Anything odd, startling, or that claims to be the best, biggest, first, last, or only, needs to be attributed to a source.

Stylistic Considerations

Newspapers have their own style, which can be very different from that of magazine feature articles. Here are some stylistic issues to consider:

- *Point of view.* Most newspaper articles are written in the third person, which means you never say "I" (except in columns and opinion pieces) or "you" (except in how-to's). Look at the paper for which you're writing to see how they handle voice, and do likewise.

- *Tense.* Most newspaper articles are written in past tense. Use "said" instead of "says," "walked" instead of "walk," etc.

- *Newspaper style.* Most newspapers use the *Associated Press Style Book* for issues of capitalization, hyphenation, dates, times, addresses, and other picky matters. If you don't have the book, at least study the newspaper you're writing for to see if you can detect trends. For example, do they write out "percent" or use %? Are dates "Dec. 25," "December 25," or "25 December"? These styles enable editors to present more information in less space, and they'll bless you if they don't have to change every date in your story.

- *Short paragraphs.* Looking at a newspaper page, you can see that the stories are set up in columns, usually five or six to a page. When forced into that format, a single sentence can take up several lines and a paragraph can go on forever. Therefore, newspaper articles are generally written in short paragraphs. A good rule is that if you've gotten to the fourth line, it's time to think about ending that paragraph and moving on to another.

- *Active language.* Active verbs are much more engaging than passive verbs and generally take up less space. Instead of "The whale was fed dead fish every morning," say "Chuck fed the whale dead fish every morning." Or better, "Every morning, Chuck dumped 10 gallons of raw fish into the pool."

- *Include sensory details.* Tell us how it looked, how it felt, how it smelled, how it sounded. Put us in the place and take us beyond mere quotes and facts.

- *Look for questions the editor might have.* Did you define any abbreviations, acronyms, technical terms or foreign words? Have you double-checked sources' names and titles? If there is something you're not sure of, do some more research or take it out. You should be able to back up every word.

Once You Have Your Foot in the Door . . .

Although the world is full of would-be writers, most editors have trouble finding writers who can actually deliver a well-written article on time. If you're one of them, you will soon be golden to those editors.

Follow-up is the key to getting more assignments and becoming a regular contributor. If an editor says no to your first idea, come up with another one. If an editor says yes to your first idea, come up with another one. Once you've sold a couple of articles to the same editor, there's nothing wrong with typing up several ideas and trying to get assignments for them all at once. Over time, you'll develop the kind of relationship where you can secure a go-ahead with a quick phone call or e-mail, and where the editor calls you with assignments. Once you make the list of proven freelancers, the editor will turn to you again and again.

If you really want to write for a particular newspaper, the worst thing you can do is disappear. If they encourage you in any way to try again, do it before your name fades from memory.

PART IV

QUERIES AND SUBMISSIONS

CHAPTER 16

The Submission Process

*D*eveloping a marketable article is only half a writer's battle. The other half is getting that article *to* the market. In this process, the *appearance* of professionalism can often count as much or more as your actual credentials; even if you've never published a single article, you can impress editors simply by providing a professional-looking submission package.

Your first step is to review a publication's guidelines. These will tell you what type of material a publication is looking for, the preferred word count, whether the publication prefers (or requires) queries or complete manuscripts, the payment rates and rights required, and whom to contact. The guidelines may also specify a publication's "response time"—which basically indicates the amount of time a writer is expected to wait before following up on a submission. Needless to say, you will demonstrate your professionalism best by following these guidelines to the letter!

Whom to Contact

While the *Writer's Market* provides a good overview of a magazine's requirements, these listings can often be out of date, particularly with respect to contact information. Before you submit, therefore, I recommend checking an online source; many publications post guidelines on their Web sites, or make them available by e-mail. The "contact us" section of the Web site will usually list the appropriate editorial contacts (including their e-mail addresses).

Generally, a publication's guidelines will specify where you should send submissions. If you're not sure, you can also check the masthead of a publication (either in print or online). Generally, you will be asked to send material to a publication's *managing editor*, who usually makes the initial decision to accept or reject an article. If there is no managing editor, you should send material either to an *associate editor* or to the *editor*.

For a publication with lots of departments, you'll generally send submissions to a *features editor* or *articles editor*. Or, you may have to send a piece to a specific *department editor*, such as a health editor, food editor, fitness editor, etc. If you can't tell from a publication's guidelines or masthead, don't hesitate to call the publication and ask!

Don't send material to an assistant editor, editor-in-chief, or contributing editor. Assistant editors have no authority over decisions; they are often little more than glorified secretaries. An editor-in-chief generally supervises a group of publications, but doesn't handle the day-to-day management of any one publication. A contributing editor isn't even a staff person; this is a title given to a freelance writer who is a regular contributor (such as a columnist).

What to Send

A publication's guidelines should tell you what to submit—and what *not* to submit. In addition to the question of whether to send a query or completed manuscript, you may also be asked to send the following:

Clips

Many publications ask a writer to "query with clips." This strikes terror in the heart of unpublished writers, who fear they can't get published without clips—or get clips without being published.

Clips are simply photocopies of published articles. Note that "published" doesn't have to mean "paid"—clips from reputable nonpaying publications are often acceptable. (This does not include high school newspapers, company newsletters, church bulletins, or self-published materials.) If possible, try to match your clips to the subject matter of the market. If you don't have "relevant" clips, use those from your most prestigious publications.

If you've been published online, a printout of the article is acceptable as a clip. If you're sending a query by e-mail, you can also reference the URLs of online publications. (Never send a clip as an attachment, unless requested.)

Unless a publication specifically states that it won't work with unpublished writers, don't let a lack of clips discourage you from approaching a market. Even publications that ask for clips will often accept other forms of credentials in their stead (see chapter 17).

Résumé

While it's not very common, some publications ask a writer to "query with résumé." Generally, this means the publication is looking for writers with relevant credentials who can be offered assignments generated by the editor. Such a market is usually not open to beginning freelancers.

Publications List

Sooner or later, you'll need to develop a publications list to send with queries. This is simply a list of the articles you've published, where they appeared, and when. You can prepare it on your regular letterhead, or create a separate sheet with your name and address and other contact information centered at the top. I recommend starting your list as soon as you publish your first article; it's easier to keep track as you go along than to try to rummage through your records later to locate article titles and publication dates.

List publications chronologically, with the most recent first. Include the article title, the publication in which it appeared, and the date of publication. If an article appeared online, you can also include the URL if you wish. Your list will look something like this:

"My Latest Article," *Dog Fancy Magazine,* June 2003
"My Other Article," *Entrepreneur,* February 2003
"Another Great Article," *Newport News Gazette,* December 2002

Eventually (yes, it will happen!) your publications list will grow too long to fit on a single page. At that point, it's a good idea to break it up into several smaller lists, focusing on particular subject areas (e.g., garden publications, pet publications, etc.). It's still advisable to keep a master list for your own records. You may also wish to subdivide your list by *type* of publication—e.g., books, magazines, newspapers, online publications, etc. You may also wish to include a section for awards and prizes.

SASE or Return Postcard

Most publications still expect a writer to include either a self-addressed, stamped return envelope[1] with submissions. Some, however, prefer a return postcard with "check-off" options. Most use a postcard for rejections, and will send an acceptance letter on their own stationery. A return postcard should look something like this:

Date: _____
RE: Article Title

☐ We have received the article [or query] listed above and will give you a decision by (date) _____.
☐ We have decided to accept the article/query listed above, and will send you a formal letter of acceptance/contract shortly.
☐ Sorry, we can't use this material.
Editor's Name: _____

You can obtain prestamped postcards at the post office. If you expect to use only a few, it's easy enough to type each one individually. (If you have an electronic typewriter with a memory function, it's easy to store your postcard text and print the message automatically.) If you plan to send lots, however, I'd recommend having them printed at a copy shop.

Bio

Usually, you won't be asked for a bio until an article has been accepted. You don't need writing credentials to produce a bio. Instead, consider what you could say about your experience or expertise that relates to your article. For example, if you've written about hiking with dogs, your bio might read:

> LilyAnne Rizzetta has hiked with her dogs in nearly twenty-four state and national parks, including Yosemite, Yellowstone, and the Grand Canyon. Rizzetta is also an accomplished backpacker and "family camper." She lives (and writes) in Alpharetta, Georgia, where she shares her home with a husband, two cats and four Samoyeds. [You might also include a Web site URL or e-mail address, if desired, to conclude your bio.]

Most publications ask for a bio of between 50 and 100 words. The bio above is 50 words; as you can see, you can pack a fair amount of information into a short space!

Publicity Photo

Again, you usually won't be asked for a photo until an article is accepted. However, it's wise to prepare for this request in advance. While you can use a snapshot in a pinch, I recommend having a professional photo taken. Keep in mind that you're trying to create a professional image; a professional photo is part of your overall business package, like your letterhead.

A publicity photo can be formal (e.g., a headshot) or candid (a shot of you at your desk, for example). It can be color or black and white; I recommend color simply because it can be reproduced in black and white if desired. Make sure the photographer has experience with publicity photos. (I don't recommend using a mall or department-store photo salon.) Keep in mind that most photographers won't give you the negatives of your photo(s), so buy several prints. Then use a scanner to create electronic files and additional copies. In some cases, you may need to provide the photographer's name for copyright purposes.[2]

Simultaneous and Multiple Submissions

One source of controversy among writers is whether or not to send "simultaneous submissions" (or "simsubs"). This simply means sending the same query or manuscript to more than one publication at a time. Since a publication can take weeks or even months to make a decision, many writers feel that sending out simultaneous submissions is a way to bypass the delays that would ensue if one sent out a submission "sequentially."

The problem is, most publications do not like simsubs, and many refuse to accept them. This means one must either limit simsubs to publications that *do* accept them, or lie to those that don't. Either way, simsubs can put a writer in the awkward position of having to say "yes" to the *first* offer that comes in, since you can't ask an editor to wait until you hear from all the other publications you submitted to. Plus, if you *do* get multiple offers, you won't look good to all the editors that you have to refuse.

Editors don't object to simultaneous submissions just to be grouchy. Many don't assign articles until they can fit them into their publication schedule. If an author comes back and says, "Sorry, I sold it somewhere else," this often leaves the editor with a hole in an upcoming issue that must be filled some other way. Rather than putting yourself, or your editors, in this position, I recommend sending submissions to your top markets first; then, you only have to worry about accepting an offer from a less desirable market if your first choices say no.

"Multiple submissions" simply means sending more than one submission (usually an article) to an editor at the same time. Some publications don't accept multiple submissions; others place a limit on how many they will review.

Waiting for an Answer

Once you've sent a submission, the next step is to wait. Typical response times range from four to eight weeks, though some publications (particularly online publications) promise to respond in two weeks—and I've seen one magazine that lists a response time of six to eight *months*. Response times apply regardless of whether you submit by surface mail or e-mail.

A published response time is not a *promise* that an editor will get back to you within that time. It is simply the amount of time a publication expects you to wait before following up on your submission. In the past, editors tended to respond more quickly with rejections than with acceptances; unfortunately, more and more editors today simply don't bother sending out rejections at all. This has prompted many writers to cease sending SASEs, reasoning that there is no point in wasting postage; however, I still recommend including at least a postcard.

Once you've waited the appropriate length of time without a response, it's time to follow up. I recommend using the same medium (surface or e-mail) that you used for your original query or submission. Your follow-up should be very polite:

> Dear Editor,
>
> I am writing to inquire whether you received my query for an article on [TOPIC/TITLE], dated July 27? In case you did not receive it, I have enclosed another copy of the query. If you did receive it, could you let me know when you might be able to make a decision on the piece?
>
> Sincerely,
>
> Moira Allen

If you're following up on a query, include the original with your follow-up letter. If you're following up on an article, however, it's generally not considered acceptable to resend the manuscript (unless the editor asks you to resubmit it).

If you still don't receive a response after, say, another two weeks, follow up again. In this case, a polite phone call is acceptable. If you still don't get a firm response, or simply don't want to wait any longer, you have the option of withdrawing your submission from consideration. This is particularly important if you've submitted a manuscript; you don't want to send it somewhere else and *then* have the first editor decide to accept it. Just send a short letter to the editor, like this:

> Dear Editor,
>
> On July 27, I sent you a query [submission] regarding an article on XXXX [titled XXXX]. As ten weeks have passed without a response to my query or to my follow-ups (dated September 27 and October 10), I have decided to withdraw this article/query from consideration. [In the case of an article submission, I would add, "Please remove this article from your files."]
>
> Sincerely,
>
> Moira Allen

Writers often wonder whether editors are annoyed by follow-ups. The answer is no. As long as you remain professional, following up on a submission will not harm your chances of acceptance.

The Editor Responds . . .

You might imagine that there are only two possible responses to a submission: yes or no. Actually, each has several variations. A rejection, for example, might take the form of "no response," or a form letter, or a "checklist" letter on which the editor can check off one or more reasons for rejection (e.g., "something similar on file"), or a personal rejection. As I said in chapter 5, a personal rejection is good news: It means that you impressed an editor enough to merit a direct response. Sometimes a personal rejection will simply consist of a few words of encouragement ("liked your style, but unfortunately, this wasn't for us"); sometimes it will include feedback on your article; and sometimes (the best news of all), it will include an invitation to submit something else. If this happens, do so!

Acceptance also comes in a variety of flavors. The simplest is a straight "yes"—either "yes, send the article" in response to your query, or "yes, we'll take it" in response to a manuscript submission. This type of acceptance letter may include the terms of purchase—for example, the amount that will be paid, the rights to be transferred, and possibly a date of publication.

When you send a query, you may receive a direct assignment—a guarantee that the editor will buy your article. More often, however, the editor will say yes "on spec"—that is, "on speculation." This means the editor wants to look at your article, but won't commit to buying it sight unseen. This is usually the case when an editor has not worked with a writer before; often, your first two or three submissions to a publication will be "on spec," after which (if the editor likes your work) you may start receiving firm assignments.

In some cases, if an editor gives a firm assignment and then decides *not* to accept your article, the publication may offer you a "kill fee"—usually 20 to 30 percent of the amount that would have been paid for the article. (This is one reason editors usually won't give assignments to new writers.) Not all publications offer kill fees, however.

An editor may also respond to a query (or even an article submission) with a request for revisions. The editor may want a shorter piece, or a longer one, or a different focus. While it's perfectly appropriate for an editor to ask for changes to an article *proposal*, it's less acceptable to ask for drastic changes to a finished article without a fairly firm commitment to purchase the piece once those changes have been made. If an editor asks you to revise an article more than once (especially if the revisions are substantial) without committing to an acceptance, you may wish to think twice before doing the requested work.

Finally, an editor may reject your submission, but ask you to write something different. Such a request is evidence that you've made a strong first impression; often, it will come as a firm assignment, and may lead to others. In this case, don't feel bad that your original piece wasn't accepted; you have your foot in the door!

After the Acceptance

Once an editor has accepted your manuscript, the next step is usually the contract. Chapter 22 discusses the types of terms you're likely to see in a contract, and how to negotiate contracts. If you've reviewed a publication's guidelines, a contract should generally not come as a surprise; however, publications *can* change their terms without notice, so be sure to read *every* contract carefully (including contracts with publications you've already worked with).

While contracts can often be negotiated, this is *not* the time to ask for more money. For example, if you already know that a publication pays 5¢ a word, don't send in an article and then ask for 10¢. Not only is it not likely to happen, it's likely to prevent you from ever working for that publication again!

If a market pays on acceptance, you should receive a check within thirty days of signing and returning the contract. (This is a good reason to have a fax machine, which can shave a couple of weeks off the process!) If you don't get paid within a month, contact the editor and ask (politely) when you can expect payment. You may also be expected to send an invoice; chapter 23 covers issues of payment in more detail.

If the market pays on publication, you won't see a check until your article is actually printed. While this may not be long when dealing with newspapers or online publications, it can be months (or even years) before a magazine publishes your article. If possible, therefore, try to get the editor to set a firm publication date. Generally, pay-on-publication markets issue checks within thirty days of the *issue* date. This means that if a magazine is published in October, checks may not be issued until the end of November, so you may not see payment until sometime in December.

Your involvement with your article often doesn't end just because you've signed the contract and gotten your check. Often, editors simply file accepted articles until they come up for publication. *Then,* an editor may decide that your piece needs revision (e.g., "please cut 500 words"), and send it back to you for more work.

You may also be asked to review and correct "galley proofs." These are copies of your article exactly as it will appear in the magazine. At this point, you may discover that the editor has made some drastic changes to the piece, but unless those changes have resulted in actual inaccuracies, or have damaged the integrity of the article, there really isn't much you can do at this stage. (Your contract will probably state that the publication has the right to edit the article as it sees fit.) Your input on galleys is generally limited to correcting factual errors and typos.

If you feel that an article *must* be changed at this point, call the editor and discuss the issue. I once found that an article of mine had been significantly rewritten simply to shorten it. Rather than accept the butchered version, I quickly rewrote the piece to the desired length, and the editor was happy to run my new version. Not all editors are this accommodating, but it never hurts to ask!

Finally, once your piece has been published, you should receive at least one complimentary copy of the issue in which it appears. Most magazines will provide two (or more) if asked; I always ask for a second copy, so that I can use one for tear sheets and file the other "whole." Newspapers will also generally send a copy of the issue, or the section, in which your article appears, while electronic magazines will send you the URL where the article is located online.

Tracking Submissions

Once you start sending out queries and manuscripts, you need a way to keep track of them. Otherwise, it's easy to forget that an editor hasn't responded to your query for six months.

While you can buy "submission tracking software," I find that a simple spreadsheet works fine (see Figure 16.1). I create a spreadsheet that lists the date I submitted an article (or query), the title of the article, and the publication. A final column shows the response. (See the sample tracking spreadsheet, below.) I also include "amounts due," so that I know when a publication hasn't paid me yet.

Some writers like to include the amount the article sells for and the rights used. Others create tracking sheets for every article they write, recording which publications each piece has been submitted to, and the results of each submission. (See Figure 16.2 for an individual tracking sheet.)

Figure 16.1: Submission Tracking Sheet

ARTICLE TITLE	PUBLICATION	DATE	ACTION	DATE	ACTION	PAYMENT	DATE
Smithfield Hist. Reprint	VA Hist. Soc. Monthly	3/12/03	Submitted	4/15/03	Accepted	$25	7/15/03
Writing a Synopsis	Byline	4/15/03	Submitted	5/20/03	Accepted	$300	6/15/03
Victorian Collectables	Victorian Cottages Today	5/3/03	Queried	6/10/03	Assigned		
5 Garden Health Herbs	Natural Health	6/1/03	Submitted	7/2/03	Rejected		
Cat Folklore	Cat Fancy	6/20/03	Submitted	8/20/03	Followed up		
Victorian Collectibles	Victorian Cottages Today	7/10/03	Submitted	8/20/03	Accepted	$250	Pending
5 Garden Health Herbs	Herbal Health Monthly	7/10/03	Submitted	8/2/03	Rejected		
5 Garden Health Herbs	Herbs for Living	8/10/03	Submitted				
Love to Write Column	Writers Weekly	9/10/03	Submitted	9/30/03	Accepted	$150	Pending
Spring garden project	Windowboxes	9/15/03	Queried				
Natural Xmas décor	Downtown News	10/1/03	Queried	10/10/03	Assigned	$50	Pending

Figure 16.2: Individual Article Tracking Sheet

Article: Five Garden Herbs You Can Grow for Your Health

PUBLICATION	DATE	ACTION	DATE	ACTION	PAYMENT	DATE
Natural Health	7/2/03	Submitted	8/1/03	Rejected		
Herbal Health Monthly	8/2/03	Submitted	8/15/03	Rejected		
Herbs for Living	8/20/03	Submitted	9/15/03	Accepted	$150	Pending

Another way to track submissions is to keep a "pending correspondence" folder. Print a copy of every query or cover letter you send out (including e-mail submissions) and place it in this file. Keep the file organized by date. When you receive a response, pull the appropriate letter and attach it. If further information is needed (such as a contract), put the letter back in the pending folder; otherwise, transfer it to a "completed correspondence" file. Every so often, go through the "pending" file and follow up on those letters on which a response is overdue. At the end of the year, just file your "completed" folder in your permanent storage (i.e., take it out of your desk drawer and stuff it in a box in the closet).

Will an Editor Steal Your Ideas?

One concern of many new writers is that if they send a query or manuscript to an editor, the editor will simply "steal" their idea and write it up in-house, or pass it off to another writer. This fear keeps many writers from even sending their work out.

Authors are also often dismayed to pitch an idea, have it rejected, and then see a similar article in the publication a month or two later. Such an occurrence often convinces them that their idea has been "stolen." In reality, however, this proves just the opposite: Since magazines work three to six months or more in advance, if the article similar to yours appears that quickly, it had to have been on file long before yours even arrived.

What writers don't realize is how many similar ideas and manuscripts editors actually receive. If you've researched a publication and come up with the "perfect" topic, chances are that several other writers have done the same. For example, a pet magazine is going to receive lots of similar pieces on training, health care, seasonal material, and more. Nor do topics have to be identical to cancel each other out. If a travel magazine has recently accepted a piece on France, for example, it may not accept another for quite awhile, even if yours is completely different from the one on file.

I was once startled to see what I thought was an article of mine under another byline. What had happened in this case, though, was that the other author had used the same *sources* I had used, thus producing an almost identical article! (The magazine had a new editor, who didn't know my article was already on file.) This can happen when writers rely on the Internet for research; two writers researching the same topic are likely to find the same sites.

Keep in mind that neither ideas nor information are protected by copyright. All that is protected is your article itself. Thus, even if an editor *does* "steal" your idea, this is not a case of copyright infringement (though it's generally considered unethical).

I won't state categorically that idea theft *never* happens.[3] I will say, however, that such theft is extremely rare. Nor is it a reason to avoid the marketplace; your goal is to be published, and you won't be published if you're afraid to send your material to an editor.

NOTES

1. Many people wonder how to *pronounce* this term: Is it "sayse" or "S-A-S-E"? The answer is: pronounce it whichever way you want. In writing the term, however, it's generally considered correct to refer to "a SASE" rather than "an SASE" (which people often write when they pronounce the letters individually).

2. For more information on publicity photos, see "Your Publicity Photo," by Patricia Fry, at *www.writing-world.com/promotion/prphoto.shtml*.

3. See "How to Protect Yourself from Editorial Theft," by Kyle Looby, at *www.writing-world.com/rights/theft.shtml*

CHAPTER 17

How to Write a Successful Query[1]

A s editors become swamped with inappropriate submissions, more and more publications are closing their doors to unsolicited manuscripts. Thus, a query letter is often the only way to break into a market.

Queries benefit both editors and writers. Editors much prefer to review a one-page proposal than a ten-page manuscript, so queries usually spend less time in the slush pile. They also enable editors to determine whether you:

* Write effectively
* Have a well thought-out idea that fits the publication
* Have a grasp of grammar and spelling
* Have read the publication
* Have the necessary credentials to write the article
* Are a professional

Queries save *you* time by ensuring that you don't waste energy writing an article that won't be accepted. As I said in chapter 5, articles are often rejected for reasons that have nothing to do with quality. If an editor already has a similar piece on file, a query will help you find this out *before* you spend time on interviews and research. (It's also easier to *get* interviews when you have a solid assignment.)

Queries also give an editor a chance to provide feedback on your idea. The editor might prefer a longer article, or a shorter one, or a different approach. She may suggest sidebars or artwork. By finding out what the editor wants before you start writing, you won't have to revise the piece later.

A query may also result in assignments you didn't expect. If an editor is impressed by your query but can't use your idea, she may offer you a different assignment. This can be the beginning of a rewarding relationship!

Elements of a Query

A successful query generally includes five basic components: the hook, the pitch, the body, the credentials, and the close.

The Hook

Your very first line must grab an editor's attention. It must demonstrate that you can write effectively, and that you understand your market. There are several ways to approach the "hook":

❖ The problem/solution hook defines a problem or situation facing the publication's audience:

> For anyone who enjoys decorating with antique or delicate quilts, care is a vital concern. Most of us realize that we can't just pop Granny's handmade quilt into the washing machine or douse it with bleach, but what are the alternatives? How can we protect fine fabrics from further dirt and damage? ("Caring for Quilts: How to Preserve a Perishable Heirloom," sold to *Traditional Quiltworks*)

❖ The informative hook presents two or three lines of information (e.g., facts, statistics), followed by an explanation of how this applies to the target audience:

> Thanks to a translation glitch, Microsoft was forced to pull its entire Chinese edition of Windows 95 from the marketplace. Microsoft recovered—but that's the sort of mistake few small businesses can afford! ("How to Localize Your Web site," sold to *Entrepreneur's Home Office*)

❖ The question, which is often a problem/solution or informative hook phrased interrogatively, such as:

> Did you know. . . ?
> What would you do if. . . ?
> Have you ever wondered. . . ?

❖ The personal experience/anecdote hook is useful for a publication that uses more personal stories, or to establish a writer's credentials:

> Last summer, our beloved fifteen-year-old cat succumbed to cancer. Along the way, we learned a great deal about this disease and how it affects cats. ("Answers to Cancer," sold to *Cats* magazine)

✦ The attention-grabber is designed to make the reader sit up and take notice—hopefully long enough to read the rest of the story. This might be a good "hook" for a query about parachuting in Yosemite:

> As I fell from the top of Yosemite's El Capitan, I wondered if my life would truly flash before my eyes—or if I would stop screaming long enough to notice.

Hooks to Avoid

Certain hooks are guaranteed to speed a query to the rejection pile, including:

✦ *The personal introduction.* Never start with a line like, "Hi, my name is John, and I'd like to send you an article about . . ." Don't offer irrelevant information, such as, "I'm a housewife and mother of three lovely children."

✦ *The "suck-up" hook.* Don't tell editors you've been reading their publication for twenty years; prove it by offering an appropriate proposal.

✦ *The "bid for sympathy."* Don't tell an editor how much it would mean to you to be published in his publication—or that your children will starve if you don't sell an article!

✦ *The "I'm perfect for you" hook.* Don't inform the editor that your article is "perfect" for his readers. Never declare that your article is "wonderful" or "fascinating." Prove it.

✦ *The "I'm an amateur" hook.* Never announce that you haven't been published before, or that your article has already been rejected by twenty other magazines, or that your friends/writing teacher/mother suggested that you send your article to this magazine. Act professionally, even if you haven't sold a single article.

The Pitch

Once you have an editor's attention, move on to the pitch. Usually, this is your second paragraph, and its purpose is to explain exactly what you're offering. If possible, your pitch should include a working title for your article, a word count, and a brief summary. For example, the pitch that followed the "Microsoft" hook went like this:

> I'd like to offer you a 1,500-word article titled "Internationalizing Your Online Market." The article would discuss how small businesses can take advantage of "localizing" agents to tailor their products and market strategies to the international marketplace.

How can you estimate word count if you haven't written the article? Simple. Find out what the magazine's preferred length is, and use that as your guide. When you write the article, you'll know how long (or how short) it has to be, based on those guidelines and what you've already pitched.

The Body

The body of your query should be two to four paragraphs that present the details of your article. Be sure you can tell the editor *exactly* what the article will cover; if you don't know yet, go back to the outline and research stages!

A good way to present your topic is to break it into logical subtopics— e.g., the types of subheads that might appear in the finished piece. The longer the article, the more subtopics you can include (though it's usually not advisable to have more than four or five). For example, a 700-word article on cancer in pets might only cover "the ten warning signs of cancer," while a 2,000-word article on the same topic might cover "common types of cancer, warning signs, and current treatment options." A good way to determine whether you have the right number of subtopics is to divide your word count by the number of topics: a 2,000 word article with five subtopics gives you a budget of 400 words per topic.

Here's how I described the article on quilt care:

> The article covers techniques of hand-cleaning delicate quilts to avoid damaging fragile fabrics and prevent fading and staining. It discusses ways to remove spot stains (including blood spots and rust stains from needles and other metal contact). It also discusses ways to mend damaged quilts without destroying the integrity of an heirloom piece. Finally, it discusses the best ways to store or display quilts in order to preserve and protect them.

Some writers like to use block paragraphs; others like to use bullets—as I did in my "Cancer in Cats" proposal:

> My article will cover:
> - The types of cancers most common in cats (including mammary tumors and cancers of the mouth, lips, and gums—some of which are preventable!).
> - How to recognize the signs of cancer early (what is that lump?).
> - The symptoms and progression of various types of cancer (weight loss, diminished appetite, coughing and wheezing can all be signs of cancer).
> - The types of treatments available, pros and cons of different treatments, how treatments can affect a cat's life expectancy and quality of life, and how to find treatment (not every city has an animal cancer clinic).

There's no rule on the best style; choose a style that makes your query visually appealing and easy to read.

The Credentials

Editors want to know why you're the best person to write the article you've proposed. The most obvious type of credential is a list of relevant publications. Note that I said "relevant": if you're proposing an article on gardening, your articles on computer maintenance may not impress an editor. If you don't have relevant publications, cite your most prestigious publications, or cite the titles of the publications rather than the titles of the articles. For example, you could write, "My work has appeared in *Good Housekeeping, Maine Parenting,* and *USA Today,*" bypassing the question of exactly *what* you wrote. Cite only four or five publications, not your entire résumé. Never cite unpublished credits, except for articles that are accepted and "forthcoming." Never cite nonprofessional credits, including articles published in your office newsletter, letters to the editor, self-published materials (such as materials you've posted on your Web site), etc.

If you can't provide a list of publication credits, don't despair. Some editors prefer other types of credentials, including:

- ✤ *Education.* A degree or other educational background in the field you're proposing is always a good credential, as long as it can help establish you as an "expert."
- ✤ *Work experience.* One of my students planned to write an article on how to avoid building safety hazards into one's landscaping. His edge: He was a lawyer, and knew what advice to offer do-it-yourself landscapers.
- ✤ *Personal expertise.* Your hobbies may also give you the background you need to impress an editor. Another student sold her first article—a lovely piece on forget-me-nots—based entirely on her own gardening experience.
- ✤ *Personal experience.* Sometimes, simply having "been there, done that" is enough to make you an "expert." Just make sure your experience sets you apart from the crowd; offering a parenting article simply on the basis of "being a parent" may not be enough.
- ✤ *Interviews.* You can often sell an article on the basis of the experts you've chosen to interview. Just be sure you *can* get the interviews if you get the assignment!

List your credentials in your next-to-last or last paragraph:

As webmaster of *www.musicphotographer.com*, it has been my job to connect music writers and photographers with the markets that need their work. This is the only site devoted to music journalism on the Web. I'm also writing the first guide on the topic. Reviews for my last book, *The Van Halen Encyclopedia*, are available at Amazon.com. (C. Chilver's pitch to Inkspot for "How to Write for the Music Market")

The Close

Use the final paragraph to thank the editor for reviewing your proposal—and nudge the editor to respond. I usually include the amount of time in which I can deliver the article if it's accepted:

> I hope this topic interests you, and look forward to your response. If you would like to see the article, I can have it on your desk within two weeks of receiving your go-ahead. Thank you for your time!

Format

The presentation of your letter can be as important as your content. A traditional (paper) query should include the following elements:

❖ A *decent letterhead* that includes your name, address, and other contact information at the top (don't type it under your signature). (See chapter 2 for more tips on designing a letterhead.)

❖ A *business-style body*. If you aren't familiar with terms like "block" or "modified block," see the sample query at the end of this chapter. Always include a blank line between paragraphs, and don't indent more than five spaces.

❖ A *formal salutation*. Don't address the editor by first name unless you know her personally.

❖ *Clean, proofread copy*. Don't rely on your spellchecker; review your query yourself.

❖ *Quality paper*. Use at least 20-pound bond paper for queries. Some writers like to use neutral-toned parchment or linen bond (I do) on the theory that it will stand out. Don't use colors, however; pink or blue paper scream for rejection.

❖ A *SASE (self-addressed stamped envelope)*. This should be a #10 (business-size) envelope, folded in thirds. Be sure it includes adequate return postage. You *can* use a "return address label" for your SASE, but I recommend printing out a larger mailing label. If you're sending a query to another country, include at least one and preferably two international reply coupons (IRCs), unless you can obtain that country's postage. (Writers outside the United States can order U.S. postage from *www.stampsonline.com*; the current rate for a letter is 60¢ from the U.S. to Canada and Mexico, and 80¢ to other countries.)

Needless to say, e-mail queries break nearly all of the rules listed above; the next chapter explains how to send a professional-looking e-query.

Multiple-Pitch Queries

A multiple-pitch query offers an editor a selection of several article ideas at once, usually with a brief paragraph describing each. Such a query can often result in more than one assignment (though an editor will rarely accept *all* the topics on your list.) Since this type of query won't provide much detail about any topic, the editor needs to know that you're capable of fleshing out those topics in an article—so this is usually *not* appropriate for an editor you haven't already worked with. Here's a multiple-pitch query I submitted to Inkspot:

> Dear Debbie,
>
> We've talked about several articles recently, and I wanted to find out whether you're interested in any/all of these:
> 1. Author chats—are they useful? I've talked to several authors who have given "chats" online. This article would discuss whether an author chat is worthwhile and how to make the best of one.
> 2. Teaching writing classes offline. This piece would discuss how to teach a writing class in a "real world" environment.
> 3. Teaching writing classes online. The follow-up to the previous article would discuss how to teach a successful online writing class.
> 4. Giving a talk—this would fall under the category of "promotion." I'd like to include information on how to prepare for a talk, and also information on the technical side—how do you give a good presentation? What will your listeners want to hear? What about handouts, outlines, charts, etc.?

An editor may respond to a multiple-pitch query with a request to pitch one or more ideas in more detail. In this case, you won't need to worry about a "hook" or "credentials" (assuming the latter have been established); instead, concentrate on explaining exactly what will be covered and how the article will be organized.

Common Query Problems

Queries fail for many reasons; here are some of the more common:

❖ *You're trying to cram too much into an article.* An editor will immediately be able to tell if you have too many ideas, subtopics, subjects, etc., for the type and length of article you're proposing. For example, I often get queries offering to explain "how to become a writer" in 700 words or less! In this case, you'll need to focus in and define the central core of your article and write around *that*, and save the other stuff for other articles (or sidebars).

❖ *You have too little to say.* Perhaps the topic is interesting, but you haven't found enough information to fill up 2,000 words. In this case, the solution might be to offer a shorter feature or department piece.

❖ *You have questions but no answers.* Beware of a query that includes phrases like, "I'd like to explore whether," or, "I will find out if," etc. If you don't know what the answers to your article's questions are, don't query until you've found out.

Queries can be sent by surface mail, e-mail, or (less often) by fax if a publication's guidelines specify that this is acceptable. Rarely is it acceptable to call a magazine editor to query (although this is sometimes acceptable to newspaper editors; see chapter 15). Magazines work months in advance, so no idea is so "hot" that it needs an instant telephone response—and if an editor thinks you're trying to "auction" an idea by pitching it to multiple editors, you'll get an even less positive response.

Sending an editor an inappropriate idea may not make that bad an impression (unless it's so far off that it demonstrates that you're *completely* clueless as to the content of the publication). Sending an editor a poorly written, badly organized, misspelled query, however, will convince that editor immediately that he doesn't want to work with you—ever. Think of your query as a letter of introduction, your first (and perhaps only) opportunity to get your foot through that particular door. If you make a good impression, you're likely to be invited back (even if your original pitch is rejected). If you make a bad impression, you may find that door forever closed.

NOTE

1. Portions of this chapter appeared in my book, *The Writer's Guide to Queries, Pitches, and Proposals* (Allworth Press, 2001).

Figure 17.1: Sample Query

SUE FAGALDE LICK
281 SE XXth Ct.
South Beach, OR 97366
(541) 555-1234
suelick@casco.net
February 22, 200_

Judy Fleagle, editor
Oregon Coast
P.O. Box 1800
Florence, OR 97439-0130

Dear Ms. Fleagle:

If the fish aren't biting, charter boat skipper Shelley Morris will pop out the door of her cabin and tell a blond joke. A while later, if things are too quiet, she'll tell another one until her passengers are laughing too hard to care whether or not they catch any fish.

Morris, the only female skipper in Depoe Bay and one of the few on the Oregon coast, won a beauty pageant in her teens. In college, she set out to be a music teacher. But along the way, she had fallen in love with salt-water fishing. After graduation, she flew to Alaska with no job, just the name of a cousin who lived there and a dream of being a commercial fisherman. For several years, she fished for salmon and kenai, ran a crane pitching crabs, and made lifelong friends among the fishermen who teased her about her height—5'1"—but respected her ability.

The Washington native had often fished out of Depoe Bay, and that was where she headed at the end of her last Alaska contract. She fished on every commercial boat in the harbor before earning her 100-ton master's license and buying her own craft, the Lady Luck, at age twenty-seven. Now she runs fishing expeditions for Tradewinds Charters.

The work is wet, cold, and sometimes dangerous, especially negotiating the narrow opening of the Depoe Bay harbor—"The saying is there's those that have hit the rocks and those that will," Morris notes. She loves fish—"You can gross out the biggest burliest guy just by kissing the fish." And she loves her job—"I am so happy when I go to work in the morning. I mean how many people can say, 'I go fishing and I get paid for it.'"

I would like to write a feature about Shelley Morris for *Oregon Coast* magazine. She is interesting on many levels, as a woman who refuses to let gender, size, or looks keep her from the work she loves, as someone who has followed her dreams and made them come true, as an expert who shares her love of fishing with visitors to the Oregon Coast. Morris and her surroundings lend themselves to color photos, which I can provide or you can assign to your own photographers. She is relatively new on the scene, so she hasn't had much coverage in the press, and I would love to give you the story.

In twenty-six years as a professional writer and editor, I have published three nonfiction books, worked on several California and Oregon newspapers, and sold freelance articles to many publications, including *The Oregonian, San Jose Mercury News, Oregon Business, Family Motor Coaching, Bay Area Parent, Byline, Writer's Digest,* and others. I am now freelancing full-time from my home in South Beach.

Please let me know if this idea interests you.

Sincerely,
Sue Fagalde Lick

CHAPTER 18

E-mail Queries[1]

W hile some editors still prefer queries sent by surface mail, an increasing number prefer e-mail queries. Among electronic publications, that preference is almost universal. E-mail queries save the writer postage and time, and many editors answer them more quickly than paper queries.

E-mail queries also have disadvantages, however. A common complaint of editors is that many writers don't bother to prepare e-mail queries carefully. Many seem to be written in haste, with little consideration for style or presentation, and no proofreading. E-mail queries are often casual, chatty, even "cute"—qualities editors rarely find endearing.

Another problem editors frequently encounter is impatience. Just because your query may arrives within seconds, that doesn't mean the editor is going to read it immediately, let alone respond within minutes. Nothing annoys an editor so much as a writer who starts nagging for a response within days (or hours) of sending an e-mail query.

While e-mail queries contain many of the same elements as traditional "paper" queries, they also contain elements that need special attention. These include:

The Header

With e-mail, you can't impress an editor with nice paper or a snappy letterhead. Instead, you must rely on your header to provide vital information about yourself and your query. Be sure to put the right information in these sections:

- ❖ To: Address your query to the right person at the right address.
- ❖ From: You wouldn't sign a traditional query with a tagline like "Crystal Windsinger" or "Rafe Moondragon." If you use such a nickname to communicate online, however, it may slip into your query by mistake. Be

sure to set up a professional "personality" in your e-mail program that includes your real name and a professional-sounding e-mail address.

❖ Subject: Include the word "query" in your subject line, along with a brief (two- to three-word) description of your proposal—e.g., "Query: Cancer in Cats" or "Query: Writing for Pet Magazines." Never leave this line blank. Avoid cuteness or excessive informality; a subject line like, "May I have a moment of your time?" looks too much like "spam" and could cause your query to be deleted.

The Text

Many writers treat e-mail queries exactly like traditional queries. Many editors, however, find that they prefer shorter queries by e-mail; generally, the less an editor has to "scroll" to read your query, the better.

Thus, more writers are turning to brief, one- to three-paragraph e-mail queries, often skipping the hook and going straight to the pitch, followed by a single paragraph of description and closing with the writer's credentials. Here's a query I received from a regular contributor to Inkspot:

> Hello! I promised you a query, so here you go.
>
> "Flash What?" is an exploration of the (at-first-glance) strange medium of flash fiction. The article does not attempt to define the form, as flash is virtually indefinable, but it does identify the many styles of flash, and its many names. I cite such writers as Lila Guzman and Pamelyn Casto and their thoughts on the form. Following this, I segue into a general how-to segment on writing flash, listing three essential questions every flash writer must ask. Once that's finished, I close out with market listings and other resources.
>
> With flash fiction becoming more and more prevalent in the literary community, especially the online publishing world (whole zines are devoted to the medium), I think that this piece is very useful to Inkspot's many readers who double as fiction writers.
>
> "Flash What?" is about 1,220 words long. I'll be happy to send along the full piece if you're interested.
>
> Thanks! Looking forward to your reply.

Give serious thought to ways that you can "condense" your e-mail query into a compact summary. Just be sure it covers all the points you wish to make!

Credentials and Clips

You can list your credentials as you would in a traditional query—or provide URLs if you have clips posted on a Web site or in online publications. For example:

My work has been published in *The Writer, Writer's Digest,* and *Byline.* You can also view two of my recent articles on writing on the Writing-World.com Web site at *http://www.___* and *http://www.___*

Some editors will check your links, others won't. Never send clips as an attachment; if editors want to see clips, they'll ask you to send them by mail.

The Address Block

In a traditional query, your name and address and other contact information would go at the top of the page or be incorporated into your letterhead. In an e-mail query, it should go at the bottom, after your signature:

Sincerely,
Jane Smith
1042 Gloriana Lane
Whippet, IL 60606
(555) 123-4567
(555) 123-4568 (fax)
janesmith@isp.com

The Signature Block

You may also wish to use a "signature block" that lists your Web site and any special credentials you'd like to list. I don't recommend putting your contact information in a signature block, as it's easy to forget to use the right "sig" for different e-mails. I also don't recommend using cute sayings, dancing weasels, or anything else "nonprofessional" in a signature block used for queries and submissions.

Removing the Gibberish

Sending a query or manuscript electronically isn't simply a matter of copying your material from a word-processing file and pasting it into an e-mail. Too often, a straight cut-and-paste ends up looking like this:

%Please don,t reject my manuscript,@ the author cried, pleading ? but to no avail, as the editor wasn&t in the mood for such %gibberish@!

Even a single line of this can be annoying; having to wade through an entire query—or worse, a manuscript—like this is beyond the patience of most editors. Kind-hearted editors will ask you to fix it; less understanding editors will simply send a rejection.

This "gibberish" is the result of transferring a word-processed document directly to e-mail without undoing the special characters and commands such a program embeds in a file. Unless instructed otherwise, for example, Microsoft Word will automatically convert dashes (--) into a special dash symbol (—), turn apostrophes and quotes into "smart quotes," turn ellipses (. . .) into another special character, and so forth. When transmitted by e-mail, these codes are converted into various odd symbols and characters, as are formatting codes for bold, italic, and underlining. Converting a document to text or RTF will remove most formatting codes but not "special character" codes.

To keep these codes out of e-mail, take the following steps:

❖ Turn off all special-character commands. In MS Word, go into the "AutoCorrect" menu under "Tools." In the "Autoformat as you type" and "Autoformat" menus, uncheck everything under "Replace as you type." In the "Autocorrect" submenu, look at the list of automatic corrections, and delete the correction that replaces an ellipsis with a special character.

❖ Replace special-character commands in existing documents. If your document already has special characters, you'll need to search and replace the problem characters with their text counterparts. Once you've turned off the "autoformat" characters, simply enter an apostrophe or a quote mark in the "find" and "replace" boxes and hit "replace all." To replace a dash with a pair of hyphens, copy and paste a dash from the Word file into the "find" box and type two hyphens (or space-hyphen-hyphen-space) into the "replace" box. Do the same for ellipses, etc.[2]

❖ Double space between paragraphs. E-mail wipes out tabs, so indicate paragraphs with two line spaces. (Simply do a search-and-replace on the "paragraph" symbol in Word and replace single paragraphs with two paragraph symbols.)

After you've made these changes, test an e-mail by sending it to yourself first. I've found that when pasting a Word document into e-mail, the double-spacing sometimes disappears between some paragraphs.

To make editors even happier, follow these guidelines:

❖ Don't use HTML formatting in e-mail.
❖ Don't use background or font colors.
❖ Do use a large, readable font.
❖ Don't send any automatic attachments, such as v-cards. Many editors will automatically delete an e-mail with *any* attachment.

The ability to contact editors electronically has made life much easier for writers around the world. To retain this ability, however, we must make sure that we make life as easy as possible for our editors as well!

NOTES

1. Portions of this chapter also appeared in my books, *The Writer's Guide to Queries, Pitches, and Proposals* (Allworth Press, 2001) and *Writing.com: Creative Internet Strategies to Advance Your Writing Career*, Second Edition (Allworth Press, 2003).

2. Mac users can insert a dash with the option + dash keys, and an ellipsis with the option + semi-colon keys.

CHAPTER 19

Formatting Your Manuscript

M anuscript format should be a fairly simple issue. Yet from some of the questions I've received, it would seem that people like to make it complicated—from editors who prefer a particular style and therefore declare that *all* editors want the same style, to writers' groups who insist that one must use this font and that layout, and so forth.

If conflicting advice on format has left you confused (and wondering if your manuscript will be rejected unread simply because you put your address in the upper-right corner instead of the left), the following tips should help clarify the issue.

Print Manuscripts: The Basics

Most editors in any genre (articles, short fiction, long fiction, etc.) want a manuscript to conform to the following basic requirements:

- Good paper (20-pound bond minimum, never erasable)
- Double-spacing
- 1-inch margins all around (at least)
- A clear, readable font (more on this later)
- Paragraphs indicated by indents (tabs), not by an extra line space

Articles should begin about halfway down the page (some folks say two-thirds). Your name, address, and other contact information (phone, fax, e-mail, etc.) should be placed in the upper-left corner of the manuscript, in a single-spaced block. The word count of the article (rounded to the nearest ten or fifty) should go in the upper-right corner. Your title should be centered on the page at the halfway point, in a larger font than the text (bold-facing is fine). Skip two lines, and center your byline (either your real name or your pen name) in a slightly smaller font. Skip another two lines and begin your article.

Running headers are expected on articles, short stories, novels, and nonfiction books. A running header should appear at the top of every page (except the first), and include the following information:

- Your last name
- The title of the article, book, or story—or a keyword from the title if the title is long
- The page number

For example, a running header for an article titled "A History of Feline Chiropractic Care" might look like this:

Allen/Feline Chiropractic/. . . 2

Contest submissions are formatted much like regular article or story submissions, with one exception: All of your contact information should be included on a cover sheet. Do not put your name or any contact information on the first page of the story/article itself, and do not include your name in the running header. The cover sheet will be removed from your submission, so that the judges do not know anything about the author of the piece. (If you see a listing that asks for work to be submitted in "contest format," this is what it means.)

Fonts and Format

People get into heated discussions over what types of fonts editors prefer. Some claim that all editors want manuscripts in Courier (which looks like a typewriter font). Lately, some editors and writers have come to prefer Arial. So what do editors really want?

The truth is, most editors really don't care, as long as the font is readable. (I can state this with confidence, having done a survey of about five hundred editors; 90 percent expressed "no preference" with regard to font.) Very few editors will reject your manuscript because it happens to be in New Century Schoolbook, Palatino, or Times Roman. Generally, it's best to use a 12-point font size, and to choose a font that doesn't squish letters together too closely.

The rationale for Courier dates back to the days when editors did an eyeball "guesstimate" of line lengths to determine exactly how much space a piece would fill in on the printed page. Courier is a "fixed-space" font, meaning that each letter takes up exactly the same amount of space. This made it easier to estimate how an article would appear when typeset. Today, however, very few editors need to do this (or even remember that it was done).

Arial is a nice, readable font—but it is also a sans-serif font, which many editors don't like. (To see the difference between a serif and sans-serif font, compare Arial to Times.) Before you use this font, be sure your editor really, really wants it.

The bottom line on fonts is simply this: If your editor expresses a preference, or if you've heard through the grapevine that this editor is obsessive over fonts (some are), use the font the editor prefers. But if your editor has no preference, don't assume that she has one—and don't agonize over the issue of font.

Electronic Submissions

Again, electronic submissions break nearly all the rules listed above. Many editors do accept electronic submissions, and some have complex guidelines as to exactly how these must be formatted. Some accept attachments (most commonly MS Word, but also RTF, ASCII text, and WordPerfect); others prefer that the submission be embedded within the text of the e-mail.

If you're sending a submission as an attachment, you can format it just as you would to print it. If you are asked to include it within your e-mail, you'll need to follow the same guidelines for "removing the gibberish" mentioned in the last chapter. Here are a few more pointers for submissions within e-mail:

❖ Don't try to double-space your text; it won't work. Just double-space between paragraphs.
❖ Include your contact information (name, address, etc.) and word count at the beginning of the e-mail, before the title.
❖ If the submission is very long, consider mailing it in two parts; some e-mail hosts truncate long messages. (At least check with the editor to make sure the entire message arrived.)
❖ E-mail the piece to yourself first to make sure it came out properly (that no paragraph breaks were lost, etc.)

Counting the Words

Another issue that confuses writers is how to estimate the word count of a manuscript. You will still occasionally read some complex formula ("count the number of lines on each page, divide by x, then multiply by . . .").

These formulas are left over from the days when we had no easy way to count the words other than ticking them off with a pencil. They are also left over from the days when editors estimated the printed length of a manuscript based on such formulas. Today, using the word-count feature of your word-processing program is perfectly acceptable. You also don't have to be precise. If your article is 1,562 words, call it 1,550. If it's 1,975 words, call it 2,000.

Other Format Issues

One Space or Two?

Those of us who are old enough to remember taking typing in high school also remember the two-space rule: Put two spaces after periods and colons. Today, we are told to leave only one space, as modern typesetting programs don't need this extra space (which was helpful when type was "nonproportional").

While many editors today prefer that you leave only one space after all punctuation, the reality is that it doesn't really matter. If you're "old school" and automatically hit that second space, it's not going to result in a rejection. It's also perfectly easy, after you've finished your manuscript, to do a global search-and-replace and replace every double-space with a single.

Should Tabs Be Five Spaces or Less?

Again, in the "old days" of typing, we were taught that tabs should be a standard five spaces. Most word-processing programs have default tab settings at every half-inch. To many writers and editors, however, such tabs look far too large. There's no longer a hard-and-fast rule on tabs: Just make sure that the editor can tell that a space *is* a tab. (I set mine at one-quarter of an inch.)

To Underline or Italicize?

The practice of underlining words to indicate italics also dates from the age of the typewriter. Word-processors enable one to indicate italics and boldface type directly. However, many editors still prefer underscoring (it often makes text easier to read), so I recommend that one use underlining to indicate italics, but boldface formatting to indicate boldface text. However, I've also never known a writer to lose a sale because he used italics instead of underlining.

One area that is particularly confusing is when one is indicating "thoughts" rather than dialogue. Although this tends to be an issue primarily in fiction, it deserves a mention. Thoughts are typically italicized in the final print version of a story or article (rather than placed in quotes); however, in your manuscript, you may wish to indicate them with underlining.

For more information on manuscript format, I recommend *The Writer's Digest Guide to Manuscript Format*, which covers different types of manuscripts, including poetry, essays, books, scripts, etc.

CHAPTER 20

Do You Need a Cover Letter?

hen you submit a manuscript to an editor, should you include a cover letter? The answer isn't always obvious. On the one hand, a manuscript stuffed into an envelope all by itself seems so—well, naked! On the other hand, stating the obvious (e.g., "enclosed is a manuscript . . . " or, "I hope you find this of interest") almost seems an insult to an editor's intelligence.

Cover letters can serve a purpose, however—and sometimes several purposes. Here are some tips on when to use them, what to include, and what to leave out.

When to Use a Cover Letter

Under certain circumstances, a cover letter can be an important addition to your manuscript. Those circumstances will also dictate the content of that letter. Such circumstances include:

❖ *When the material has been requested.* It doesn't hurt (especially if you're a new writer for the publication) to remind the editor that this is requested rather than unsolicited material. Simply state something along the lines of "Enclosed is the manuscript you requested in your letter of (date) [or "that we discussed in our conversation/e-mail/whatever of (date)"], titled (title)."

❖ *To provide supplementary information.* You may wish to note that you can provide photos, illustrations, contacts, or sources of additional information. If a publication wishes to "fact check" your article, a cover letter is a good place to list your sources.

❖ *To provide information about yourself.* If the article is unsolicited, use your cover letter to list your credentials, expertise, or other qualifications for authoring the piece. Or, you may wish to list the credentials of the experts you've interviewed for the article.

Moira Allen
1234 Mystreet • Mytown, VA 20151
(XXX) 555-1234 • (XXX) 555-1235 (fax)
moirakallen@writing-world.com

March 15, 200_

Editor's Name
Publication
Address
City/State/Zip

Dear Mr./Ms./Editor Jones:

Enclosed is a manuscript of XXXX words, titled [whatever] for your consideration. A SASE is enclosed for your response; the manuscript itself need not be returned. Thank you for your time and consideration. I look forward to hearing from you.

Sincerely,
Moira Allen
Encs. (optional)

❖ *When you write under a pseudonym.* A cover letter is the place to provide your real name and address, along with the pseudonym you wish to use as your byline.

❖ *To provide a biographical sketch.* Usually, your bio sketch should be no more than 300 words (and more likely around 100 words), and relate to the content of the article if possible. (See chapter 16 for information on creating a bio.)

❖ *To provide a record of your name, address, and article information.* Your manuscript may be passed from one editor to another, and the cover letter gives an editor an easy way to find your name and address even when the manuscript isn't on his/her desk.

❖ *To indicate whether the manuscript should be returned.* While the size of your SASE should be an indication of your intentions (a large SASE indicates that you want the manuscript returned, while a #10 envelope indicates that it can be discarded), some editors prefer an explicit statement of your preferences. (Editors have received angry notes from authors who wonder why their twenty-page manuscript wasn't returned in their #10 envelope.)

❖ *When you have been referred to the editor.* If you have been referred to an editor by someone the editor knows (such as a regular contributor), mention this in your cover letter. For example, you might say, "Sue Jones, your nutrition columnist, suggested that I send this piece to you."

❖ *To offer supporting material that isn't included in the package.* For example, I recently submitted an article to a U.K. market, and promised to provide a sidebar listing various resources mentioned in the article—*if* the article was accepted. Since the task would have required extra time and research, I didn't want to provide it until I knew it was wanted.

If none of these circumstances apply to you, but you still prefer to include a cover letter, just keep it simple and professional and don't worry about redundancy. Your cover letter should be prepared in a standard business format (block or modified block), as shown on the next page.

Nine Things to Leave Out of Your Letter

While a professional cover letter usually can't hurt you, an unprofessional letter can. Avoid, at all costs, a letter that might prejudice an editor against you, or convey the impression that you're anything less than a professional writer. That means avoiding the following topics:

❖ *Irrelevant personal information.* One of the cover letters that has stuck in my memory from my editing days is the one that began: "Dear Editor, I am an unpublished mother of three. . . ." Don't offer information about your age, gender, family status, or anything else that does not relate to your article. (If it *does* relate, it should be part of your credentials.)

❖ *Announcements of your unpublished status.* If you have never been published before, that's fine—but the editor doesn't need to know this. Don't try to play on an editor's sympathies by explaining that this is your first article, or that you hope it will be your first publication.

❖ *Hype.* Don't tell the editor that your article is brilliant, thoughtful, exciting, inspiring, or "sure to please." Editors prefer to make these decisions for themselves.

❖ *Apologies about your article (or yourself).* Some writers actually "apologize" for flaws they perceive in their articles or in themselves: "I realize I'm not a professional wordsmith, but I hope you will like this piece," or, "I'm sorry if my style doesn't exactly match your publication, but I hope you'll take the time to read this." If your article is flawed, don't send it—

fix it! If your article is fine, but you have doubts about your abilities anyway, keep them to yourself.

✤ *Explanations of why you're sending material that doesn't match the publication's guidelines.* If your article is 2,000 words longer than the stated word limit, or written from the first-person POV of your dog, or typed on pink paper, don't explain. Rewrite.

✤ *An explanation of why the article differs from your assignment or proposal.* Sometimes a change is appropriate (you find new information, or you can't contact an expert you hoped to speak with). These changes should never come as a surprise, however. If you must change the focus of an article after it has been assigned, discuss this with the editor in advance.

✤ *Demands.* Don't tell an editor what you expect to be paid, or what terms you will offer—especially if those differ from the payment or terms specified in the publication's guidelines. (One of my favorite cover letters was a 3 × 5 card with the typed phrase, "I am a professional and deserve your HIGHEST RATES!") If you wish to negotiate payment or contract terms, do so before you submit the finished article (or after you become an established contributor).

✤ *Opinions of your family, friends, or writing teachers.* Editors really don't care what these people thought of your work!

✤ *A list of prior rejections.* Never tell an editor that a submission has already been rejected five times. Editors are likely to assume there was a good reason! And *never* imply that you hope this will be the "smart" editor who is able to see the merit of your work that others have overlooked!

A good cover letter won't sell your manuscript, but it also won't hurt your chances of acceptance. A bad cover letter, on the other hand, may shoot down your submission before the editor even reaches the first page. So by all means, cover your work—and yourself—by keeping your letter short, sweet, and professional.

PART V

RIGHTS AND CONTRACTS

CHAPTER 21

Understanding Rights and Copyright

ne of the most common questions I hear is, "How do I copyright my work?" Copyrighting your work is actually the easiest part of writing, because your work is automatically protected the moment you write it down. Under current law, copyright on any work you've created since January 1, 1998 is good for your lifetime plus seventy years.[1]

I also get questions along the lines of, "I have this great idea for a story; how can I copyright it so that no one else will write it?" The answer is, "You can't." Ideas cannot be protected by copyright. Copyright covers your "intellectual property," which means your actual written material. Similarly, the information that goes into your written material—dates, facts, figures, etc.— is not protected by copyright; anyone else has just as much right to use that same information in their own work.

You do not have to register a copyright for your work to be protected, and most writers do not register copyrights for their articles before submitting them. Copyright registration *is* necessary prior to filing an actual copyright infringement suit[2]—but the chances of needing to do this when sending your work out for publication are extremely slim. (Most such suits result from infringements of work that has *already* been published.[3])

You have undoubtedly seen articles claiming that mailing an article to oneself counts as a form of "copyright protection" (the theory being that the postmark on a sealed envelope "proves that you wrote the material prior to that date). According to Illinois copyright lawyer Charles Petit, this is not true. "Poor man's copyright" is not a substitute for actual copyright registration and has no value in a court of law.

The cost of registering a copyright is currently $30. However, you can also register collections of material (e.g., a compendium of all the articles you wrote within a given year) for a single registration fee. For more information or to download registration forms, visit the Copyright Office at *http://lcweb .loc.gov/copyright*.[4]

You can also post your own copyright notice on your material, by including the following information at the beginning or the end of a document:

Copyright © [year] by [your name]

It was once common practice for writers to put such a notice on any material they submitted for publication. This is now considered amateurish; editors are aware that you own the copyright to your work, and consider this notice a statement of a writer's insecurity. However, if you plan to distribute your material to friends, especially by e-mail (and most especially if you plan to send it to an online discussion group or critique group), a copyright notice is highly advisable. While editors understand about copyright protection, average readers may not, and often pass on works they receive by e-mail without realizing that they are infringing upon the author's copyright.

A Writer's Rights

"Copyright" refers to your right to claim ownership (and authorship) of a particular piece of work. It also means that no one can reproduce, sell, or distribute that work without your permission. You have the ability to grant that permission through "use rights." Licensing the right to *use* your work does not mean that you give up ownership of the copyright, unless you actually transfer that copyright through a contractual agreement (such as a work-for-hire contract).

Rights are generally transferred through a written contract. In the absence of a contract, a publisher cannot claim any rights beyond first or one-time use. For example, a print publisher does not have the right to post your article online unless you've signed a contract transferring electronic rights. Nor does it have the right to reprint your article in another publication or an anthology unless you've authorized reprint rights. Most importantly, a publisher cannot claim to own the *copyright* to your material unless this has been specifically transferred in a contract. (Chapter 22 looks at contracts in more detail.)

Following are the types of rights most often used by periodical publishers:

- ❖ *First North American Serial Rights (FNASR).* This gives a periodical publisher (e.g., magazine or newspaper) within North America (including Canada) the right to be *first* to publish your work. It authorizes a publisher to use your work once only; it does not authorize a publisher to reprint your work in another publication (such as an anthology) or on a Web site. Note that you can only sell this right once (because only one publication can be "first"); thus, this is considered an "exclusive" right.
- ❖ *First Rights.* This term is usually used in combination with a specified

medium or location—e.g., "first print rights" or "first English-language rights." It indicates that the publication has the right to the first use of your material within the specified medium or distribution area. Note that you can sell different subsets of "first" rights, such as "first print rights" to one publication, and "first electronic rights" to another. Each sale of a first right (in any medium) is an "exclusive" sale of those rights, but such sales do not preclude the sale of other types of "first" rights.

❖ *One-Time Rights.* This grants a publisher the *nonexclusive* right to publish your material. This means that you can sell the same material to other publishers at the same time. This right is often used for reprints, and for columns licensed to multiple publications (such as newspapers).

❖ *Second or Reprint Rights.* Once you've sold first rights in a medium, your next sale of the same material will generally be regarded as a reprint and thus a use of "second" or "reprint" rights. Second rights are generally *not* associated with a specific medium, and are generally considered nonexclusive (meaning that you can market the same reprint to different markets simultaneously).

❖ *Electronic Rights.* Most print publications now want some form of electronic rights, usually to post material on their Web site. Some try to claim that electronic rights are included in FNASR, but this is not true. Many don't offer additional payment for electronic rights, even though by using those rights, they prevent you from selling "first" electronic rights to an online publication. Some offer a percentage of the original fee (e.g., 25 percent) if the work is used on the publication's Web site. (See below for more details about electronic rights.)

❖ *All Rights.* This means everything: first rights, second rights, print rights, electronic rights, even movie rights. Once you've sold all rights to a publication, you've lost all further use of that material; you may not even be entitled to post it on your personal Web site. Many writers argue that one should never sell all rights, while others maintain that there are circumstances in which it is acceptable (such as when the material isn't suitable for reselling, when the fee is high enough, or when the publication—e.g., *Reader's Digest*—is prestigious enough to offset the loss of rights). Some publications will license back certain rights to authors, such as the right to sell reprints.

❖ *Work-for-Hire.* Originally applied to work created as an employee, a work-for-hire agreement not only transfers all rights to your material, but also its copyright. Thus, you are no longer legally the "author"—a publication can remove your byline, change the material, or even run it under another name. In addition, if you write a substantially similar or "derivative" article, you could actually be liable for copyright infringement.

❖ *International Rights.* In addition to FNASR, you can sell rights to other regions, based either on geographical boundaries or on language. For example, you could offer "first British rights," "first Japanese rights," etc. You can also sell "first German-language rights" or "first Japanese-language rights," which limits distribution by language but not by geographical boundaries. (Note that a license of "first English-language rights" is actually more inclusive than FNASR, as it would include the right to distribute in the UK and any other English-language-speaking country.)

Many writers are confused by the practice of some e-zines of posting a copyright notice at the end of every article or page on their site, and are concerned that this means the publication is claiming the copyright of the article itself. Actually, this type of notice is a publication's announcement of its "collective copyright" over the issue as a whole—*not* over individual articles or other materials within that issue. Each issue of any periodical is covered by the publisher's *collective copyright*, which gives the publisher the exclusive right to publish and distribute that issue *as an entity*. It does not give the publisher the right to use or sell portions of the issue in other ways.

Electronic Rights

This catch-all phrase can cover anything from publication on a Web site to inclusion in an online database to publication in a CD-ROM or other electronic medium. The term has become increasingly associated with some form of "Web" publication, however, including publication on a print magazine's Web site, in an e-zine, in an e-mail newsletter, on a "content" or catalog site, or in an online database.

Web publication rights are generally considered to be "worldwide," as a publisher can't control where an online publication is read or "distributed." (Geographical rights refer to where a publication is read, not where it is published.) Thus, terms like FNASR don't apply to Web publication. Nor are you likely to see a contract that asks for "first British electronic rights," or something similar.

Common electronic rights clauses include:

✤ *First (or First Worldwide) Electronic Rights.* This usually applies to publication on the Web or in an e-mail newsletter.
✤ *One-time Electronic Rights.* Like one-time print rights, this is a nonexclusive clause that generally applies to Web or e-mail publication.
✤ *Web Publication Rights.* This specifically indicates that the material will be used online, not in a CD-ROM or as a download (such as an e-book).
✤ *Archival Rights.* This gives a publication the right to archive material (such as the back issues of an e-zine or newsletter) online, sometimes for

a specified period of time but more often "indefinitely." Some publications grant an author the right to request the withdrawal of an article from the archive after a specified period of time.

✜ *Electronic Distribution Rights.* This gives a publication the right to market (distribute) your work to *other* electronic publications. For example, many print publications request this right so that they can sell articles to online databases (generally without passing a penny of the profit back to you!).

✜ *All Electronic Rights.* This transfers all *electronic* uses to the purchasing publication, but leaves the author free to market print rights.

While a print publication has a specific "lifespan" (e.g., a monthly magazine is deemed "out of print" once the month has passed), material that is posted online remains available to readers indefinitely. Thus, most electronic rights clauses include a specified *duration.* For example, an e-zine might request "first electronic rights for ninety days," which means that the publication will have exclusive use of the material for ninety days after it is published. Thereafter, the writer can offer it to other electronic publications. Some publications specify archival rights for a period of one year; others request such rights "indefinitely."

Most electronic rights clauses also specify whether those rights are exclusive or nonexclusive. Print publications, for example, often request *nonexclusive* electronic rights, giving them the right to post an article on their Web site. Archival rights are generally nonexclusive. Most electronic publications may ask for exclusive *first* electronic rights, but do not ask for print rights, which means that you can sell the material to a print publication at the same time.

Exclusivity can be a tricky thing. While a nonexclusive contract can mean that you can offer the same material to other publications, you must make sure that none of *those* publications want exclusivity. For example, if you sell an article to an e-zine that wants nonexclusive archival rights, you could not sell the same article to a print publication that wants any form of *exclusive* electronic rights.

Use versus Payment

Many authors are confused over what constitutes a "use of rights." I often get questions like, "How can a magazine own my rights if they didn't pay me?" or, "How can putting something on my Web site be a use of first rights?" The answer lies in the issue of "usage." When you create something (such as an article), you own the copyright to that creation—which means that you have a bundle of "rights" to "use" that material in various ways. You can *sell* or *give* those rights to others, or you can use them yourself.

I always get a laugh out of guidelines that state that "all rights revert to the author after publication." This sounds nice, but isn't precisely true. If you allow another publication to publish your material, you have given up certain use rights—usually "first publication rights," whether you're paid or not. The only issue is whether the material has been *published*—if it has, then no other publication can ever be "first" to publish that work. A publication may give up any *future* claim to a piece, but the rights that have already been used can't be reclaimed by the author.

Using a piece of writing yourself can also use up certain rights. For example, if you post an article on your Web site, many believe that you're "using" the "first publication rights" to that article. (More and more publications regard this as "prior publication," and treat such material as a reprint rather than a first use.)

Showcasing your unpublished works on a Web site is poor policy for other reasons as well. The main reason is that it can make you appear to be an amateur—someone who can't "get published" any other way. Contrary to the hopeful opinions bandied about in some writing circles, editors do *not* surf the Web looking for promising material on personal Web sites, and posting your unpublished material online is *not* an effective way to get it "picked up" by a publisher. Nor are editors interested in queries that invite them to read your available articles online: First, they don't have time, and second, such a query makes it clear that you're offering generic articles rather than material tailored specifically for the publication.

It's much better to post *previously published* material on your site, if you retain the reprint rights. (If you've sold all rights to a piece, you won't be able to do this.) Once you've sold an article or story, you can post it on your site with a notice as to where it was previously published, and use this as an online "clip." This can be a useful promotion tool, for it shows that you're a *published* writer—not just a hopeful wannabe.

Protecting Your Rights

Knowing your rights is the most important step you can take toward protecting your work in today's competitive marketplace. But can you do more?

Some writers' advocacy groups say that you can. Such groups recommend "boycotting" publications that insist on all-rights or work-for-hire contracts, or that demand ill-defined electronic rights or lump those rights under terms such as FNASR. If you're faced with such a contract, such groups suggest that you take your work elsewhere.

Unfortunately, such tactics have little effect. With thousands of freelance writers competing for the same markets, publications have no incentive to change policies just because one or two writers decide to go elsewhere. No editor is likely to lose sleep over the fact that you, or any other writer, is "boycotting" that publication.

What you can do is negotiate, as tactfully and firmly as possible. If an editor seems unclear on the definition of a particular rights clause, educate that editor—but do so politely. If an editor claims that he is unable to alter a contract, don't assume this is a lie; in many cases contracts are developed by a publication's legal department. If you can't persuade an editor to change the contract, attempt to negotiate a higher fee, or a specific "exception" to the rights (e.g., the right to use certain portions of the material elsewhere in a noncompeting market).

In the end, it becomes a matter of personal choice. In every contract decision, you must weigh what you stand to gain against what you stand to lose. Don't let another writer (or group) tell you what you must or must not do. Only you can determine what is best for you and your writing career.

NOTES

1. Copyright terms for materials produced prior to January 1, 1998 vary. Material written before 1923 is now in the public domain; in addition, some materials written or published between 1923 and 1998 may also be in the public domain, depending on various factors. (Anything published between 1923 and 1963 on which the copyright has not been renewed, for example, is now in the public domain.) For details on when copyright expires on materials produced prior to 1998, see *www .authorslawyer.com/c-term.shtml*.

2. If one hasn't registered a copyright before filing an infringement suit, one can only collect "actual" damages, which translates into the amount that an infringement actually cost you (e.g., in lost revenues). One cannot collect statutory damages or attorney fees. Statutory damages can range from $750 to $30,000, and up to $150,000 if the infringement was found to be deliberate.

3. Traditionally, it was believed that a magazine's "collective copyright" notice counted as copyright registration in the case of an infringement suit; however, this is not always the case and can't be counted on.

4. Canadian writers should check with the Canadian copyright office (CANCOPY) at *www.cancopy .com/welcome.html*. British writers are not able to actually register their copyright with a government agency; however, there are private copyright registration firms in Britain.

CHAPTER 22

Understanding Contracts

contract does not have to be printed on stiff paper with gilded edges to be binding. Nor does it have to be packed with legal jargon. A contract can be any form of document that spells out the terms of a sale, including:

- A preprinted legal document, with blanks for the name of the author, the title of the material being sold, and the fee.
- A letter of agreement. This may be an original letter tailored for a particular sale, or a standard form letter, or even an e-mail.
- A "fill in the blanks" or "check the boxes" form.

A contract must be negotiated *before* the ownership of the material actually changes hands. In the past, some publishers attempted to claim rights by stamping a "rights transfer" clause on the back of a writer's payment check, indicating that by endorsing or depositing the check, the writer was transferring the rights indicated. In 1997, a judge ruling on the Tasini decision (regarding questions of electronic rights) ruled that such a stamp did *not* constitute a legally binding contract, and could not be used by publishers to claim rights. (If you should ever receive such a check, you can sign it without hesitation, as the stamp means nothing.)

Contracts may be transmitted by fax or e-mail. Faxed signatures are generally considered legally binding. E-mail is trickier; it may lack the editor's signature, and you'll have to print it out to sign it. While agreements may be negotiated entirely via e-mail (without signatures), doing so depends on a degree of trust between author and publisher.

Understanding Terms

Any agreement between a writer and a publisher should contain, at a minimum, the following information:

- The title of the material being purchased.
- The rights being purchased—e.g., first rights, FNASR, one-time rights, reprint rights, electronic rights, all rights, etc. (For more information about rights, see chapter 21.)
- The medium (or media) to which those rights apply, or in which the work will be published. Some rights apply only to print publication (such as FNASR); others apply to electronic publication; others apply to all forms of publication. Watch out for clauses that attempt to give a right more "meaning" than it customarily has (e.g., by claiming that FNASR also includes the right to publish material online).
- Payment, including the exact fee offered for your material and when you can expect to receive it (e.g., within thirty days of acceptance or publication).
- Your obligations and liabilities. Some contracts address issues of accuracy, originality, and libel. Make sure that such clauses don't demand assurances that you can't reasonably provide. When in doubt, insert the phrase, "to the best of the author's knowledge" after such clauses.

Most contracts also include the following clauses:

- A statement that the magazine is entitled to edit the material. This is standard, and most publications understand that it means "within reason." A publication typically has the right to do any amount of editing as long as the basic substance and meaning of the article remain unchanged. Some editors take this as a license to rewrite your piece from top to bottom; if this happens, there is honestly very little you can do about it.
- An indemnification statement. You'll often see a long block of text about indemnification issues. These are provided to ensure that if someone wants to file a suit about the article, it is filed against *you* rather than the publisher. Such suits don't happen often (in fact, I've never heard of one happening at all), but it's the sort of legal protection lawyers like. Again, if the statements aren't clear, insert the line, "to the best of the author's knowledge."
- The right to use the material for promotional purposes. Most contracts give a publication the right to use some or all of an article for promotional purposes.
- A statement that the article is original and your property. This protects the publisher from a lawsuit if someone claims that you stole his or her article. Again, this doesn't happen very often!

Negotiating Contracts

If you don't like the terms of a contract, it's always appropriate to ask whether negotiation is possible. Always be polite and reasonable. Before you attempt to negotiate, be sure you know what you hope to achieve. What do you actually want out of the negotiation? What are you prepared to offer? Are you willing to sell the range of rights requested for a higher fee? Or are you simply not prepared to give up the requested rights?

Keep in mind that the editor may actually not be empowered to negotiate a contract. In larger publishing/media companies, the contracts are often drafted by the legal department, and the editors have no authority to change them. If this is the case, you're pretty much stuck—but even then, some editors may be willing to negotiate while others won't. Again, it never hurts to ask, but if an editor says he can't, and seems firm on this, there is little point in pushing. Never hassle an editor or lose your professional cool; this will only result in costing you a potential market.

If the editor won't negotiate, it's up to you to make a decision. Will you accept a contract you don't like—or will you withdraw the article? Only *you* can make this decision. Don't let anyone else make it for you. You'll read lots of articles by writers who urge everyone to walk away from all-rights contracts. That's easily said, but if you're trying to earn a living as a writer, you may find that you aren't willing to do so. Your choice is your own: Do not let someone else pressure you or make you feel guilty about your decision.

Understanding Your Position

❖ Do not assume that you have to accept what a magazine offers/demands. Many new writers feel that their first acceptance is their *one big chance* to make a sale. They don't want to blow that chance by getting picky over a contract. So, if a magazine asks for all rights, they'll take the deal. The reality is that if you're *any* good at all as a writer, you'll have other chances. You do not have to accept the first offer that comes along. If it isn't good, you can always walk away.

❖ Do not assume that a publication will blacklist you (or worse, spread the word that you're a "difficult" writer) if you try to negotiate a contract. Actually, editors are well aware that it is the *more* professional writers who try to negotiate (because they are more knowledgeable), so politely attempting to negotiate a contract will not harm you. You may not succeed, but it won't make you "look bad."

❖ Do not assume that you will never use a piece again. It's very easy to think that you have no other possible markets for an article, so "why not sell all rights"? I've done this myself—and every single time I've been convinced that I would never use a piece again, a market has come up for it. Granted, you may be able to rewrite those articles for a new market—but that's extra work.

✤ If you don't understand what rights are being requested, ask. I've seen some weird phrases—e.g., "multi-use rights"—that aren't intuitively obvious. Don't worry about appearing ignorant; chances are, the ignorant person is the one who made up the terminology in the first place!

What Isn't a Contract

Certain things do not constitute a legally binding agreement, including:

✤ A stamp on the back of a check indicating something like "Endorsement or deposit of this check transfers all rights to your material to MegaPublishers Inc."

✤ Writer's guidelines, whether published in a guide such as *Writer's Market* or distributed by the company itself. Guidelines can be changed without notice, and are superseded by a written contract.

✤ Your own notation on a manuscript indicating the rights you're offering. Many writers like to put a notice at the top of a submission stating something like "Rights Available: FNASR." This means nothing; you should know *before* you submit a piece what rights the market requires. If you aren't willing to sell those rights, don't submit.

✤ A verbal agreement. In theory, such agreements are binding—but they're hard to enforce in court. It's wise to back up any oral agreement with, at the least, a memo or letter confirming the terms.

✤ An altered document that has not been cosigned or initialed by both parties. If you want to change a contract, you must obtain the agreement of the publisher; it isn't enough to simply mark out or revise unwanted clauses.

In addition, certain rights can be transferred *only* through a written agreement. If you have no contract with a publication, that publication cannot claim that it owns "all rights," or that your work was "work-for-hire." According to copyright law, if no contract exists, the only rights a publisher can claim are first rights (e.g., FNASR) or one-time rights.

Never let a publisher try to bully you into believing that it owns more rights than it does. (I once received a letter from a writer who was informed by his publisher that "collective copyright"—i.e., the copyright applying to the publication as a whole—meant that the publisher owned the copyright to the individual articles in that publication. It doesn't.) Many publications offer contracts stating that they are purchasing FNASR, but then go ahead and post material on their Web sites without any additional compensation for the writer. This is a contract violation; if you find that someone has posted your work online in the absence of a contract specifically transferring some form of electronic rights, you're entitled to ask the publication to remove the work or provide additional compensation.

Making Your Own Contract

If a publication offers no contract, it's wise to protect yourself by offering your own letter of agreement. Keep this as simple as possible, spelling out the terms you're willing to offer and nothing more. Such a letter might read something like this:

> Dear Editor:
> Thank you for accepting my article, "[title]." I have received your check in the amount of [$], in payment for FNASR. I look forward to seeing my article in the [date] issue.

If no publication date has been confirmed (and especially if payment is contingent on publication), you can use this letter to inquire about the anticipated date of publication. While such a letter may not be as binding as a cosigned document, it does provide a written record of the terms you have authorized.

Another good time to send your own contract is when you've been promised a contract by an editor, but haven't received one yet. If the promised contract never materializes, your letter of agreement should stand as the "accepted" contract; if the publisher later tries to disclaim that agreement, you can simply point out that no *signed* contract exists to supersede it.

Some Tricky Contract Issues

While some contract issues are straightforward, others are more complicated. Here are a few of the more difficult contract questions I've heard:

Is It Ever Too Late to Get a Contract?

Many writers ask whether it is too late to get a contract *after* a piece has already been published (and, hopefully, paid for). Technically, the answer is yes. However, in this case, the absence of a contract won't hurt you, and may actually be better for you than getting a contract "ex post facto." In the absence of a contract, the only rights a publication can claim (especially once they've already used your article) are "first" or "one-time" rights. Even if a publisher *tries* to claim (or use) additional rights, it has no legal basis for doing so, and you're legally free to re-use or resell your material.

What If the Publisher Never Uses My Material?

One frustrating situation that often occurs is when a publisher buys an article, pays for it, but never actually publishes it. Many writers wonder whether they have the right to resell that piece if it is never published by the original buyer. The answer is "it depends"—specifically, on the rights the publisher has bought.

If, for example, a publisher has bought (and paid for) all rights to your work, then you don't have the right to use it elsewhere, *whether the publisher ever publishes it or not.* By buying all rights, a publisher has also bought the right, in effect, to *not* publish your piece. Sometimes, for example, an editor buys something and then simply can't find a suitable place for it. In other cases, a magazine changes editors, and the new editor doesn't want to use the material purchased by the old one. When this happens, it's frustrating (after all, you want to see your work "in print"), but there's really nothing you can do.

A more frustrating situation is when the publisher has bought *first* rights, theoretically leaving you free to sell reprint rights. However, you can only do this once the material has been published the *first* time—and since the publisher holds the right to be the *first* to use the piece, you can't sell it anywhere else until that first use has occurred.

If, however, a publisher contracts for your work but has not actually *paid* for it (e.g., the publisher pays on publication rather than acceptance), then you may have an opportunity to reclaim that work if a significant period of time elapses without publication. Keep in mind that a pay-on-publication market *can* take as long as two years to actually print a piece (and pay for it), so don't expect to be able to reclaim your work after just a few months. When dealing with a pay-on-publication market, I recommend asking the editor to include a clause that indicates *when* the piece will be published. (Most reputable pay-on-publication markets now schedule articles before issuing contracts, to avoid the "to be published whenever" problem.) If the piece is *not* published on the specified date, you can then (a) ask the editor for a new publication date, or (b) ask for payment in advance, since the contract date has come and gone.

If no publication date has been scheduled and you've waited a year or more for the piece to appear, then you may wish to approach the editor and ask to withdraw the article from inventory. Since the publication has not paid you, it has not fulfilled its half of the contract, and you're within your rights to request to have the article back so that you can resell it. Keep in mind that not every publication will say "yes," but it's certainly worth a try.

Finally, if the publication was supposed to pay you (i.e., on acceptance) but hasn't done so, *and* it hasn't published the article, then, again, it has not met its side of the contract. In that case, you're again within your rights to formally withdraw the article from the publisher's inventory.

In many cases, however, the sad fact is that you simply *don't* have any recourse when your article isn't published. If you've been paid, and you don't have the right to reuse the article, then often the only thing you can do is sigh and move on.

Can a Publisher Ask for Additional Rights to Previously Purchased Articles?

A new, and nasty, tendency in the publishing industry today is to issue *retroactive contracts*. A retroactive contract is one that claims rights to *previously* published articles that were originally covered under different contract terms. Generally, a retroactive contract is issued when an author submits a new article—and is told that before the publisher will accept the new piece, the author must agree to sign over rights to earlier materials. Often, regular contributors are told that if they want to keep working for a publication, they will have to sign a retroactive agreement and give up their rights to older materials.

The trend toward retroactive contracts was launched when Jonathan Tasini, et al., filed suit against several major publications (including the *New York Times*) over the issue of electronic rights. The suit, filed in 1993, stated that the *NYT* and other defendants had sold electronic rights to various articles written by Tasini and others without their permission or a contractual agreement transferring such rights. The publications had a practice of selling their articles to various electronic databases (or, in one case, of putting out an electronic edition). Tasini et al. contended that this was an unauthorized use of the material. In 1997, a judge ruled against Tasini, but in 1999, an appeals court overturned that decision, and in 2001, the Supreme Court ruled seven to two that newspapers and magazines could not sell freelance contributions to electronic databases without the permission of the writers.

Tasini, who heads the National Writers Union, heralded this decision as a victory for writers. The effect in the real world, however, was simply to motivate more publications to either institute all-rights (or work-for-hire) agreements—or, worse, to institute retroactive agreements that required writers to sign over all rights to all articles they had previously sold to the publication, regardless of the rights that the publication had originally purchased. In many cases, publishers told their contributors that any future sales were conditional on signing such a contract.

So far, no one seems to have challenged the legality of such a contract, even though it violates the basic principle of contract law: that a contract must *precede* the exchange of goods and services. The issuance of retroactive contracts has proven a major source of controversy for writers. By signing them, writers give up a huge chunk of rights—but by refusing them, writers risk losing important markets for their work. This is another one of those issues where there is no "right answer"; the answer depends on what is most important to you, in your personal situation as a writer.

Can I Get My Rights Back If a Magazine Folds?

Once again, the answer to this question is "it depends." If an independent publication folds, then chances are you can reclaim any rights that you originally sold to that publication. A contract ceases to be valid if one party to that contract ceases to exist.

A key question, however, is whether the publisher has actually ceased to exist. Many magazines are owned by a larger publisher—often, a media conglomerate that owns dozens or hundreds of magazines. In this case, your contract is not with the magazine itself, but with the publisher of that magazine, who continues to exist (and hold your rights) even if the magazine itself has closed. If a magazine folds, therefore, check your contract to see who actually owns your rights: the magazine, or some larger publishing entity.

If a publisher has bought all rights to your article, it will continue to own those rights even if the magazine it bought them for ceases to exist. However, such a publisher *may* be agreeable to a request to return those rights, particularly if the article has not yet been published. (For example, when *Cats* magazine folded in 2001, its owner, Primedia, returned the rights to any unpublished articles to the authors.) If the article *has* been published, a publisher may be more likely to hold on to any rights it still owns, as it still might wish to produce a compilation of "best articles," or a CD-ROM of back issues, or some similar product.

If a publisher has not fulfilled its part of a contract—i.e., it hasn't paid you—at the time that a magazine folds, then you're in a much stronger position to request a return of your rights. A publisher is far less likely to want to pay you on behalf of a publication that no longer exists. If the work was to be paid for on publication, and has not yet been published, then the publisher would be unable to fulfill its agreement with you, and you should have little difficulty reclaiming your rights. If the work *was* published, but was not paid for, then the publisher would be in violation of its side of the contract, and should either pay you or return your rights.

In any case, the best approach in this type of situation is to *ask*. Many writers are afraid to ask publishers for their rights, for fear that somehow they will be blacklisted in the industry. This simply doesn't happen, and you won't get *anything* from a publisher that you don't ask for!

What Happens to My Work When a Magazine Is Sold to Another Company?

Magazines change hands with frightening regularity these days, especially as the larger media conglomerates gobble up smaller, independent publications. Sadly, many of these buyers are interested only in the bottom line—bringing lots of money in while paying out as little as possible. When a magazine changes hands, its contributors are often left in the lurch.

For example, when the online publication Allpets.com was sold in 2002, its new owners informed contributors that they would not be paid for any outstanding invoices. Many columnists were owed for two or three back issues, and were left with no means of collecting payment. The new owners claimed that they had purchased only the *assets* of the publication (i.e., the columns that had been published) but not the *liabilities* (i.e., the payments due to contributors).

I don't know if it's legally possible for a new owner to purchase only a company's assets and not its liabilities as well. However, I *do* know from experience that trying to collect payment when a publication changes hands is virtually impossible. In a situation like this, contributors have no leverage over the new owner; generally, the amounts involved don't justify taking any sort of legal action (in the Allpets case, for example, I was owed a whopping $50).

The same is true when a publication goes bankrupt (as *Themestream* did in 2000): Contributors are generally going to be the *last* "creditor" to get paid, if they even manage to file a claim against the company to begin with. In a bankruptcy case, even if a contributor *does* file a claim, one can hope at best to gain only pennies on the dollar.

In cases when a writer needs to take steps to obtain an overdue payment, or to regain a set of rights, a contract can be both an enemy and an asset. A bad contract can be nearly impossible to overturn; but at the same time, *no* contract can make it virtually impossible for a writer to claim a debt. A writer's best protection is to be able to understand and negotiate a contract— and, when necessary, to "cover" one's assets by writing one's own.

CHAPTER 23

Setting Fees and Getting Paid

ne question commonly asked by new freelancers is, "How much should I charge?" The short answer is, "It's not your choice." While most forms of self-employment enable an individual to set his or her own rates, freelance writing is an exception. In this business, rates are determined by the market, and freelancers have very little control over what they are paid. In addition, most markets are notoriously inflexible; if a magazine pays 10¢ per word, don't expect to persuade it to give you 25¢ per word.

There are other ways, however, to determine your "preferred" rate of pay, even if you can't convince editors to loosen their purse-strings.

By the Word versus by the Hour

If you've come to freelancing from a "normal" job, you're probably used to a paycheck that was based on an hourly rate. Converting to an accounting system that is based on the word or the project can be confusing.

As you choose and plan your projects, however, it's a good idea to keep that hourly rate concept in mind. By determining the hourly rate you would prefer to receive, you can determine what publications to approach, what projects to accept, and how much time to invest in each project.

Determining that rate is a highly individual decision. If you're trying to support yourself entirely through freelancing, you'll need to set it fairly high (especially as you must take into account the number of hours spent on non-paying projects, such as queries, researching markets, basic accounting and administrative tasks, etc.). On the other hand, if you're just trying to "break in" and don't need to earn a living wage, you can set a lower rate.

The next step is to determine how long a particular project is likely to take. In the beginning, this may not be easy; tasks such as interviewing, research, and revision may take longer than you expect. As you become more experienced, however, you'll be able to estimate a project's requirements fairly accurately. Then, "setting your rate" becomes a simple matter of dividing a magazine's fee by the estimated number of hours to see if it meets your hourly requirement.

Suppose, for example, that a magazine offers $100 per feature article, and you've decided that you want to earn no less than $20 per hour. In that case, you'd only pitch an article idea to this magazine if you were certain you could complete the entire piece in five hours or less. On the other hand, if a magazine offers $1,000 per feature, you'll be willing to invest considerably more time and effort into that market. Similarly, you'll soon realize that a single $1,000 article actually "pays" considerably more than ten $100 articles, given the same rate of effort per article.

Another way to look at your rate is by averaging it across assignments. Suppose you accept a $100 assignment, but spend ten hours completing the project. You've earned only $10 per hour, or half your goal. On the other hand, another article may bring you $600 for ten hours' work, giving you a total of $60 per hour. On the average, you're now earning $35 per hour, which exceeds your goal (and also helps compensate for all those hours when you aren't earning a penny). Often, "averaging" is a more accurate method of determining how much your time is actually worth.

When Time Isn't the Only Factor

Money is nice, but it may not be the only consideration when choosing whether to seek or accept a particular assignment. Some factors may be worth more than cash, including:

✿ *Credentials.* If you're just starting out, your first goal may be to build a portfolio of clips. In the early stages of freelancing, "getting published" is often more important than "getting highly paid." In the beginning, a track record of success and acceptance can be more important than the actual fee.

✿ *Practice.* Some writers believe that every word they write makes them better writers—and is therefore worth the effort. Writing for lower-paying markets can provide an opportunity to build and hone your skills, and prepare you for the demands of the "big time."

✿ *Reputation.* Some markets pay little, but offer extra rewards in terms of recognition and reputation. This is especially true online, where your work may be viewed by readers from around the world. Writing for a low-paying publication that will put your name in front of thousands of readers (and quite possibly a number of editors) can be worth more than the higher paychecks offered by comparable print publications, and lead to bigger and better markets down the line.

✿ *Love.* Sometimes you may choose to write about a particular subject, or for a particular publication, simply because it's what you want to do. In many cases, passion counts for more than cash. Many writers would rather get paid a little for writing about what they love than get paid big bucks for writing material of no personal interest.

Conversely, you may also discover that some projects aren't worth doing, no matter how much they pay. Some factors outweigh the potential financial benefits of a piece, including:

❖ *Difficult editors.* Some editors provide unclear guidelines, then expect the author to keep revising a piece until it seems "right." Some are impossible to please, even when you've provided exactly what was asked for. Some drag out the process by constantly asking for one more thing—more information, another interview, another sidebar, another revision, etc. Others won't answer your questions, provide clarification, or even return your calls or e-mail. Whatever the problem, a difficult editor can outweigh the benefit of a check.

❖ *Unacceptable alterations.* Few things are as frustrating as writing an article, and then finding that the published piece bears little or no resemblance to your work. Perhaps it was edited by someone with no concept of basic grammar, resulting in a piece that you'd be ashamed to send out as a clip. Perhaps it was cut to half its length, wasting your work. Or perhaps material has been added—not only material that wasn't your work, but worse, material that actually contradicts the point of your article. If this happens, it's wise to avoid that market in the future, unless you really don't care what appears under your byline!

❖ *Unfair terms.* Only you can decide what terms you're willing to accept when negotiating a contract. Keep in mind, however, that even a high rate of pay may not fully compensate for the loss of your rights. Be very sure, when giving up all rights or signing a work-for-hire contract, that you have absolutely no chance of selling that material elsewhere.

❖ *Damage to your reputation.* Will an article make you look good—or bad? Sometimes the very context in which an article appears may damage your reputation in a particular field. If the publication itself is not reputable within a field in which you hope to sell more work, then selling to that publication could damage your career. It's also important to avoid assignments that might cast you in a negative light (e.g., that present an argument you don't actually agree with). What you say in print will be taken as representing your point of view, even if it doesn't. Your good name is worth more than any paycheck, and losing it can make you "poor indeed."

The bottom line is that "the bottom line" for a writer can be influenced by a number of factors, of which money is only one. By considering those factors carefully, you *can* set the rates you desire—rates that not only improve your bank account but contribute to your ongoing career goals.

Handling "Pay on Publication" Markets

Many writers refuse to write for "pay-on-publication" markets. This type of market pays the writer only when the piece is actually published or printed. Typically, payment is issued at the end of the cover month or the beginning of the following month. Thus, if you send in an article in April, and it is scheduled for October, you won't see a check until sometime in November, or even December. Since most print publications schedule material at least six months in advance, and often as much as a year in advance, this means a writer can wait a very long time indeed to get paid.

However, pay-on-publication markets are often more open to new writers (perhaps because more experienced writers prefer not to work for them!). So it may not be realistic to recommend that you avoid such markets altogether. If you do write for such markets, here are some ways to protect yourself:

✤ Try to get a commitment as to when the article will appear. Ask the editor to specify a publication date in your contract.

✤ Ask for a time limit. If you can't get a specific issue date, consider having a clause inserted into your contract that specifies that the article will be published *within* a certain time limit (e.g., two years). If possible, try to include a kill fee if the material is *not* published within that time; for instance, if it isn't published in two years, rights revert to you and you will receive 25 percent of the promised payment. Not all magazines will do this, but *it never hurts to ask*.

✤ Keep following up on the piece if it doesn't appear. I'd contact an editor at least every six months to inquire about the "anticipated publication date." Keep in mind that as long as this article isn't published, not only are you not getting paid, but you're also constrained from reselling the article anywhere else.

✤ Withdraw the piece if it remains unpublished. If your article is not published within a year, you may wish to consider withdrawing the piece from the publisher's inventory. I would give the editor one more opportunity to either schedule the piece, or pay you for it in advance. If the editor is not willing to do either, then you can send a polite "withdrawal" letter stating that you wish the article to be removed from the publisher's inventory, and for all rights to revert to you. Since you have not received any payment for the article, the publisher has not yet fulfilled its side of the contract, which makes it easier for you to cancel your side.

Asking for More Money

While publications generally quote a specific payment rate in their guidelines, the reality is that most publications offer a *range* of rates—and the quoted rate is often the lowest end of that range. Editors and publishers know that *most* writers will never bother to ask if they can get paid a higher rate. Many writers, indeed, are afraid to ask such a question; they're afraid that it will make them look difficult, or demanding, or unprofessional.

Of course, asking for a raise *can* make you look unprofessional if you do it at the wrong time, or in the wrong way. Here are some *bad* times to ask for more money:

❖ When you contribute your first article to a publication. When you first submit to a publication, an editor expects you to have reviewed the guidelines and to be aware of the pay range. If the publication doesn't offer as high a rate as you want to receive, don't write for them! It's not considered professional to demand a rate higher than the posted range on your very first submission.

❖ When you've accepted an assignment and your article is due. As an editor, I've had more than one experience with a writer who promises to provide an assigned article—only to call on the due date to explain that he or she feels that she should get more money for the piece. Editors have a word for this: It's called "blackmail." Essentially, the writer is threatening to hold an assigned (and possibly scheduled) article "hostage" for more pay. Occasionally, a writer may get away with this once if the editor absolutely *has* to have the article for that issue (if, for example, the cover has already been printed with a blurb advertising the article). However, you can be sure that if you try this approach, you'll never write for that publication again!

❖ When you find that an article is taking more work than you expected. When you agree to write an article, you agree to the terms. If you find that an article is requiring more work than you anticipated, that's your problem, not the editor's. Telling an editor that the article is "harder than you thought" is simply going to look like bad planning on your part.

The time to start asking about higher payments is after you've sold your second or third article to the same publication. By this time, the editor should be familiar with you and your work, and you may even be considered a "regular contributor." If you're a reliable contributor, an editor will generally want to keep you happy—and one way to do so is to increase your rate.

Before you ask for a raise, however, take a look at what happens to your work after you submit it. Are your articles printed just as you write them, or are they substantially revised and edited? If an editor has to invest a lot of work in your contributions—particularly if the editor needs to clean up your grammar, spelling, and punctuation—then the editor may not be enthusiastic about giving you more money. Editors generally pay higher rates to the contributors who need the *least* amount of editorial work.

You also need to know the criteria for different rate levels. Some publications offer higher rates for articles that are more "difficult"—those that involve more research, interviews, or in-depth knowledge. For example, a publication may pay more for an article that requires interviews with four or five technical experts than for a light, personal experience piece that you could write "off the top of your head." If you're writing "easy" pieces, start asking for more difficult assignments—and then ask for more money. For example, you might approach the editor with a statement like this:

> As you can see, this piece required considerably more research than some of the previous articles I've written for you. It involved several interviews, and a lot of fact-checking. Consequently, I feel that it might be worth a higher rate than you have paid in the past. I note that your pay range is between XXX and XXX—any chance that you could bump this one up a bit on the scale?

Another approach is to ask the editor to move you from the "new contributor" pay range to the "established contributor" range:

> I notice that your guidelines indicate that you have a pay range from XXX to XXX. I assume that the lower end of this range is the rate you offer writers who are new to the publication. As I've now contributed [X] articles, I'd like to think I've moved up to the status of regular contributor. Any chance that my pay could be adjusted to reflect that?

Yet another approach is to ask, flat out, what the criteria are for higher payments:

> I notice that your guidelines specify a pay range of XXX to XXX. Can you tell me what the criteria are for the higher rates? I'd like to offer you the best possible product, and knowing exactly what you're looking for will help!

Keep in mind that not all editors control the pay rates. If a range is specified, however, chances are that the editor has a voice in what writers are paid, and it never hurts to ask. Again, don't let fear stand in the way. The key is "professionalism."

Getting Paid

"Selling" your article is often only half the battle. The other half involves getting your check.

Some publications offer payment once they have received a signed contract. Others, however, require an invoice from the writer. I recommend sending an invoice even if it is *not* required: It provides a good record for you, both in case you need to take further action to get paid, and so that you can monitor which payments are still outstanding.

An invoice can be a very simple e-mail statement, or a more complicated form. You can purchase invoice blanks at an office-supply store, but the easiest way to create an invoice is to simply design one in a spreadsheet program (such as Excel; see Figure 23.1). This way, you can print off your invoice and mail or fax it to the editor, or you can send it as an e-mail attachment (with the editor's permission).

Here's an example of a simple e-mail or text invoice:

INVOICE

DATE: (Date of invoice)
TO: (Contact name, publication, address)
FROM: (Your name, address)

FOR: (Article title)
(If the person you're invoicing handles several different publications, you might also wish to list the title of the publication the article has or will appear in, and the issue date.)

AMOUNT DUE: $XXX
(If the payment rate is per word, include the word count here; for example, "2,000 words @ 5¢/word = $100")

SSN: Your Social Security number; this will be required by U.S. publications of any author who is a U.S. citizen, even if you're not a resident of the United States. If you don't want to provide this information by e-mail, then send an invoice by fax or surface mail.

Send the invoice to your editor. Your editor is responsible for getting this information to the accounting department. If you don't receive your payment, contact the editor directly. The editor may tell you to send your invoice directly to the accounting department; if so, do this, but remember

Figure 23.1: Sample Invoice

Moira Allen

1234 My Street, Somewhere, VA 20000

(123) 555-1900 • (123) 555-1901 (fax)

Sold To: Universal Magazine Publishers	**Invoice#** 03-1011
1234 Somewhere Drive	**Date:** 9/15/03
Music Beach, FL 33443	**P.O. #**

Project Description	#	Total
Example 1: Flat-fee project		
"World of Cats" article (Sept. 2003)		$500.00
Example 2: Project billed at hourly rate		
Book manuscript editing @ $35/hour	10 hrs	$350.00
Example 3: Project billed by the word		
"Writing a Synopsis" @ 5¢/word	1500 wds	$75.00
Social Security Number:		
Total:		$925.00

that it is *still* the editor's responsibility to make sure that contributors get paid. (Most editors are required to submit a payment list to the accounting department for every issue.)

But what if you don't get paid? If a significant amount of time goes by and you haven't seen a check, start following up. While a phone call is one way to follow up, I recommend *always* following up with a written request—either by e-mail or by surface mail. It's important, at this point, to establish a paper trail that indicates your efforts to obtain payment. Make sure that you (a) have a contract or some letter of agreement indicating what you're supposed to be paid and when, and (b) an invoice indicating that you've made an attempt to collect that payment. Save a copy of any correspondence you send thereafter. Submit regular invoices to the accounting department, and indicate the amount of time that has elapsed (e.g., thirty days, sixty days, etc.) from the date of the first invoice.

Most publications honor their commitments to contributors. Some, however, are slow payers, and respond only after a fair amount of nagging. And now and then, you're bound to run into a publication that doesn't pay at all, no matter how much you follow up. When this happens, and you've done everything you can do, you may be able to get assistance from a writer's organization such as the National Writers Union (*www.nwu.org*) or the Author's Guild (*www.authorsguild.org/welcome.html*). Unfortunately, you have to be a *member* of such an organization before you can turn to their legal department for help, and membership dues for many authors' groups tend to be high. If, however, you're trying to claim a payment of $500 to $1,000, a membership fee of $100 will be well worth the cost.

It's also wise to check out publications *before* you write for them. You can find lists of problem markets on the National Writer's Union Web site (*www.nwu.org/alerts/alrthome.htm*) and also on WritersWeekly.com (*www.writersweekly.com/warnings/html*).

Finally, until you're familiar with a market and know that it pays in a timely fashion, never submit a *second* article until you've been paid for the first! I've heard from writers who have submitted as many as five articles (and even had them published) before getting a check for their first submission. Having a publisher express interest in your work is great—but make sure that interest is backed up with cash.

The sad truth is that there will be times when, even when you do everything you can, you will get stiffed. It happens. Sometimes publications change hands, and the new owners refuse to honor the contracts or invoices of previous contributors. Sometimes a publication shuts down or goes bankrupt, and though writers can submit their invoices to the court for collection, they're likely to be the last creditors paid—and may receive only pennies on the dollar. And sometimes you run into a publication that simply doesn't honor its agreements.

When this happens, there is very little you can do. Generally, the amounts are not sufficiently large to justify hiring a collection agency or filing a lawsuit. The one bright spot to consider is that if a publication fails to pay, it has failed to honor its side of your contract—which leaves you free to market the material elsewhere. The best response to nonpayment (after you've exhausted every collection means within your power) is to move on, and to avoid agonizing over the loss.

CHAPTER 24

Handling Income and Expenses

*A*ny income that you make as a writer is taxable—including article sales, book royalties, advances, etc. This means that you need to know how to keep accurate records of that income, and of your expenses that relate to writing. Generally, this income falls into the category of "self-employment." (The exception is if you work as a contractor for a company for which you are doing business or technical writing, and receive a paycheck from which taxes are withheld. In this case, you would treat that income as "wages" rather than as self-employment income, even though you may technically be considered a private contractor rather than an employee.)

If you don't expect to do a great deal of writing, or to earn much money from writing (e.g., less than $1,000 a year), you do have the option of treating your writing income as "hobby" income. Hobby income must be reported to the IRS on the "Other Income" line on your 1040 (line 21). Hobby expenses (e.g., paper, postage, etc.) are deductible only if (a) you itemize deductions, and (b) those expenses exceed the 2-percent-of-income minimum. The only advantage of considering your writing a hobby is that you don't have to worry about such matters as saving receipts, keeping good records, etc. If you honestly don't mind giving the IRS more money, this is certainly an option.

If you consider yourself a "serious" writer, however—if you write frequently, and if you're hoping to increase your skill, your output, and your income—you need to think of your writing as a business. This is in your best interest even if in the beginning you do not make a great deal of money. After all, your goal is to make more later, so it's best to get into the habit of thinking (and acting) like a professional as soon as possible.

NOTE: The information in this chapter applies to writers who pay U.S. taxes. If you're not a U.S. citizen, or liable for U.S. taxes, you'll need to check with the tax agency of your country of citizenship or residence for information on how to handle your writing income.

One way to qualify as a business is to make a profit in three years out of five. Even if you do not, however, you may still qualify if you can demonstrate that you have made a reasonable effort to (a) make a profit and (b) conduct your business in a professional fashion. That means being able to demonstrate that you:

❖ Spend a significant amount of time writing, or engaged in writing-related activities. Your business does not have to be "full-time," but you should be producing work regularly.

❖ Actively attempt to market your work. This means seeking appropriate markets and submitting to those markets (even if you're rejected). The best way to prove this is by keeping track of your submissions and responses.

❖ Keep accurate and businesslike records. This includes records of your income and expenses, and records of your work itself (e.g., tracking submissions, time spent, etc.).

Even if you're making no money whatsoever right now, these are good habits to get into, because they'll protect you once you *do* begin earning an income.

Tracking Your Business

In the "business" of writing, good records are important in two areas: to track your work, and to track your income and expenses. Tracking your work means keeping copies of your submissions, cover letters, queries, and responses (see chapter 25). It's also a good idea to keep a running log of submissions that notes what the item was (e.g., a query or article), when it went out, to whom, when a response was received, and what the response was. This log will also help remind you to follow up on items that have received no response.

Tracking your income and expenses can be just as easy as tracking your submissions. No fancy filing system or advanced bookkeeping degree is needed for this. All you need is a few folders or envelopes, and some method of keeping a running account of your financial transactions (see below).

To track your writing income and expenses effectively, you'll need to keep them separate from your personal finances. This means getting into a few simple habits:

❖ Purchase writing supplies (such as paper, printer cartridges, and postage) separately from other supplies. If you're making business and personal purchases in the same store, pay for them separately.

❖ File business receipts separately from personal receipts. My method is to stuff each month's receipts and canceled checks into an envelope that is clearly labeled with the month and year. When the month is over, I close the envelope and (hopefully) forget about it. If I need an old receipt, I know where to find it. At the end of the year, I move that year's envelopes to a storage box in the closet and start a new set. Record project titles on your receipts, if appropriate. This isn't necessary for office supplies, but is useful for travel and entertainment expenses.

✤ Store (and use) writing supplies separately from business supplies as much as possible. Granted, you probably won't swap "business" paper for "personal" paper in the printer just because you're writing a letter to your sister, but be realistic. If you attempt to deduct the cost of fifty manila envelopes and you can show that you've sent out forty-five man-uscripts, no one is likely to ask about the other five. But if you write off fifty and have sent out five manuscripts, that could raise eyebrows in an audit.

✤ Open a separate checking account. This isn't a "must," but it's helpful. It needn't be a business account (which often costs more and may require a business license); your best bet may be a personal account that charges no fee if you maintain a minimum balance. Find out if you can get your checks returned (some banks charge a small fee, such as $1 per month, for this service); while canceled checks aren't an absolute necessity, they provide added security.

✤ Consider investing in a separate telephone line, especially if you conduct a lot of writing business (such as interviews) by phone. Again, this need not be a business line. If you use a separate line for business, the entire cost of the line is deductible; if you use your personal line, you can only deduct the cost of the calls themselves. (A separate line also enables clients and editors to reach you even when you're surfing the Web or checking e-mail.)

✤ Maintain an ongoing record of your income and expenses. This can be as simple as a handwritten ledger (though I recommend using a comput-erized spreadsheet). At the minimum, your record should contain four entry categories: Date, Item, Income, and Expense. Whenever money goes in or out, enter the amount in the appropriate category. If you'd prefer to save time and effort at tax time, it's helpful to include addi-tional columns that correspond to the numbered categories on the Schedule C (or at least those categories that you expect to use). If you use this method, it's best to "double-enter" your expenses: once under the generic "expense" column, which will give you an ongoing total of your expenses, and once under the "category" column (such as "office" or "utilities"), which will give you a total for that particular category (see Figure 24.1).

✤ Keep your records (correspondence, tax forms, and income and expense receipts) for at least five years; some sources recommend seven or ten. While the IRS technically won't go back more than three years unless they suspect fraud, keep in mind that an audit may not be initiated until a year or more after a return is filed. (You can also scan records such as receipts; I recommend this approach for storing older files.)

Why All This Trouble?

Why is all this record keeping important? After all, you got into this business to write books, not keep them! Some writers fancy that "words" come from one side of the brain and "figures" from the other—and those of us who are good with words just don't have a head for figures. That's about as logical as saying "girls can't do math." Besides, we have computers to do the hard work for us!

Getting into the "habit" of good bookkeeping is important for several reasons. Here are the top five:

❖ *Good bookkeeping can protect you from an audit.* If your tax figures make sense, your return is less likely to raise a "red flag" at the IRS. When you track your income and expenses over the course of a year, you can recognize areas where your expenses are outstripping your income, and make the necessary adjustments. For example, if you're hoping to show a profit (and thereby demonstrate that you're truly a "business"), remember that there is no law against *not* claiming all your deductions, even if you're entitled to them. (You can also "postpone" some deductions until the following year.)

❖ *Good bookkeeping protects you if you* are *audited.* I know; I've been there. Thanks to the fact that I had all the records I needed to support my claims (and knew exactly where those records were), my audit was neither scary nor particularly costly. I didn't have to waste time wondering whether the IRS was going to "uncover" some ghastly accounting or reporting error. Believe me, there's nothing like the confidence good records give you when an audit notice arrives in the mail!

❖ *Good bookkeeping can help you determine how successful your various writing ventures are.* By tracking income and related expenses, you can determine which projects are profitable, and which are actually costing you money. (For example, if you pay a $50 phone-interview bill for a $25 article, you may want to rethink your marketing strategies.) Good records will also show you areas in which you may be overspending: If you're like me, for example, you may find that you're spending a lot of money on writing-related books that you don't have time to read.

❖ *Good bookkeeping is essential if you have to pay estimated taxes.* This occurs if (a) you have a tax liability (you owe money) and (b) no taxes are being deducted from your income to cover that liability. When you receive a paycheck, your taxes are deducted each time you are paid; when you're self-employed, however, you have to make that "deduction" yourself—often long before you actually receive the money you're expecting. Good records are essential to help you figure out how much money you're likely to receive in a given quarter, and how much tax you're likely to owe.

✦ *Good bookkeeping drastically reduces your stress level at tax-time.* When you've kept a record of your income and expenses throughout the year, all you have to do is plug the totals into your tax form and you're done. Then you can get back to your real job: writing.

Preparing Your Taxes

Believe it or not, declaring your writing income and expenses really isn't that complicated (most of the time). Let's start with the simple stuff, then move on to the exceptions.

When you operate a sole-proprietor business (such as writing), you declare income and expenses on the Schedule C. (If you have no more than $2,500 in business expenses, only one business, no depreciation or amortization, and do not claim the home-office deduction, you may be able to use the Schedule C-EZ.) The Schedule C is remarkably straightforward (for an IRS form); it asks a few basic questions, offers a few categories to fill in, and you're ready to go.

First, you'll be asked to fill in your name, address, social security number, and "Principle Business Code." For writers and artists, that's 711510. Your principal "business or profession" is "writing" (or "author"). Your accounting method will be cash; that means you claim expenses when you pay them (by cash, check, or credit card) and income when it is received. Did you "materially participate" in your business? Yes—unless someone else is doing your writing for you!

Next you'll list your income, which is all the money you've received from writing during the year. This includes royalties (don't be confused by Schedule E, which involves a completely different kind of "royalties"). You'll almost certainly enter the same amount on lines 1, 3, 5, and 7; ignore the other lines. (By the way, don't assume the IRS doesn't know how much you earned: If you received more than $600 from any single source, that source will file a Form 1099 with the IRS declaring that income.)

Deducting Expenses

Now for the fun part: expenses. Fortunately, you can deduct any expense that is directly related to your writing efforts, including (but not limited to) the following:

- Office supplies, such as paper, envelopes, postage, printer cartridges, pencils, pens, computer disks, etc. (You can deduct these under "office" or under "supplies.")
- Printing and photocopying, such as tear sheets, business cards, etc.
- The expense of an Internet connection, if it is used primarily for business. If you "share" your connection with other family members, figure out the percentage of time spent on business and prorate the expense accordingly.
- Telephone calls related to writing, such as calls to editors, interviews, etc. If you have a separate line, you can deduct the entire cost of the line (under "utilities"); if not, you can only deduct the cost of the calls themselves. If you have extra services related to writing, such as a "distinctive-ring" number for your business or fax, you can deduct that as well.
- Books, magazines, and similar materials that relate to writing or research. This includes sample magazines for market research, and subscriptions to magazines relevant to your field or to writing in general (within reason). Books are a tricky issue: If a book is for short-term use only (e.g., if it is for research for a one-time project, or if it is an annual such as *Writer's Market*), it can (possibly) be deducted under "miscellaneous." If, however, you keep the book as part of your "professional library," it must be amortized or "expensed" (see below).
- The cost of attending a writer's conference, including 50 percent of your travel and meal costs.
- Business fees, bank fees, professional fees (such as the cost of an accountant or lawyer), fees paid to an agent, etc.
- Dues paid to societies and organizations that are related to writing, or to a specific area of expertise that you write about.
- Taxes, such as state and local taxes incurred on your writing income, and sales tax on large purchases.
- Repairs to office equipment, and rental of office equipment (such as a postage meter).
- Classes, reference materials, and other resources that are designed to improve your skills in your existing profession are deductible. Thus, once you have decided to establish yourself as a "professional writer" (even if you have made no sales as yet), you can deduct the cost of writing classes, reference books, magazine subscriptions, etc. However, if you have not yet begun to do any actual writing, you may not be able to deduct the cost of a course designed to get you started as a writer.

These are the simple deductions. Now let's look at some of the more complicated expenses you may incur as a writer.

Mileage

Certain auto expenses are deductible. If you can claim a home-office deduction, for example, then you can also deduct the cost of using your car to drive from that office to, say, the office-supply store, or an interview, or whatever. If, however, you do *not* claim the home-office deduction, then you can't claim the expense of driving from home to a work-related location. However, you may be able to claim the cost of driving from one work-related location to another. For example, if you drive from home to the office-supply store, and from there to the post office, and from there to an interview, you could deduct the cost of driving from the store to the post office and from the post office to the interview—but *not* the cost of driving from home to the store, or from the interview back home again. (The drive to and from your home is considered a "commute.")

For those mileage costs that you can deduct, you can either deduct "actual expenses" (by prorating the costs of maintenance, gas, etc.) or "mileage." Check with your accountant for the current per-mile rate, as this changes from year to year. (Auto expenses are handled on Form 4562.)

Depreciation, Amortization, and Expensing

Some expenses cannot be deducted directly. Items that have a long "lifespan," such as equipment, furniture, autos, etc., generally must be depreciated or amortized. This requires a separate form and some rather complicated calculations. In brief, some of the types of expenses that must be depreciated include:

❖ Computer hardware, including monitors, keyboards, printers, scanners, modems, etc.
❖ Office equipment, such as fax machines, copiers, telephones, answering machines, etc.
❖ Furniture, such as chairs, computer desks, carpeting, lamps, etc.
❖ Computer software (unless updated annually, like a phone disc or tax software); this must be amortized.
❖ Books that become a part of your permanent professional library.

The good news is that you may elect to "expense" many of these items rather than depreciate them over the course of three to seven years. You can "expense" up to $17,500 of depreciable equipment (but not items that must be amortized) by using Section 179 of Form 4562. The amount you expense, however, cannot exceed your total writing income.

I've heard varying opinions on whether books should be expensed or amortized. My own accountant claims they must be amortized, but others say they can be expensed. When in doubt, discuss the question with an accountant (or two). So far, every accountant I've talked to agrees that computer software *must* be amortized *unless* it is something that you have to replace every year.

Travel

Some travel and entertainment expenses are deductible. However, this deduction is shrinking fast. Also, the IRS frowns on deductions that look like, "I took a $5,000 dream vacation to France, and now I think I'll see if I can sell a $100 article on it." If you're going to deduct travel, you'll do better if you have an assignment in hand before you leave (then you can claim that you're traveling for business purposes, not trying to wring a business deduction out of personal travel).

The Home Office Deduction

Writers are entitled to take the home-office deduction, which is the "cost" of the space you use for an office. You can deduct a percentage of your rent or mortgage, based upon the percentage of space used by your office. For example, if your home is 2,000 square feet and your office takes up 100 square feet, you can deduct 5 percent of your mortgage (or rent) plus 5 percent of your utility bills. To claim this deduction, however, several conditions must be met.

❖ Your office must be a clearly defined location, such as a bedroom, an attic, a nook, a closet, etc. You cannot deduct "a corner of your living room" or "10 percent of the kitchen."

❖ Your office must be used exclusively for business purposes. Pay your personal bills somewhere else, and don't use that space for personal storage. Clean the games off your computer!

❖ Your home-office deduction cannot be used to create a loss. For example, if your total deduction were to come to $2,000 per year, but your writing income is only $1,000 and you have $400 in other expenses, the maximum home-office deduction you will be able to claim is $600.

It has been said that the home-office deduction "raises red flags" at the IRS and makes an audit more likely. Most business magazines, however, say that the IRS encourages this perception to discourage people from claiming deductions to which they are entitled, and that one shouldn't forego this deduction out of fear of an audit. If in doubt, it would be wise to get the advice of an accountant.

If you plan to sell your home, and you have been claiming a portion of it as an "office" on your taxes, you may find that you have to pay taxes on a portion of the income of your home sale. Since you have declared a portion of your home to be "business property," when you sell your home, a corresponding portion of the revenue from the sale is now "business income" (i.e., income that you gained by selling the "business" portion of your home). If you anticipate moving or selling your home, talk to your accountant about this issue before declaring a home-office deduction.

Estimated Taxes

While we all dread April 15, the truth is that taxes aren't actually due on that date. They are technically due *when your income is earned.* When you earn a paycheck, your taxes are deducted automatically. When you work for yourself, however, you don't have that advantage, and chances are that you will have to pay estimated taxes not only to the IRS but also to the state.

According to the IRS, you are expected to pay estimated taxes if your anticipated tax liability for the coming year is $1,000 or more. For example, if, in April 2003, you were required to pay $1,000 or more in taxes for the year 2002 (over and above the taxes, if any, that were deducted from your paycheck), then you will probably be required to file estimated taxes for 2003, *beginning* in April 2003. (In other words, you'll be filing last year's taxes *plus* the current year's estimated taxes for the first quarter at the same time.)

Estimated taxes are due quarterly, beginning in April. The problem, of course, is that you must pay them in advance—i.e., before you actually know what your income will be. As a writer, it's often difficult to predict one's income from one quarter to the next, but that's exactly what you're expected to do. It's better to overestimate than underestimate; refunds are better than penalties.

If your writing is not your sole source of support, or if you or someone else in your household is earning a paycheck, one way to reduce your estimated tax liability is to increase the withholding tax on that paycheck. While that may mean slightly less cash now, it can help offset your tax burden later.

According to the IRS, you can also pay your self-employment tax (another little goody you'll be hit with when you make a profit as a writer) through estimated taxes.

Surviving an Audit

The thought of an audit seems terrifying, but in fact they are not that common. Audits are more common in some regions than in others (Las Vegas and Los Angeles are high on the list). Don't let the fear of an audit prevent you from establishing a writing business. And even if you are audited (as I have been), the event is not as terrifying as you might think. Your best defense against an audit is good records.

- Keep all expense receipts; never claim a deduction you can't verify.
- Make sure you know where your receipts are. File receipts by month and by year.
- Keep copies of all writing correspondence, which proves that you are "working."
- Make sure your ledger numbers are accurate.
- Don't make stupid claims, like huge travel expenses that will get an auditor's attention.
- Don't give an auditor more than she asks for. Simply provide the requested receipts.
- Don't panic!

Get an Accountant!

When it comes to the more complicated aspects of tax preparation, such as depreciation, amortization, mileage credits, the home-office deduction, etc., there is often no substitute for a good accountant. Yes, an accountant costs money. On the other hand, so does an audit (usually), and an accountant is usually far more friendly than an IRS agent. The IRS is also (theoretically) somewhat less likely to audit small business returns prepared by an accountant, because these are (theoretically) less likely to contain errors than returns prepared by the taxpayer.

Notes on Figure 24.1

Categories listed on this spreadsheet are: Office/Supplies, Postage, Internet, Utilities, Dues/Publications, Professional, Books, Miscellaneous., Hardware, and Software. You may find that you need to add other categories, or that some of these aren't useful to you. A good way to choose categories is to check the expense items listed on the Schedule C; however, for a writer, many of these don't apply, and so many typical "writing" expenses fall under "miscellaneous" that it's useful to break them out into separate categories.

Year-end totals are achieved by totaling each column. The Profit/Loss for the year is, of course, the total income minus total expenses.

It's not necessary to subtotal each month; however, I find this a good way to track my progress over time.

I also run a "check sum" figure at the end of the spreadsheet. This figure is a sum of the totals of each individual "expense" column. Compare this figure to the total of the main expense column to make sure they match; if they don't, an item has been entered incorrectly in one of the expense columns.

Figure 24.1: Sample Income/Expense Tracking Spreadsheet

JAN-03	ITEM	INCOME	EXPENSE	OFFICE	POSTAGE	INTERNET	UTILITIES	DUES/PUBS	PROF.	MISC.	HARDWARE	SOFTWARE	BOOKS
5-Jan	"Love to Write" column	$300.00											
6-Jan	Paper		$25.60	$25.60									
8-Jan	Cox Cable		$49.95			$49.95							
15-Jan	Tuscarora Times article	$30.00											
16-Jan	Eudora 5.0		$45.00									$45.00	
20-Jan	Cats of the World	$400.00											
21-Feb	Writing for Money		$15.00										$15.00
25-Jan	Office supplies		$65.32										
26-Jan	Telephone expenses		$9.70										

$730.00	January Income		
$210.57	January Expenses		
$519.43	January Balance		

FEB-03	ITEM	INCOME	EXPENSE	OFFICE	POSTAGE	INTERNET	UTILITIES	DUES/PUBS	PROF.	MISC.	HARDWARE	SOFTWARE	BOOKS
2-Feb	Postage		$65.00		$65.00								
3-Feb	"Love to Write" column	$300.00											
5-Feb	Travel Writing Guide		$25.00										$25.00
8-Feb	Travel Writers Memb.		$80.00					$80.00					
8-Feb	Cox Cable		$49.95			$49.95							
10-Feb	New Writers Market		$49.95										$49.95
10-Feb	Book shipping		$3.95		$3.95								
15-Feb	Scanner		$100.00							$100.00			
15-Feb	Accountant fee		$350.00						$350.00				
16-Feb	Travel		$150.00							$150.00			
20-Feb	Toner cartridge		$89.95	$89.95									

$300.00	February Income		
$963.80	February Expenses		
($663.80)	February Balance		

Y2003	YEAR-END TOTALS	INCOME	EXPENSE	OFFICE	POSTAGE	INTERNET	UTILITIES	DUES/PUBS	PROF.	MISC.	HARDWARE	SOFTWARE	BOOKS
($144.37)	Balance 2003	$1,030.00	$1,174.37	$115.55	$68.95	$99.90	$0.00	$80.00	$350.00	$150.00	$100.00	$45.00	$89.95

CHAPTER 25

Keeping Records

One thing you're bound to produce as a writer is *lots* of paper. Forget the concept of the "paperless office": While you may find that you can store *some* records on your computer, you're still going to amass large quantities of files.

Sooner or later, you're going to start asking yourself how much of that paper you actually need to keep. The quick and easy answer is: every file that relates directly to your writing business. That includes the following:

Contracts and Letters of Agreement

Whenever you sell a "work" (an article, story, poem, book, whatever), you should have some sort of written agreement with the purchaser. Sometimes this will be a formal contract; in other cases, it may be little more than a letter saying, "Thanks for sending this; yes, we'd love to use it." If you don't receive even that much, create your own letter of agreement specifying the rights you're licensing. For the greatest degree of protection, ask your editor to countersign a copy of this letter and send it back to you.

Such contracts and agreements may be your only evidence in later years that you sold (or did *not* sell) a specific set of rights. If you have no record of the terms under which your material was published, it will be very difficult for you to prove the terms of that agreement.

Keep these contracts *forever*. You don't need a fancy filing system for them; a simple folder marked "contracts" should be enough. If you have lots of contracts, consider investing in an expanding "pocket" folder with alphabetical dividers, so that you can file your contracts by publication name. Never assume that you won't need a copy of that contract in later years. I found material of mine posted online (without my permission) that I'd sold fifteen years earlier.

Correspondence

Granted, a lot of your writing correspondence looks pretty trivial: "Do you want to buy this article?" "No." Even rejection letters are important, however. If nothing else, they demonstrate to the IRS (in case of an audit) that you really are attempting to conduct a writing business. Acceptance letters are even more important: Often, they spell out the terms of the sale. If so, put them in your "contracts" file.

While it may be tempting to set up alphabetical files for your correspondence, I've never found this necessary. My own system originally consisted of two folders: "Pending" and "Completed." Once a response arrived to a letter in the "pending" file, I'd staple it to my outgoing letter and file both in the "Completed" file. At the end of the year, I label the Completed folder for that year (e.g., "Correspondence 2002") and store it in a file box in my closet. If my correspondence becomes too much for a single folder, I subdivide it into "acceptances," rejections," and "everything else," all of which get stored in the box at the end of the year. You may never have to touch these files again—but you never know! (A note for those who live in wet climates: Don't store your files in a garage, cellar, or other noninsulated room. Keep them where they won't be damaged by damp.)

Invoices

If you regularly send out invoices to editors, you may want to store these separately from your regular correspondence. You may also want two folders: one for pending invoices, and one for paid invoices. If you want to subdivide these alphabetically, fine; otherwise, a single "paid" folder will usually suffice for a single year of invoices.

Clips

Rare is the writer who doesn't preserve copies of everything he or she has ever published! This is your "clip" file, which you can use both as a portfolio and as a way to store and file clips that you want to copy and send with queries. I recommend getting a nice leather binder (found in the briefcase section of office-supply stores) for your "display" portfolio—this will be the place to file your best (and most recent) clips. Eventually, it will overflow, and you can store older and less prestigious clips in regular binders.

Use plastic page protectors—the kind that have an extra strip on the side for the binder holes—to store your clips. If these include newspaper articles, I recommend cutting out the article and arranging it so that it will fit on one or more sheets of regular paper; then, photocopy it. Photocopies last longer than newspaper clippings, and this will make your article easier to read and copy. Then, when you need to make a copy of a clip, you can photocopy it directly through the page protector. (I don't recommend bothering with color copies unless the article includes your own artwork or photography.)

In addition, you may want to keep copies of the actual magazines in which your work appears. I always ask publications to send *two* complimentary copies; I pull my clips from one and store the other whole as a backup. Store your magazines in magazine holders, or in a file box; you can also purchase individual plastic magazine protectors at a comic book store.

Many writers like to post clips on their Web site. This is fine if you still own the electronic rights; if, however, you've sold all rights, or all electronic rights, you technically no longer have the right to do this. Clips are best posted as HTML files, *not* as scanned images. If you do want to scan your clips and save them as image files, save them as Adobe PDF files, which editors can either download from your site or request by e-mail. This also makes a handy way to store your clips permanently on CD-ROM as an extra backup. (When sending out copies of your clips, however, use photocopies rather than printouts of electronic files, as photocopies will be easier to read.)

Manuscripts

Should you keep your old manuscripts forever? A few days ago, I might have said, "don't bother." Then I realized, as I contemplated submitting a fairly ancient reprint, that I have only the published version of that article—a version that was butchered by a grammatically challenged editor. Since I no longer have the original, I can't resubmit what I actually wrote—I have to reconstruct it from memory.

Fortunately, most of our manuscripts are electronic these days, so we don't have to worry about saving boxes and boxes of published (or unpublished) works. Just be sure to back up your manuscript files on disk periodically, or a computer crash could wipe out your life's work in a blink of an electron.

Keeping Electronic Records

Chances are, most of your writing and much of your correspondence is handled electronically nowadays. That's great from the standpoint of saving trees (and space in the back of your closet). However, it does present a risk: A computer failure can irretrievably wipe out your most important records. It can also be difficult to locate important correspondence in a confusion of e-mail folders.

The key to keeping good electronic files is to resist the temptation to purge them. It's very easy to think that you'll never need a particular e-mail record—only to find, months later, that it had a vital bit of information that is now lost to you forever. If nothing else, keep an "archive" folder in your e-mail system that stores copies of every writing-related bit of e-mail you send or receive.

Did I mention the importance of *backing up* these files on disk periodically? While I often fail to practice what I am about to preach, I cannot emphasize enough the importance of making regular backups of *everything* that might be relevant to your writing records.

Unfortunately, backing up everything on floppy disks can be a tedious chore, and disks aren't always reliable; just when you think you have everything nicely saved, you insert a disk and find that the computer suddenly can't read it, or that there is a "disk error" in the middle of your most important document. I recommend that you invest in a CD-ROM writer. CDs now cost $1 apiece or less—a small price to pay for the ability to easily back up all your writing files in ten minutes or less, every week or so. (CD-ROMs are also more reliable for backup than Zip disks.)

Scanning Files

Another way to keep electronic files is to scan your paper files. It is acceptable, for example, to store some of your back tax records as scanned electronic files. You can save your expense receipts, cancelled checks, stubs from payment checks, and tax forms as scanned files; over time, this can save a lot of closet space. I usually take some time at the beginning of each year to scan my tax records from three years earlier, so that I'm only keeping three years of actual *paper* copies on file. You can also scan correspondence and other paper files that you want to keep indefinitely, but that are taking up too much storage space. Some writers also scan copies of their clips. Scanned files also give you a backup in case something happens to your paper files. For example, you can make several backup copies of your records on CD-ROMs, and store one or two *away* from your residence (at your office or your spouse's office, or with a relative or friend). Then, if something disastrous happens to your records (such as fire or flood), you'll still have the electronic version.

Keeping good records isn't just a matter of saving what you're working on today. It's a matter of recognizing that you have no way of knowing what will suddenly become vitally important to you *tomorrow*. It can be so tempting to throw out that e-mail, that unsold article, those old letters. But we are entering an era when an increasing number of threats to our rights (and our livelihood) are coming down the pike—threats we can scarcely anticipate today and probably couldn't have imagined yesterday. Good records are your best (and only) form of self-protection. When in doubt, *don't* throw it out!

PART VI

EXPANDING

YOUR

WRITING

BUSINESS

CHAPTER 26

Selling Reprints

ou've probably read articles on the wonders of selling reprints. A lot of them sound something like this: "I've sold the same article 462 times, and netted thousands of dollars!" Such pieces tend to make one feel like a total slouch for having sold a piece only once.

Are reprints really an untapped goldmine for writers? Can you make your fortune reselling work you've already published? The answer often depends on who you ask—and also on what you write. The following questions and answers will give you an idea of the basics of the process.

Q: What is a reprint?
A: Publications consider an article to be a reprint if it has been previously published and remains substantially unchanged from that previous publication. Many publications do not accept reprints at all. Others pay a lower fee for reprints than for original material. Within these broad guidelines, however, you can find a host of variations and exceptions.

Q: When is a reprint not a reprint?
A: When you sell simultaneous, nonexclusive, or one-time rights to a piece of material. "Reprint" terms apply when you're marketing to publications that use "first" or "second" rights. When you sell first rights to your article, typically any subsequent sale would be of "second" or "reprint" rights. However, in some markets you can sell the same material to several different publications, either simultaneously or sequentially, by offering "one-time nonexclusive" rights. This gives every publication who buys your work the right to use it once, but not the right to use it "first," and not the right to be the only publication to use it. A good example of this type of use would be a column distributed to several newspapers or similar publications.

Q: When can I sell a reprint?

A: If you have sold first rights to an article, you generally cannot offer (or sell) reprint rights until that material has actually appeared in the original publication. "First" rights means the publication has the right to use it first, so if you were to sell reprint rights before the first article appeared, you could be in violation of your original contract. However, once the article has appeared in print or online, or wherever, generally you're then free to offer reprint, or "second" rights to other publications.

Q: Do all articles make good reprints?

A: Some articles have good reprint potential; others don't. If you have tailored an article toward a specific audience and publication, it may be difficult to remarket that material elsewhere without doing a substantial rewrite. If you're writing for a very narrow market niche, you may not find many markets for reprints. If a small number of publications are competing for the same market share (as is common in the pet-magazine market), you may find it difficult to find a "noncompeting" market to buy a reprint.

Time-sensitive articles generally don't work well as reprints. If the subject you're covering will be old news once the article hits print, if the material is outdated, if things have changed substantially, or if interest in the topic has waned, your chances of reselling the material are low. Similarly, material of purely local interest may be difficult to resell to a different regional market. The focus or slant of your article may also hinder its resale potential.

Q: Where should I market reprints?

A: The most important rule to follow when looking for markets for reprints is to look for "noncompeting" publications. If two publications serve the same market or audience, each is unlikely to accept material that previously appeared in the other. For example, the magazine *The Writer* is not likely to purchase an article that formerly appeared in *Writer's Digest,* and vice versa. The key lies in finding a noncompeting market—either a publication that addresses an audience with different interests, or a publication that has a very different regional distribution.

Many authors do well selling reprints to noncompeting regional publications, such as magazines that serve a single city, county, region, or state. Even though the general "focus" or content of each magazine might be substantially similar, the audience is limited to a particular region, and therefore the publications are "noncompeting." By the same token, it is often possible to sell reprints of your work overseas. Print publications will sometimes accept material that has appeared electronically, and vice versa.

Q: How do I find markets for reprints?

A: The first step is to identify likely customers. It's actually a good idea to consider this step before you actually start writing your article; then, you can determine whether you need to gather additional information for revisions and retailored articles while researching the original. Brainstorm the potential markets for your topic, and jot down any ideas that come to mind. For example, if you're writing an article on natural health care for women for a major women's' health care magazine, consider the potential for reselling the same article (or a retailored version of it) to other markets, such as:

❖ Women's health care magazines in other countries
❖ General women's magazines
❖ Magazines targeting specific age groups (e.g., teenagers, older women)
❖ General interest publications (especially if you can develop a newsworthy slant)
❖ Local and regional publications (especially if you can link the material to a local source or expert)
❖ Local, regional, and major metropolitan newspapers (target their "lifestyle" sections)
❖ Publications that address some subset of the topic, such as herb publications, natural health magazines, or New Age/spiritual magazines
❖ Online/electronic publications in any of the above categories

Once you've developed a list of potential markets, start hunting down information in the latest *Writer's Market* or online. Use an online newsstand or a guidelines database to gather more information about potential markets. If you can't find out from the listing whether a market accepts reprints, send a brief e-mail to the editor and ask, or make a very brief, courteous phone call. Choose the markets that offer the highest pay potential first, and work your way down the list.

Q: What rights can I sell?

A: Whether you can sell a reprint at all depends first and foremost upon the rights you sell to the original article. If you sell "all rights" or produce an article as "work-for-hire," you cannot sell reprint rights, as you no longer own those rights. This doesn't mean that you should never sell all rights; however, if you do, be sure you're sufficiently compensated for the loss of potential future reprint income, or that no likely market for reprints exists.

If you sell "first" rights of any kind (e.g., first North American serial rights, or FNASR, first electronic rights, etc.), you can then sell "second" rights to the same type of market (e.g., a North American publication), and in some cases you can sell "first" rights to a different market (e.g., a British publication). For example, if you've sold FNASR, you may be able to sell the article as a "first" to an overseas publication (although you'll find that many prefer to handle such material as a reprint anyway). If you've sold first print rights, you can still sell first electronic rights, and vice versa. Regardless of the actual rights you've sold, however, many publications will still regard previously published work as a "reprint" (and treat it as such) even if some area of "first" rights is still available.

When selling the reprint itself, you will generally offer nonexclusive "second" rights or "one-time" rights. "Second" serial rights can be sold over and over; the term simply indicates that the publication is no longer "first." (In other words, you don't have to worry about keeping track and offering "43rd serial rights.") Most reprints are sold "nonexclusively," which means that you can sell the same reprint to more than one publication, often at the same time. Sending out "simultaneous submissions" of reprints is also a little more acceptable than sending out simsubs of an original article; just be sure that the reprint isn't going out to competing markets.

When offering a reprint overseas, be sure to address issues of regional rights and language rights in your sale. For example, you might want to sell a reprint to a British publication, but hold onto the rights to sell the same material in English to another European country, as well as the rights to sell the material in other languages.

Q: If I rewrite an article, does it cease to be a reprint?

A: There is no hard-and-fast rule about how much "editing" or "revision" is required to change a reprint into a new, original piece. The keyword is usually "substantially"—i.e., the piece needs to be "substantially" different. If you just change a few words here and there, add a paragraph, or drop a sentence, this generally isn't enough to make a piece "new."

Rather than selling reprints per se, many writers prefer to tailor the same information to several different markets. For example, if you were writing a piece on relocating to a new city, you could slant one article to a business audience, another to a financial publication, another to a woman's magazine, and yet another to a parenting publication. Each piece would have a focus specific to the market you're targeting, each would qualify as "original"—yet each is drawn from the same pool of research information. This is often the best approach, as many publications prefer that material be tailored directly toward their audiences.

The best way to test whether something is rewritten sufficiently to be considered a new article is to put yourself in the reader's shoes. If you read the two articles in two different publications, would you think they were different articles? Or would you regard them as being the same? If you would regard them as the same (or regard one as being an excerpt of the other), then they are, essentially, the same. This means they are the "same article" with respect to the rights you're selling; you won't be able to satisfy one editor's request for, say, "first" rights or "exclusive" rights to a piece if you're selling a portion of that identical piece to someone else.

That being said, you can submit the same article to two different publications *if* those publications are willing to accept nonexclusive one-time rights to the material. If, however, either publication (or both) wants first rights, or exclusive rights (e.g., exclusive electronic rights), then you can't. You have to honor whatever rights you're offering—and that usually means the rights that are requested by the publication (which you'll know by reading its guidelines).

Since most publications that deal with a specific topic are likely to be competing, this is even more reason *not* to try to pitch the same article (or very similar articles) to two at the same time. Most likely, each will get wind of the fact that you've sold something similar to a competitor, and that would be enough to make each editor decide never to work with you again.

Q: Do I need to query for reprints?

A: Generally, one doesn't bother to query on a reprint, as you have already written the article, so you're not really looking for an "assignment." Queries are more to save you time by preventing you from going to the trouble of writing a new article before you know that it will be accepted. Since a reprint has already been written, it's usually best to send it directly, with a cover letter. Just be sure that the publication accepts reprints, and that your material wasn't originally published in a competing magazine.

Q: Should I tell a publisher that a submission is a reprint?

A: It is considered proper to inform a publisher of any previous publications of a manuscript, regardless of the rights. A previously published piece is considered a reprint, whether you have the rights back or not. Otherwise, you would be (falsely) giving the publisher the impression that they are buying "first" rights. (By the way, if something has been previously published, you no longer have "all" rights to the work, as "first" publication rights, at least in a particular medium or area, have already been used and are, basically, gone forever.)

Q: Should I send the published article or the manuscript?

A: There are two schools of thought on this. Some people prefer to send a copy of the published article as it appeared in print. However, that doesn't really give the next publisher anything to work with—i.e., it can be difficult to convert a tearsheet into a usable manuscript. So others prefer to send manuscripts.

My own preference is to send both: a copy of the published article, and a copy of the original manuscript. (If your manuscript was heavily edited by the first publisher, *and* you believe it was improved by the editing, you might want to simply retype the piece.)

If photos are involved, you can send them just as you would with an original, or let the photos that were published with the first publication stand as "examples" of what is available. If the reprint is accepted, the new publication may want to select different photos. (Of course, if you're sending a black-and-white photocopy of the article, the quality of color photos may not be easy to see, in which case you might want to send prints or just indicate that photos are available.)

Q: How much time should I spend marketing reprints?
A: That's up to you. As you build a collection of material, you'll probably find that some pieces are more appropriate for reprint sales than others. Don't waste a lot of time on those that aren't—and don't waste too much time on those that are! For example, you may not want to invest the same amount of time and money on "sample copies" for potential reprint markets as you would when researching markets for original articles; the return on your investment often won't be worth the effort.

Reprints can provide a viable source of income. However, to be able to market reprints successfully, you must first build a supply of "original" published articles. Never spend so much time trying to resell old work that you stop writing new material!

CHAPTER 27

Selling Photos

It has been said that a picture is worth a thousand words. In the world of publishing, this is not simply a parable, but the absolute truth. Magazines aren't simply a verbal medium; they are also a visual medium. That means that for every 1,000 great words an editor receives, she will need at least one great picture.

If you have a knack with a camera, you may be able to make your editor's day—and increase your writing income—by offering packages of text and pictures. You don't have to be an experienced photographer to sell your photos. Granted, tourist snapshots of your trip to Rome won't make it into *National Geographic*, but they may be just what a smaller travel publication or your local newspaper travel section needs.

Photo "Ops"

Many editors make their purchasing decisions based on whether the author can provide photos. Keep this in mind, therefore, when you plan future articles. While some articles don't lend themselves to easy illustration, others are "naturals" for accompanying photographs, including:

❖ *Travel articles.* Whenever you travel, take your camera along, and use it. Don't worry about the cost of film or development; just snap every shot that looks remotely worthwhile. The results may surprise you! While major travel publications accept only top-quality professional photos, many smaller publications welcome clear, focused shots that illustrate the sights described in your article.

❖ *Profiles.* Bring your camera when you go on an interview. Try to get a few "candid" shots of your subjects, in different types of light. If you're interviewing an artist or craftsperson, take photos of the person's work. If your interviewee has special interests, include those in the session. Also, ask your interviewee if he has publicity photos that you could include with your article. (Be sure that your subject is authorized to use this photo for publication; remember that the copyright of a professional or publicity photo is usually owned by the photographer, and the photographer's name should be listed in the credit line if known.)

❖ *How-to articles.* Suppose you want to pitch an article on administering first aid to an injured pet. While your words may be vivid, nothing will get the idea across like a series of photos that demonstrate exactly how to apply a bandage, where to apply pressure, and so forth. The next time you prepare a how-to piece, consider setting up a "photo shoot" in which a friend or family member demonstrates the techniques you're describing while you take pictures. (Or, if your friend is the better photographer, reverse the process!)

❖ *Craft projects.* Many magazines decide whether to buy instructions for a craft project based on a photograph of the finished result. They may not buy the photo itself; most will want to take their own photos of the finished piece. Your photo of "how it will look," however, can be the key to selling your idea.

❖ *Events.* Photographic coverage of a newsworthy event can make all the difference between a sale and a rejection. Try to avoid static "grip and grin" shots (where two people shake hands and smile at the camera), or dull headshots. Instead, try to capture people in motion, with natural poses and expressions. Experiment with different angles and lenses (a telephoto lens, for example, can help you zoom in on individuals or zoom out for crowd shots).

Basic Equipment

I won't try to tell you how to take great pictures. To learn more about photography, check with your local photo shop or adult education center; you may easily earn back the price of a class with your first photo sale.

Nor will I try to tell you what kind of camera to buy, except that you need something better than a basic "instamatic" or Polaroid. (Magazines won't accept Polaroid prints.) You'll also need film. Keep in mind that the higher the speed rating of the film, the more likely your pictures are to develop a "grain" that detracts from the image. (Never use that film commonly advertised in newspapers as providing "prints and slides from the same roll"; this film has very large grain that could detract from a picture's salability.)

Many magazines still require slides (though more and more now accept prints). If you use slides, you may want to buy an inexpensive light box to help you sort and select photos. If you don't want to invest in a light box, drop by your local photo shop and borrow theirs.

Slide users will also want to buy a "loupe," a small but powerful magnifying glass that editors use to review slide submissions. By viewing your slides through a loupe, you'll be able to determine whether your photos are sharp enough to be enlarged to magazine size. Loupes are available at photo shops and art-supply stores.

You'll also want to pick up some plastic photo-protector sheets corresponding to the size of the slide or print you use. These sheets not only protect your photos during shipping, but also provide a safe way to store them; most are "archival quality," which means that they don't contain acids that can damage your film over time.

Finally, you'll want to start saving 8" × 10" sheets of cardboard, such as the backs of notepads, so that you'll have something to further protect your photos during shipping.

Submitting Photos

While your manuscript may be "disposable," you'll usually want your photos back in good condition. To ensure that they remain undamaged, follow these packaging steps:

❖ Put your name and address on each photo. The easiest method is to attach a return address label to the back of each print, or to the cardboard mount of each slide.

❖ Number each photo. Do not write on the back of a print with a ballpoint pen or ordinary market, as the ink will smear (and if you stack prints, it will come off on the face of the photo beneath). Use a permanent marker to number prints (and write small), or print off labels that include the number of the print and the caption information.

❖ Send slides and prints in plastic protective sheets. These protect your photos from handling and postal damage. Editors can view slides through the sheets, and will only remove those they actually plan to use. (This also helps keep your photos together.)

❖ Send proof sheets of black-and-white photos, rather than making expensive enlargements.

❖ Prepare a caption list that corresponds to the numbers of your photos. Don't worry about inventing clever captions (the editor will do that). Just record essential information, such as the subject of the photo, and anything else the editor might need to know (the location, date, etc.).

❖ Obtain model release forms for your photos, if necessary. This is particularly important when photographing children; editors are very wary of publishing child photos without a parent's permission. You may need a model release when photographing individuals, or even when photographing private property. (For more information on the legal aspects of photography, see *Every Writer's Guide to Copyright Publishing Law*, Second

Edition, by Ellen Kozak; *Business and Legal Forms for Photographers*, Third Edition, by Tad Crawford; or *The Law (In Plain English)*® *for Photographers*, Revised Edition, by Leonard D. Duboff.)

❖ Package your photos securely. Put at least one sheet of cardboard into the envelope (usually your manuscript will be sufficient protection on the other side). Include a SASE with enough postage to cover the return of the photos, whether or not you want the manuscript returned.

Digital Photos

This business of prints and slides and plastic sheet protectors and manila envelopes may sound rather low-tech in this day of digital, but it is still the preferred method for most publications. While many editors are willing to receive queries and solicited manuscripts via e-mail, very few will want to receive photo submissions in the same way. Photo files tend to be large, and make cumbersome attachments. It's usually easier to flip through a stack of prints than to view electronic files; plus, prints and slides can be more easily handed around to other editors and art directors.

There are exceptions, however. For example, an electronic publication will almost certainly want electronic files of your photos. If you expect to submit photos to e-zines, therefore, you might wish to invest in a good-quality color scanner and a program such as Photoshop, so that you can convert your prints to gifs, jpegs, or other desired formats.

Kodak now offers the option of receiving a photo-CD when you have prints developed. Such a CD usually holds one roll of film, and costs around $15 (over and above the cost of the prints themselves). It doesn't take too much math to realize that you will probably save money in the long run by buying a scanner (or digital camera) of your own! Scanners are also available to convert slides as well as prints. Scan photos at a resolution of at least 300 dpi (you can always scale this down when submitting photos, but some publications won't accept anything less).

The output of digital cameras is now becoming virtually indistinguishable from that of traditional film cameras. While most print publications still don't accept digital camera photos, most online publications do—and in another two or three years, I suspect that the quality will be sufficient for many print publications as well.

Electronic submissions work best for photos that have been specifically requested or previously approved. For example, after you send a batch of prints to an editor for review, the editor may request that you submit certain photos electronically. One way to assist in the electronic screening process is to load your scanned photos onto a "private" Web page (one that is not listed from your Web site's main directory) and invite the editor to review them online.

Finally, it's a good idea to keep a scanned photo of yourself available in several formats (e.g., gif, jpeg, tif, etc.) so that you can provide it to editors who want a photo to accompany your bio or byline. In this case, editors are often happy to work with an electronic file that they can load directly into the text of your article. Consider having a professional portrait shot taken that you can scan and reduce to the appropriate size (2" × 2", for example); you might also want to have one black-and-white and one color portrait available. Again, scan your photo at a resolution of at least 300 dpi.

Obtaining Photos from Other Sources

If you despair of taking good photos yourself, that doesn't mean you have to despair of *offering* photos to editors. It simply means that you'll have to find another source.

One approach is to find a photographer that you can work with, and sell a package deal to the editor. In this case, you'll have to work out an arrangement with the photographer with respect to who gets paid what—particularly if the publication offers a single rate for the entire text-photo package. It's a good idea to write up a brief contract up front, so that everyone knows what they can expect when the check arrives.

However, you may also find free sources of photos. When I write for pet magazines, for example, I'll often put out a call for photos on topical mailing lists (such as a cat-writing list). Generally, these photos won't be professional quality, and I usually don't offer the contributor any payment for them. Sometimes the magazine will use them, sometimes they won't. If payment *is* involved, I simply pass along the name of the photographer to the editor and let the editor handle payment for the photos separately.

When you're writing travel articles, check with tourist organizations for photos. Many tourist agencies offer free publicity photos, which will enhance your article without costing the editor another penny.

Submitting Photos without Manuscripts

If you can take high-quality photographs, you can also sell them independently, without an accompanying article. Many magazines buy shots of their basic subject matter year-round. For example, pet magazines always need generic photos of veterinarians examining animals, animals involved in various activities, animals interacting with different types of people (e.g., seniors, children), seasonal shots, and so forth.

You don't have to simply guess what editors are looking for. Many magazines offer photographer's guidelines that list upcoming articles and the types of photos that will be required. For example, a pet magazine may list the breeds it will cover over the next six months, plus special articles like "puppies" or "senior cats." These guidelines will tell you when photos must be submitted for each issue. By tailoring your photo shoots to these "need" lists, you'll have a better chance of breaking in.

You may even make more money by selling your photos separately than if you combine them with an article. While some editors pay the same amount for an article with or without photos (or add only a small bonus for the photos), they also have standard rates for photos alone. For example, a magazine might pay $50 per photo for inside use, and anywhere from $100 to $500 for a cover shot. Larger magazines pay more, of course, but also expect top quality. Smaller publications may pay $10 to $15 per shot. (To find out which magazines take independent submissions, and how much they pay, see *Writer's Market* or *Photographer's Market.*)

Finally, you may find that a photo submission can lead to an article assignment. If an editor falls in love with your photos, but has nothing on hand to use them with, she may ask you to write a piece to accompany them. Remember, editors think in two media—verbal and visual—so by sending a package that combines both, you stand a better chance of selling your work. (Oh, and if a magazine pays 5¢ per word and $50 per photo, one picture really is worth a thousand words!)

CHAPTER 28

Selling (and Syndicating) a Column[1]

f you specialize in a particular subject area, or have an area of expertise that you'd like to write more about, you may start thinking about launching a column. A column is a great way to establish yourself as an "expert," and offers a steady income. Opportunities for columns can be found in magazines (usually monthly), newspapers (generally weekly but sometimes daily), and Web sites (most often weekly, monthly, or bimonthly).

While magazines generally offer the best pay rates for columns, this market also tends to be the most difficult to crack, as magazine space is the most limited. When a column opening comes up, most editors will turn to existing contributors—which means that the best way to get a shot at a magazine column is to become a regular contributor to a publication. Once you've sold several articles to a magazine, you might wish to pitch a column idea; even if it's not accepted, it will let the editor know that you're interested in a columnist position in case something opens up in the future. Magazines generally offer the highest pay rates for columns—anywhere from a few hundred dollars to $1,000—but also generally expect exclusive rights.

Newspapers represent the largest market for columns. Even the smallest regional papers typically run a few columns, often by local authors. Larger papers run a mix of local and national (syndicated) columns. Daily papers usually offer a mix of daily and weekly columns; weekly papers usually offer weekly columns. Weekend editions often have their own set of columns, often including review and "local event" and entertainment sections. Newspapers also offer the widest variety of content opportunities, as regular sections may cover health, cooking, lifestyles, women's issues, fashion, entertainment, sports, business, real estate, home décor, and more. Papers may also offer columns of specific regional interest. The downside is that the pay scale tends to be lower (anywhere from $10 to $50 in smaller papers); however, you can often "self-syndicate" your column to more than one regional. (Most national papers buy exclusive rights, but also offer a much higher fee.)

Electronic publications offer excellent opportunities for columnists, as such publications have fewer space constraints. A Web-based publication could have any number of regular columns. An e-mail newsletter, on the other hand, will tend to have only one per issue, as most e-mail newsletters prefer to place limits on their lengths (however, a newsletter might feature links back to columns on a Web site.) Many commercial and "catalog" sites use columnists to offer material intended to attract visitors (and hence customers), and can often pay more than an independent zine. Columns are usually archived, so that readers can access not only your current column but also all previous columns. Most electronic publications want exclusive rights, or at least exclusive *first electronic* rights, to a column, making it less likely that you'll be able to market the same column to more than one online publication (although you may be able to market the same column to an online publication *and* a print publication). The downside, again, is that most electronic markets pay less than print markets, except for those that are affiliated with commercial enterprises, print publications, or other media.

Choosing a Column Topic

Magazine columns are generally governed by the same principles that apply to magazine articles, with "how-to" and informational columns being the most common. The easiest way to determine what type of column you might pitch to a magazine is to look at its regular content and choose a topic that could be covered on a monthly basis. Magazines may also feature editorial/opinion columns, news roundups, review columns, and regional coverage (e.g., local restaurants, night spots, entertainment, events, personalities, etc.). Another popular type of column is the "advice" format, in which the columnist answers questions from the magazine's readership. (A pet magazine, for example, might have a medical or behavioral "advice" column, while a women's magazine might have an advice column on relationships or parenting.)

To write a magazine "how-to" column, you need to have some personal expertise in the field. Unlike a single feature article, where you can interview experts, a monthly column will be drawing on *your* knowledge of a subject, and a successful pitch will be based on your credentials. Don't try to pitch a gardening column, therefore, if you don't know a rake from a hoe! Similarly, if you want to pitch an advice column, you'll have to demonstrate that you have the credentials to *answer* those questions.

Newspapers may offer a similar array of columns, but will focus more on a general readership than on the "subject-specific" readerships you'll find with most magazines. Since daily newspapers typically offer a different "special-interest" section each day, these offer a wide range of column possibilities. If your expertise is real estate, consider pitching a column about tips on buying and selling homes, or dealing with your local real estate market. If you have business expertise, consider pitching a column for the business section—and so on.

Newspapers also generally offer a variety of "op-ed" and "personal" columns. Op-ed columns typically focus on a perspective or viewpoint, such as liberal, conservative, feminist, minority, etc. To pitch an op-ed column, you'll need to persuade the editor that your opinion is worth hearing, and is likely to reflect the views of a substantial portion of the newspaper's audience. "Personal" columns tend to focus on a "slice of life" approach, again often focusing on local issues or on lifestyle topics that will be common to a large portion of the newspaper's readership. Some "slice of life" columns are humorous, but others are completely serious.

Newspapers also offer a range of review columns, covering movies, books, products (including high-tech products and computer games), entertainment, local events, restaurants, nightlife, and more. A newspaper's travel section might include reviews of travel destinations and accommodations. The best way to break in with this type of column is to pick a topic that isn't already being reviewed, and offer a convincing argument as to why the paper should cover this topic. This type of column often requires no special expertise or credentials (though if you're going to review something like computer equipment, you'll need to convince an editor that you understand technology). Such columns also tend to blur the line between information and entertainment; review columns are often chosen as much for the writer's style and voice (and wit) as for the reviews themselves. The bad news is that for this very reason, review columns are often the first thing amateur writers try to pitch, the most common being book reviews. To earn a space, therefore, you'll have to be able to ensure that your column rises above the competition.

It's also important to understand that a review column doesn't necessarily mean free tickets to movies, free dinners, free travel, or free books. I get lots of letters from writers who want to know how to get on a publisher's "list" for free books to review. Publishers, however, rarely send books directly to individual reviewers; instead, they tend to send them to *publications,* who then pass them along to established reviewers. The way to get "free books," therefore, is to become a regular book reviewer for a publication.

Newspapers also run humor columns, but as you have probably already noticed, these tend to be few and nationally syndicated (e.g., Dave Barry). This type of column is very difficult to sell (let alone syndicate), because the market for pure humor is limited—partly because a lot of people aren't nearly as funny as they think they are, and partly because newspapers devote only a limited amount of space to this type of column.

Pitching Your Column

Once you've chosen a topic that you feel would make a good column, you need to develop a proposal that includes the following elements:

❖ A catchy column title. (Keep in mind that the editor may *change* that title once the column is accepted, but you still need to develop one that will get an editor's attention.)

❖ An overview of the column's general subject area, e.g., what the column will cover over time, why you feel that this coverage is important for the publication, and what the general "purpose" of the column will be.

❖ A list of topics. If you're pitching a monthly column, you'll need to provide at least six months' worth of topics; if you're pitching a weekly column, try to develop topics for two to three months.

❖ Three to six sample columns.

❖ A list of your credentials (including an author bio and, optionally, photo). This may also include your publications list and, if appropriate, your résumé or curriculum vitae.

While it *is* possible to pitch a column by e-mail, you'll generally want to put together a physical package that can be sent by surface mail. Most columnists recommend assembling these materials in a pocket folder, perhaps with a label bearing the name of the proposed column and your name on the cover.

Your package will include a basic query letter, which will be structured much like an article query. However, instead of proposing a single piece, you're proposing an ongoing series—so the goal of your query should be to present a rationale for why the target publication would want to cover your subject on a regular basis. Instead of going into detail about any single column, your query should present an overview of the nature and purpose of the entire column. Describe the subject, and explain why this subject is of sufficient importance (or interest) to merit ongoing coverage.

Any of the types of hooks mentioned in chapter 17 will also work for a column. For example, if you were proposing a column on natural health alternatives to a general-interest women's magazine, you might try any of the following hooks:

❖ *Problem/Solution:* "Many women today are becoming increasingly frustrated with the limitations of 'traditional medicine.' Often, traditional techniques—or harried HMO doctors with not enough time—just don't seem to answer women's questions or meet their needs. More and more women are seeking alternatives—and seeking accurate, helpful information to guide them toward those alternatives."

✦ *Informative:* "Natural remedies have become big business. No longer confined to strip-mall 'health stores,' they now line the pharmacy shelves of every supermarket. Now, more than ever, women are in need of accurate, reliable information on the products competing for their health dollars—and on how to safely incorporate natural health care into their lives."

✦ *Question:* "Are you bewildered by the array of natural products on your local supermarket shelves? Do you wonder whether these products are safe, whether they can actually meet their claims, or how to choose between them? If so, you're not alone: Thousands of women face the same decisions every day."

✦ *Personal Experience/Anecdote:* "When I had my first baby, I wasn't prepared for the violent reaction I would have to XXX drug. Yet it was all my doctors could offer. The next time, I vowed to be prepared: I studied alternatives, and found natural solutions that eased my pain without ruining my health. Since then, I've talked to many women who wished they had the same options. . . ."

✦ *Attention-Grabber:* "Nature can be the death of you—even when it's attractively bottled in a supposedly 'safe' product on your supermarket shelf. While natural remedies offer a host of helpful alternatives to traditional healthcare, it's vital to know what you're doing—what's in that bottle, how much you can safely take, whether it actually works, and how it might react with other natural products."

Your hook should lead directly into your pitch, which will include not only the title of the column, but also its length and frequency (unless this is predefined by the frequency of the publication). If you're pitching to a newspaper, mention the section in which you believe your column should appear. A good pitch to follow the hooks above might read:

> I'd like to offer you a [monthly, weekly] column covering the many facets of natural health care. Titled "Natural Health," this column would fit well within your "To Your Health" section. It would run between 750 and 1,000 words, and cover such topics as: . . .

Follow this with the body of your query, in which you'll list a selection of topics that will be covered in the column. A bullet list often works well for this:

✦ Traditional home remedies: which ones work, and why.
✦ How to read and understand the labels of "natural" products.
✦ Why "natural" doesn't necessarily mean "safe," and how to use such products safely.

- ❖ Understanding the health claims of natural products: What they're based on, whether they're true.
- ❖ Product interactions: knowing which natural products can be taken together, and which can be harmful.
- ❖ Teas, tisanes, and distillations: how to best prepare a natural remedy.
- ❖ Natural remedies for pregnancy and childbirth problems.
- ❖ (etc.)

Finally, close with your credentials: the personal skills, expertise, education, job experience, or whatever, that qualifies you to write this column—or to dispense advice to the publication's readers. Since an inaccurate column can damage the credibility of the entire publication, an editor will want to be sure that you're the right person for the job.

The closing paragraph of your query should offer a potential start date for your column, and may also be the place to specify your terms: the rights you're offering, and, if appropriate, the fee you would like to receive. Unless you're self-syndicating the column, however (see below), you'll generally leave these items for subsequent negotiation.

While you'll be sending sample columns with your proposal, you may also wish to include relevant clips that support your credentials and demonstrate your ability to write on the chosen topic. Be sure to reference any articles you've written for the publication you're pitching to! Clips from professional or academic journals can help establish your expertise and experience writing on your chosen topic, but they will generally *not* reflect the style you'd use for a consumer publication, so be sure to balance them with clips that show your ability to write for a more general audience. A published book also makes an excellent "clip," and is a great way to establish your expertise. If you can, send the publisher a copy of the entire book—or, photocopy one or two relevant chapters and copies of some favorable reviews.

Again, you'll generally submit this package by surface mail. If you're submitting a proposal to an electronic publication, however, you may need to put these materials into an e-mail. If so, find out from the editor whether you can send any of the materials (such as your résumé and publications list, and sample columns) as attachments, or whether you need to place everything in the body of an e-mail. If you must put everything in a single e-mail, then you should limit that e-mail to a basic query, a list of topics, and *one* sample column; offer to send the editor additional materials (such as more columns, publications list, or clips) on request.

Self-Syndicating Your Column

Since newspaper readership is generally based on geography rather than on subject matter (as is the case with magazines and electronic publications), it is often possible to "self-syndicate" a newspaper column to more than one publication. You can sell the same column to newspapers in different states (provided that it applies to the area), or even to papers in different counties or cities in the same state, as long as those papers have little or no reader overlap.

Reader overlap is not necessarily determined by location. It is also determined by the size and distribution of a paper. While readers of a local paper in one town or county may not read a similar paper that is published in the next town or county, they *may* read a larger city paper that is distributed to *both* towns. For example, residents of Olympia, Washington, may read the local *Olympian*, but may also read the larger *Tacoma News Tribune* and the national *Seattle Post-Intelligencer*—but may *not* read a paper published in nearby Tumwater.

To self-syndicate your column, you must have a topic that "travels" well. You're not likely to be able to syndicate a local "review" column, for example, that focuses on purely regional subjects. Nor would you be able to syndicate a column that might have broader regional appeal but that won't be useful to readers in a completely different climate (e.g., gardening in the Pacific Northwest). Columns on more universal topics, however, such as home décor, real estate, parenting, health, fitness, cooking, etc., can be distributed to a wide range of papers. Your column must also offer something unique; while you may be the only person writing about parenting for your hometown paper, thousands of other writers cover this topic in other regions, so your column would have to offer something special in order to compete.

Finding Markets

You can locate newspapers through one of more than a dozen electronic "newsstands" on the Web. Many of these, however, simply provide a title and URL for a paper; you'll have to dig deeper to locate the names of appropriate editors, and their address or e-mail. Nor do most of these sites offer information about a paper's distribution area or circulation; some won't even tell you if the paper is daily, weekly, or monthly. (For a list of online "newsstands," see *www.writing-world.com/links/magazines.shtml*.)

You can get more detailed information from the *Gales Publication Directory,* which you'll find in the reference section of any library. Gales offers information about circulation, frequency, and staff. If, for example, you've decided you want to target daily newspapers with a circulation of over 20,000, you may wish to turn to Gales. You don't, for example, want to waste time submitting your column to weekly "shoppers," or to papers with no budget for freelance material.

Another resource is the *Annual Editor and Publisher International Year Book,* also available in most libraries. This lists addresses and editors of U.S.

and Canadian dailies, along with alternative and specialty papers. It also provides information on circulation figures, the paper's weekly sections and special editions, and whether it has a Sunday magazine.

If a region is served by several local papers and a larger state or big-city newspaper, you'll need to decide which to target first. This decision may not be as easy as it sounds. While a big-city paper may pay more (and will reach a larger audience), it is also likely to demand more rights (or even all rights). It is also more likely to want to post your material on its Web site, which can further limit your ability to distribute that column elsewhere. Smaller papers, though offering lower pay, may be less demanding of rights and less likely to have a Web site (or to put all their material on such a site).

Protecting Your Rights

Rights are a key issue in self-syndicating a column. Indeed, you should start thinking about "rights" long before you consider self-syndication; you should think about this issue when you sell your very first column to your very first paper. More and more publications (including small-town newspapers) want writers to sign over all rights to their columns, or even produce them as "work-for-hire" (which means that the newspaper owns the copyright to the material from the beginning). You may find that publications that pay as little as $10 to $50 per column still expect you to fork over all rights to that piece.

If you have any intention of selling your work elsewhere, you must ensure that you retain the rights to do so. Typically, you will want to offer a newspaper "one-time nonexclusive rights" to your column, perhaps with the guarantee that the column will not appear in a competing publication. An alternative is to offer "exclusive regional rights," and define "region" as narrowly as possible. The region should be limited to the area of the newspaper's general readership; if, for example, the paper is read only in Yakima, Washington, don't let it restrict you from selling the same column to another paper in Seattle or Tacoma.

In some cases, a newspaper will want "first" rights. This may work if your first column sale is to your local paper—it gives you the ability to resell that column a week later to all your other markets. Since only one publication can ever be "first," however, think carefully before granting this option.

Don't be tempted to accept more money for "all rights." The goal of self-syndication is not to earn a huge amount from any single publication, but to gain the widest possible distribution for your piece. Payment for columns is always fairly limited; you're not likely to get an offer above $500 from even the largest paper. If you can sell the same piece to twenty newspapers that offer $50 apiece, you've already doubled that figure—and quite possibly doubled your readership as well. (If you have hopes of moving on to national syndication, readership figures will be vital to your success. It is better to be read not just by a large number of people, but by a large number of people distributed across a wide range of markets.)

Finally, you'll want to determine a minimum rate that you're willing to accept. Some small newspapers still offer as little as $10 per column—but that amount can add up quickly if you can sell your column to several papers. Some columnists set a fee based on circulation, such as 50¢ per 1,000 subscribers.

Preparing Your Package

Self-syndication has one downside: expense. Most newspapers still prefer receiving column proposals by surface mail rather than by e-mail. This means that to pitch your idea to a wide range of markets, you'll have to invest in postage, printing, and envelopes.

Your submission package will be much the same as that described in the previous chapter, including a cover/query letter, three to six sample columns, a list of topics, your credentials, clips, and a SASE or a self-addressed, stamped postcard with "check boxes" for an editor's response. Newspaper editors often prefer a postcard to a SASE, as it enables them to check the appropriate response rather than having to write an acceptance letter. Your postcard might read something like this:

Date: _____

Dear (Your Name):
    Thank you for submitting your proposal for a column titled "Natural Health Tips for Seniors."

☐ We would like to use this column on a weekly basis. We will pay you a fee of $_____ for one-time, nonexclusive rights (per your guarantee that the column will not appear in a directly competing publication).
☐ We regret that we cannot use your column.

(Signed) _____
Editor's Name: _____

If you plan to submit your column to a large number of newspapers, you'll probably want to have all of your materials printed in bulk. Have your cover letter printed on good-quality paper stock; your clips and column samples can be printed on plain 20-lb. bond. Most print shops will also be able to print your return postcard. To save costs (and weight), print your clips double-sided.

It *is* possible to pitch a newspaper column by e-mail, though it is more difficult. First, you'll have to build a list of e-mail contacts. As with pitching a regular column, you won't be able to send as many materials as you would by surface mail; usually, you'll be limited to a *short* query letter, a brief list of topics, a description of your credentials, and one sample column. Offer the editor the opportunity to receive more materials either by mail or e-mail if interested.

Don't be surprised if you never hear anything from the majority of the editors you query. Most newspaper editors don't bother with rejections; they respond only if they are interested in a submission. While you can certainly follow up on nonresponders, your follow-ups may not produce a response either. If you don't hear from a market, just drop it from your list and move on.

When an editor *does* respond, don't be surprised if he or she wants to modify your terms, perhaps by suggesting a different word count or a lower price. It's up to you to decide whether to accept editorial changes. If you're distributing your column to a large number of publications, it's usually easier to send the same column to everyone (and let individual editors make their own changes or cuts) than to try to tailor several versions for different markets. On the other hand, if you're working with only a few editors, this can be a good way to build a better relationship with them—and possibly gain other assignments in the future.

Self-syndication is a wonderful way to build your portfolio. Be sure to ask for copies of the issues in which your column appears, or at least for a tearsheet of your column. Once you have a regular column with a local paper (even if it's not local to *you*), you can list yourself as a "contributor" or "stringer" to that publication. This may be just the stepping-stone you need to propel your column into the big leagues—such as national syndication.

NOTE

1. Parts of this chapter appeared in my book, *The Writer's Guide to Queries, Pitches, and Proposals* (Allworth Press, 2001).

CHAPTER 29

Writing (and Selling) a Nonfiction Book

A t some point in your writing career, you're probably going to say, "Wow, I could write a book about that!" Unfortunately, many writers stop at that point, intimidated by the prospect of writing something as large as a book—or by the horror stories they've heard about the difficulties of getting published.

Writing a nonfiction book doesn't have to be an intimidating process, however. Often, it's the logical "next step" in your career, and can provide a number of benefits. While articles are often forgotten once a magazine or newspaper hits the recycle bin, people keep books on their shelves for years. A book is considered a more significant "expert" credential than an article. And if a book stays in print, you could receive royalty checks for years to come.

The market for nonfiction books is huge. Walk into any bookstore and you'll see that the nonfiction titles vastly outnumber the fiction titles—and that's not counting the "specialty" bookstores that focus on a particular topic, such as travel, self-help, military history, crafts, and so forth. There are also more nonfiction publishers than fiction publishers, ranging from huge commercial concerns to smaller "niche" publishers that focus on a particular topic or region. Nor is it that difficult to get a nonfiction book published. (Most of the horror stories you've heard relate to fiction.) It rarely requires an agent, and you can often sell your book before you write it.

Writing a book involves most of the same basic skills required to write and market nonfiction articles: the abilities to develop and refine a topic, organize your subject matter, conduct research and interviews, and write and polish your material. It also requires much the same credentials. Plus, any articles that you've already sold on a topic will help you "prove" your ability to write a book about that topic.

These are all reasons why I've referred to writing a book as a "next step." I don't recommend attempting to *start* your writing career with a book. Even if you've got the "perfect book idea," keep it "on hold" until you've mastered the process of writing (and selling) articles. Don't tackle something as significant as a book project until you're thoroughly comfortable with the writing process, and feel sure that you won't mind spending several months writing and researching a single topic. A book project is a great way to apply and expand the skills you've developed as a freelance writer, but isn't the best place to try to *learn* those skills.

Why Write a Book?

Writers choose to branch out to book-length manuscripts for a variety of reasons, including the following:

❖ *To share your knowledge or expertise.* If you're an expert in a particular subject, chances are that you're already writing about it. You may have found, however, that there are only so many articles you can sell on the topic—and so much more that you want to say. A book may be the ideal way to get this information across.

❖ *To fill a niche.* Frequently, as you conduct research on a topic, you find a "gap" that is just begging to be filled. For example, at the time of this writing, I've noticed a sudden influx of books covering *women* in the Civil War—an area that has been neglected amid the flood of books addressing battles, leaders, and so forth. Your inability to find information can be an incentive to provide that information yourself.

❖ *To help people.* Many books are written out of a desire to help people with a particular problem. For example, I wrote my first book, *Coping with Sorrow on the Loss of Your Pet*, after discovering through a magazine survey that hundreds of pet owners felt they were "alone" in their grief. The desire to reach out to others can be a powerful motivation to write a book.

❖ *To bring your written work together in one place.* Many writers compile collections of columns or articles into a book. Mary Emma Allen, for example, turned her series of columns on Alzheimer's into *When We Become the Parent to Our Parents*. The book you're reading is based on the columns and articles I've written for various writing-related publications.

❖ *To ensure that an important event or person is not forgotten.* Autobiography, biography, and genealogy are all potential sources of material. I know of one writer, for example, who is working on the history of an ancestor who was a Buffalo Soldier. Many writers want to ensure that future readers will be able to know "what happened" or "what life was like when."

Note that one motivation I *didn't* list is "to make lots of money." While some nonfiction books earn a great deal of money, others earn only a few thousand dollars in royalties. Most writers find other incentives more powerful than the lure of cash.

Getting Started

It may seem like a big jump to go from writing 2,000-word features to writing a manuscript of anywhere from 60,000 to 100,000 words. The first step, therefore, is to stop thinking about your project as a "book" and start thinking about it as a series of "chapters." Then think of each chapter as being equivalent to a 2,000- to 5,000-word article. If you already know that you can write an article a week, then you know that you can write a book chapter a week. If you have twenty chapters, your book will take about twenty weeks, not counting research time. While a book may actually take anywhere from six months to three years to write, most contracts anticipate a delivery time of one year.

Choosing a Topic

Choosing a book topic is similar to choosing a topic for an article. Once again, you may start with a general subject (e.g., dogs) and move to a more specific topic (e.g., health). Then, begin brainstorming subtopics. The difference is, when you're writing a book, each subtopic may become its own chapter.

When you choose a topic, you may find that you have either too much information, or too little. For example, a subject like "dogs" is too broad for an article *or* a book. A topic like "canine health," however, is too broad for an article, but *could* be turned into a book. Narrowing that topic still further—e.g., "natural health care for dogs"—will make your book even more focused, and thus more marketable.

A book that targets a more specific market niche is often more marketable than a more "general" book. For example, a book that focuses on "how to have a healthy dog" might have a broader market appeal (for "all dog owners") than a book on "how to care for the older dog." However, it will also have more competition. Your book on older dogs may have a smaller audience, but it may also stand out as the only book of its kind on the shelf.

Focusing on too narrow a topic, however, can leave you with insufficient information to write an entire book, and too small an audience. For example, it might be difficult to write a book about "chiropractic care for dogs." However, you could expand that topic to "holistic health care for dogs," covering not only chiropractic but also acupuncture, Reiki, massage, herbal therapies, and so forth. This will expand your book *and* your market.

Organizing Your Book

When you start writing a book, you face that same question you faced when writing articles: "Do I need an outline?" The answer is "yes"—if only because you'll need a chapter-by-chapter outline when preparing your proposal.

Fortunately, the techniques I recommended in chapter 9 apply just as well to books. The difference is that each subtopic is likely to be an entire chapter. For example, if you're using the "logical sequence of events" approach (this happened first, this happened next . . .), each major event may be a chapter. Your introduction and conclusion, instead of being limited to a few paragraphs, will be chapters in their own right.

Once you've developed a basic chapter structure, use each chapter "heading" to organize your research. Many writers set up a file folder for each chapter, and use it to store research information. If you find that a chapter has too much information, you can always split it; if a chapter is too short, you can often combine it with another chapter.

Another common question is whether to write your book from beginning to end, or whether you can write a chapter here and a chapter there. The answer, of course, is: Use whatever method works best for you! Some people like to write the easiest chapters first, then progress to the more difficult ones, and finally tie it all together. Others prefer to write chapters sequentially, particularly when it's important to know what you've "already covered" in earlier parts of the book. If you find that one approach isn't working for you, try the other.

Write, then Revise

Your writing can bog down if you attempt to edit your book as you go. It's usually better to simply try to "get it all down" first—even if the end result is considerably longer than your allotted word count. Once you've written a first draft, it's easier to determine where to make cuts or add information. It's also easier to "polish" a manuscript all at once rather than a piece at a time.

Most writers recommend giving yourself a "cooling off" period of at least a week before attempting to edit or polish your manuscript. Then, you'll find it easier to approach your words from the perspective of the reader, rather than as a parent trying to edit a beloved "baby."

This can be essential when you discover, for example, that your book is 20,000 words longer than the limit. At first glance, you may not be able to imagine how to cut 20,000 words. After a break, however, you may find that you can manage to part with a paragraph here and a minor concept there, or even a chapter that seemed interesting but isn't vital to the whole. You may also find that you can cut words by creating contractions (e.g., changing words like "you are" to "you're" and "you will" to "you'll"). You'll also be amazed to find how easy it is to tighten up phrases and paragraphs. For example, if your book is 2,000 paragraphs long, you only need to cut an average of ten words per paragraph!

Finding a Publisher

As I said earlier, it's often possible to sell your book before you write it. To accomplish this, you'll need to submit a proposal to an appropriate publisher.

The first step, of course, is *finding* an appropriate publisher. Don't just grab a directory of markets and look in the topic index for, say, publishers who handle books on "dogs." Instead, try these steps:

❖ *Check your bookshelf.* Who publishes the books *you* refer to on this subject? Would your book fit into their line? Take note of any publisher who appears more than once on your shelf.

❖ *Check a bookstore.* Which publishers are offering similar, or complementary, titles? Do you find that you're picking up books by one publisher more often than others? This could mean that your interests mesh with those of that publisher. While you're browsing, ask yourself these questions:

- Do you like the look and feel of the publisher's products? Is the paper high quality? Do you like the cover? Is the type easy to read? Would you like your book to look like this?
- Does the publisher offer the type of book you're planning? Does it have the same depth of content? If the publisher uses lots of color photos, can you provide them? Conversely, if you're planning to use lots of artwork, does the publisher support it?
- Do the books match your style? If you write in a "conversational" style, don't pitch to a publisher who offers highly technical or academic books.
- Are your credentials comparable to the publisher's other authors? Do you need a special degree or professional experience?
- What is the price range? Does it match the likely budget of your audience? You may like the *idea* of having your book published in glossy coffee-table format, but will your audience shell out $30 or more for it?

❖ *Review the guidelines.* You may find these on the publisher's Web site, or in a guideline directory. (You'll find lists of book publisher sites at *www.writing-world.com/links/bookpubs.shtml.*) Also, try to find the publisher's current catalog; this will tell you what books have recently been published. If a publisher has recently published a book similar to the one you're proposing, it isn't likely to want another—but a competing publisher might! Make sure your book matches the publisher's requirements, including length, illustrations, etc. Finally, make sure you know what terms the publisher offers, including royalties, rights, etc.

Chances are, your research is going to turn up more than one "appropriate" publisher for your book, and that's good. You will want a backup plan if your first choice doesn't come through. The question is, can you submit your proposal to more than one publisher at a time?

There is no clear answer. Some publishers still resist "simultaneous submissions," but others acknowledge that when it can take six months or longer to review a proposal, it's asking a lot to expect authors to submit proposals "sequentially." One approach is to submit simultaneous *query* letters, asking whether you may follow up with a proposal and sample chapters. If a publisher says "yes," you can then ask whether the proposal must be "exclusive" (sent only to that publisher) or whether you can send it to other interested publishers. A book query is functionally the same as a magazine query (see chapter 17), and you can often send it by e-mail.

Preparing a Proposal

Once you've found a publisher, you need to develop a professional proposal that includes the following elements[1]:

The Overview

The overview of your proposal is presented in narrative format, and may have several sections, including:

TITLE

A title helps establish the concept of your book in the editor's mind. Amy Shojai, author of *New Choices in Natural Healing for Dogs and Cats,* points out that a title "must not only describe the book and/or concept, but be that illusive thing that editors/agents describe as 'sexy'. The title must strike an instant chord of recognition with the editor." At the same time, she notes, "don't get too attached to titles. Editors change them all the time, often for something that's boring."

CONTENT

Your overview should offer a general summary of the content. Don't go into excessive detail; instead, try to convey the general focus and purpose of your book, including the benefits it will offer to readers. (The concept of "benefits" is key: Your overview should clearly indicate what readers have to gain from your book.)

The overview for my proposal for *Writing.com: Creative Internet Strategies to Advance Your Writing Career* (Allworth Press, 1999), for example, defined the content of the book through a series of questions likely to be asked by readers, beginning with "What do writers want to know about the Internet?" The overview continued with this promise:

Writing in Cyberspace [my original working title] is designed to answer these questions, and more. It is divided into three sections that correspond with the way most writers "experience" the Internet: *Exploration* (research), *Interaction* (using e-mail and networking), and *Creation* (establishing an online presence). Each chapter highlights a particular aspect of the writing business and how that aspect has been affected (or can be improved) by the Internet.

RATIONALE

Your overview should also explain who will buy your book (and why that audience will want to buy the book *now*). "Back up the need for the book with stats," says Shojai. "Editors want numbers; don't just say 'everybody who loves pets will buy my book.' Tell them how many owners there are who have dogs who chew used bubblegum and would benefit from your book, *12 Steps to De-Gumming Da Dog.*"

When pitching her book on natural healing, Shojai began with broad statistics to define the potential market: the fact that Americans own 66.2 million cats and 58 million dogs. She then narrowed that audience to those who "welcome pets into their hearts and homes as full members of the family. This pet-generation is eager to provide quality care for their furry families." She explained the timeliness of her proposal by noting the "national obsession with health and fitness."

COMPETITION

Which books will you be competing against, and *how* will you compete? To answer this question, of course, you must first *research* the competition— something that, hopefully, you did before you started writing. Says Shojai, "The competition section is probably the most important part of any proposal. I try to *never* slam the competition, but to put my proposal in a favorable light compared to whatever might be out there. In this case, I felt that some of the competition was quite good—just way, way out of date, which meant my proposal was timely. Of course, I added lots of new elements the competition didn't have, too."

Your discussion of the competition should list specific titles (including author, publisher, and publication date). It should then explain how your book differs from those titles: how it improves, diverges from, or goes beyond what has been written before. For example, Shojai listed several representative titles in her proposal, then noted that while most of her competitors focused on single therapies, her book would present a range of approaches.

What if you can't identify any competition for your book? This is not necessarily a good thing! Shojai notes, "If there is no competition, find some. Put something in, even if it's a stretch, because if nobody has done the topic before, the publisher/editor will figure . . . it's not a saleable idea. You *want* books on your topic to be out there and successful; that means you have a ready-made market. Then it's a matter of making your book different enough . . . to make the idea viable."

FORMAT

This section should list the book's title and subtitle, the number of words you anticipate, and any other information relevant to the production of the book. Mention whether your book will include any graphics (tables, charts, figures, diagrams) or illustrations (photos, line drawings, etc.), sidebars, appendices, and so forth. Indicate whether the publisher will need to assist with artwork or whether you will be providing it yourself. If color artwork is included, make sure you provide a rationale for the cost.

MARKET

Explain how your publisher can reach the book's target audience. List magazines in which the book should be reviewed, organizations and groups that might be interested in the book, specialized bookstores or other market outlets, etc. Note whether the book could be used as a classroom text. (You'll be asked for this information anyway once your proposal is accepted, so start gathering it now.)

Chapter-by-Chapter Summary

Most publishers expect to receive a list of proposed chapters, with a brief (one- to two-paragraph) summary of each. If you haven't written your book, you may not know exactly how many chapters it will contain, but you should be able to flesh out a summary from your basic outline. This information isn't "set in stone"—you can always change the number of chapters, or their organization, later. There's no "right" number of chapters; however, a book with too few chapters (e.g., less than five) may seem too "light," while one with too many (e.g., more than thirty) may seem unwieldy.

Some publishers will also ask for sample chapters. If so, find out whether they need to be sequential (e.g., the first three), or whether you can send the most *representative* chapters.

Author Bio

What are your qualifications for writing this book? Your bio should answer this question in the space of (about) a single page. It should be written in narrative format, and in third person—e.g., "John Smith is an award-winning decoy carver who has practiced and taught the craft for more than twenty years." As with magazine publishers, a book publisher is likely to expect credentials in one or more of the following areas:

- Educational background
- Professional background
- Personal experience/expertise
- Previous writing credits

Be sure you know what credentials are expected of you by the publisher and by the market you are attempting to target. If your book focuses on "scholarly" information, chances are good that you'll be expected to have academic credentials. If your book focuses on business or technical information, you may be expected to provide relevant professional experience. If your book addresses more popular "how-to" or "self-help" topics, you may be able to market your proposal on the basis of professional *or* personal expertise.

Personal experience can be tricky. It is, of course, essential for a book that is an *account* of your personal experiences, but is usually less helpful in marketing how-to or self-help titles. The more impact your book might have on a reader's well-being, the more credentials you will be expected to have. While you might sell a book on fly-fishing on the basis of a weekend hobby, you may have trouble selling a book on childcare if your only "credential" is being a parent.

Writing credits are useful if they are relevant. If you have published other nonfiction books, for example, this demonstrates that you can finish *and* sell a book-length manuscript, even if it's on a completely different topic. Articles will also help demonstrate your skill and marketability, though publishers often aren't impressed by articles on an unrelated topic. Fiction credits may not impress an editor at all. Keep in mind that you're not just trying to prove that you can write; you're also trying to demonstrate that readers should believe what you say!

Supporting Materials

You may also wish to include the following materials:

- Résumé or curriculum vitae, if it supports the credentials listed in your bio.
- Publications list that cites *relevant* publications (and any books that you've already published).
- Writing samples. Some publishers like to see writing samples, others don't. Check the guidelines first, and send no more than three (relevant) samples.
- Business card, so that a publisher can easily contact you.
- SASE. Unless you have an overwhelming reason to want the publisher to *return* your proposal, simply send a #10 SASE.
- Reply postcard. If you want to be informed that your proposal was

received, include a self-addressed, stamped postcard that the recipient can toss in the mail. The postmark itself will give you the delivery date.

Don't send your photo (you'll only need to provide this *if* the proposal is accepted), testimonials or reviews (especially from friends and family), irrelevant writing samples, copies of other books you've written, or "imprinted" business products (such as personalized pens, card-magnets, calendars, etc.). Most of all, never send anything that would appear unprofessional!

The Publishing Process

Selling your proposal is just the beginning. Here's what happens next:

The Contract

The first step in the publication process is the contract. Read it carefully; if there is anything you don't understand, ask for clarification. Be sure you know what rights you are giving up (don't sign a "work-for-hire" contract by mistake!), what royalties you'll receive, and the basis for those royalties. Some publishers pay royalties on cover price, others on "net" price (after bookstore or distributor discounts, which can be as high as 60 percent). This can make a significant difference in what you're paid; for example, while 10 percent royalties on the *cover price* of a book priced at $15 would be $1.50 per book, 10 percent of *net* on that same book might be as low as 60¢. Find out what you'll be paid for "subsidiary" sales, such as electronic or audio editions, translations, or movie rights (the standard rate is 50 percent).

The Advance

Once you've signed and returned the contract, you should receive a portion of your advance. Most publishers pay 50 percent on signing the contract and 50 percent on delivery of an "acceptable" manuscript; some, however, pay the advance in thirds. If you fail to deliver the book, or if it is not considered "acceptable," you may have to return the advance.

The Author Questionnaire

At about the same time as you receive your advance, you may receive a (long) questionnaire asking you to describe possible marketing outlets for the book. The publisher will use this questionnaire to guide the book's promotional campaign, so be as thorough as possible!

The Manuscript

Your contract will specify a delivery date for the manuscript, and the form in which it is to be delivered (e.g., hard copy, disk, etc.) Your publisher will announce a publication date and begin promoting the book long before you deliver it, so meeting that deadline is important. (If you can't meet it, contact your publisher as soon as possible.)

First Review

Once you've delivered the manuscript, it must be reviewed by the publisher before you receive the second half of your advance. Often, this takes one to three months, so don't expect a check immediately. I recommend following up six weeks after delivery.

Editing

First, your book will be reviewed for content issues, and you'll be asked to clarify anything that seems unclear, or perhaps to add (or cut) information. (This is a great time to reread the manuscript yourself and make any necessary editing changes.) Next, your book will be copyedited, and you'll be asked to review and approve suggested changes. You may be given only four or five days for each review.

Galley Proofs

Once the book is typeset, you'll be sent "galley proofs" for a final proofreading review. Your job now is simply to make sure that no typos or errors have been introduced in the typesetting process; the publisher will *not* appreciate editorial corrections unless you spot a major error. Again, you may have less than a week to review galleys.

Indexing

At the galley stage, you may be asked to create an index for the book. (I have found that the easiest method is to sit down with a notepad and go through the book page by page, jotting down terms that should be indexed with the corresponding page numbers.) If you don't want to index the book yourself, the publisher will arrange for indexing, but will usually charge the cost (typically around $3 per galley page) against your first royalty check.

Printing

Your book may go to press anywhere from six months to two years after you deliver the manuscript. When it does, you'll receive the number of author copies specified in your contract (usually ten). You'll also have the option of buying more copies at a discount (usually 40 percent); however, you will *not* receive royalties on copies you buy. You may also have the option of pre-ordering a quantity of books at a higher discount (e.g., 60 percent); this is useful if you expect to sell books at talks, classes, or other personal appearances.

Royalties

Most publishers pay royalties twice a year, based on royalty periods beginning in January and June. If your book is published in June, your first royalty period would end in December, and you'll see your first statement around February or March. You won't actually receive royalties, however, until your book has sold enough copies to "earn out" the advance you've already been paid. For example, if your book is priced at $15, your royalty is 10 percent, and your advance was $3,000, you'll have to sell 2,000 copies of the book ($3,000 ÷ $1.50) before you receive additional royalties.

A Final Word on "Doing It Yourself"

Many authors, frustrated by the time-consuming process of submitting a proposal and waiting a year or more to see their book in print, are tempted to "do it themselves." And many have made a success of self-publishing.

Before you venture down the "do it yourself" road, however, be sure you understand what is involved. Becoming your own publisher means moving beyond being a writer—it means becoming your own marketer, administrator, bookkeeper, designer, editor, distributor, and more. You should also be aware that it is extremely difficult to get a self-published book into bookstores, and that many publications won't review them.

It's also important to understand the difference between "self-publishing" and "subsidy publishing." While both involve "paying" for publication, there is a distinction. When you self-publish, you retain all rights to your books, you own the physical books that you produce, you can set your own prices and discounts, and you receive all revenues. When you subsidy publish, you often give up the same rights you'd give a commercial publisher, you do *not* own the published books, you can't set your own rates, you have to pay for any books that you send to reviewers, and you receive only a portion of revenues in the form of royalties. In addition, subsidy-published books are generally regarded with even less respect than self-published books (and most bookstores won't stock print-on-demand books at all).[2]

Whether you self-publish or sell your book to a commercial publisher, the final thing you need to be aware of is that your job isn't "over" when you deliver that manuscript—or even when that box of "author copies" arrives at your door. Your job as an author may have ended—but your job as a promoter has just begun. The more you're able to participate in marketing your book, the more successful—and profitable—that book will be![3]

NOTES

1. To view examples of successful book proposals, see *www.writing-world.com/publish/samples.shtml*.

2. For more information, see "Subsidy vs. Self-Publishing: What's the Difference?" at *www.writing-world.com/publish/subsidy.shtml*. For information on self-publishing, visit *www.writing-world.com/self-pub/index.shtml*.

3. Needless to say, Writing-World.com also has a section on promotion: *www.writing-world.com/promotion/index.shtml*.

CHAPTER 30

Writing for Businesses

by Peter Bowerman

A marketing communications firm, a regular client from way back, called me on a Thursday—in a bind and a bit frantic. They needed an 800-word article for their client, and they needed it by Monday. They provided the source material and a contact phone number for the one interview I needed to do. My fee: $1,000, including a 25 percent rush fee. Fine with them.

Over the next five weeks, I'd work on four more articles, averaging 800 words and approximately $850 each. Plus promotional posters and flyer copy for $950. Two roughly twenty-four-page benefits guides averaging $3,300 each. Step-by-step "walk-through" sales sheets for their Internet sites netted me an additional $850. Six sales letters for $1,500.

Then I got a call from my big telecommunications client, checking on my availability to work on a job right away. Not needing the work, I tried to discourage them by bumping my then $85 hourly rate up to $95 (what I currently earn). They said, "Fine." That turned out to be seventeen hours for a little over $1,600. When it was all said and done, I earned close to $16,000 in six weeks. No, probably not typical. But it's not rare either. This is the potential of the commercial writing business.

In the last decade, and certainly the past few years, the twin trends of downsizing and outsourcing have permanently altered the business landscape. Corporate America is doing more with less—fewer people, less resources, smaller budgets. The creative, marketing, and communication departments are being scaled back or eliminated altogether.

As a result, many organizations rely heavily on freelancers to get their work done—and for some good business reasons: They provide no salaries, benefits, and vacations. They pay only for what they need when they need it. They get a broad range of talent. They enjoy fresh "outsider" perspectives. And as budgets shrink, the same company that couldn't afford to keep on full-time staff or hire an expensive agency or design firm may now find the freelancer option a lot more economically attractive.

No, it's not always as easy or rosy as the "$16K in forty-five days" scenario described earlier. You'll have your share of $500 weeks and, in the beginning, you'll be working a lot more for a lot less. This is *not* a "get-rich-quick" scheme. But develop the right work habits early and you'll be surprised at how soon you'll be having some pretty lucrative stretches. Most projects are done within a few weeks, you're generally paid in thirty days, and chasing your money is the very rare exception, not the rule.

Why Pursue Commercial Writing?

- ❖ *You like to write and are good at it.* (Just making sure. . . .)
- ❖ *The time is right for freelancers.* Downsizing, outsourcing, etc. (see above).
- ❖ *Easy low-overhead start-up.* As writing fields go, commercial writing is one of the easiest to break into and, for even a moderately talented scribe, one of the most lucrative. And given that you're probably already set up with a computer, fax, and Internet access, the overhead is one of the lowest around.
- ❖ *No special skills.* My major in college? Russian Studies—not English or Journalism. I'm a good writer. I'm only a passable grammarian. Remember, I had no writing background whatsoever. You don't need special credentials. Clients want good reliable writers who're creative, strategic, competitively priced, and who will deliver good work—on time and on budget. They don't care what you studied in college or even if you went to college. They don't care what your work background is, unless it's relevant to the specific project.
- ❖ *Brilliant writing not required.* You *do* have to be a good writer, but incredible talent is not necessary. There are plenty of industries, such as health care, banking, manufacturing, insurance, high technology, and many more that need oodles of clear, concise copywriting that effectively conveys information but doesn't have to be a work of art. If you are "crackerjack," you'll get into the fun creative arenas like ad copy and direct-mail writing, among others.
- ❖ *Unlimited work.* Marketing brochures, corporate-image pieces, advertisements, newsletters, direct-mail campaigns, industrial-video scripts, trade articles, press releases, case studies, executive profiles, educational/industrial CD-ROM scripts, radio spots, TV commercials, event scripting, business letters, sales-promotion material, marketing manuals, technical manuals, corporate profiles, annual reports, product documentation, product spec sheets, proposals—shall I go on? Every single one of these has to be written by someone.

  There are three main arenas of work: "B-to-C" (Business to Consumer), which are the things you as a consumer see; "B-to-B" (Business to

Business), which you usually don't see, except in your own business; and "internal" communications—the projects that exist only within the "four walls" of a corporation and for "their eyes only"—a *huge* segment.

To see samples of the types of projects you might be doing, visit my online portfolio at *www.wellfedwriter.com* (click "WriteInc."). It might also give you some ideas for putting your own commercial-writing Web site together.

❖ *Be your own boss.* In the 9 to 5 working world, you've pretty much got to march in lock step with the rest of the troops. Want to sleep from 2 to 9 A.M.? Go for it! Of course, in the beginning, you'd better be meeting clients when and where they want.

❖ *Variety of work.* Over the years, I've written about UPS's Canadian operations, BellSouth's product line, Coca-Cola's alliance with The Boys & Girls Clubs of America, how one company would design an entertainment pavilion for the Olympics, the charitable activities of a prestigious Chattanooga hospital, and on and on. Every day is different!

❖ *Finance your writing "bliss."* Maybe you think there's something mercenary about writing for Corporate America. But, what's the point of being a writing "purist" (books and articles) if you end up moonlighting to make ends meet? Why not write and earn $50 to $75 an hour? That'll give you the time and space to pursue your "bliss"—that future Oscar, Pulitzer, Emmy, or Tony-award-winning masterpiece.

❖ *Healthy income.* If you have even a modicum of intelligence, ability, and drive, I'd say you can sleepwalk your way to $30,000 a year. If you're reasonably aggressive about getting the word out, you should easily top $50,000. I know a healthy number of commercial writers grossing $100,000+ a year. Interested in part-time? Once established, making $2,000 a month part-time is very doable.

❖ *Use your background.* What's your industry background or work experience? High-tech? Finance? Healthcare? Advertising? Wherever you come from, approach them first. Chances are excellent that they have writing projects for someone who knows the ropes.

❖ *A nice life.* Good money, flexible hours, stimulating work. Go to bed when you want, get up when you want (most of the time), wear what you want, take vacations when you want, shower and shave when you want. Sure, getting established takes some effort, but it's not nearly as difficult as you'd think, and depending on your present situation, you could be halfway there right now.

Building a Portfolio

How do you get work when you have nothing to show? Start with any projects you've done in a past or present job: marketing manual, brochure, press release, newsletter, sales sheet, speech, article, etc. If the job-related "pick-ins'" are lean, try doing some pro bono work for a charity or startup. It could be the Arthritis Foundation, a hospital, a group like the Sierra Club, a political organization, a small theater group, etc.

Possible projects? Simple trifold or more complex brochures, newsletters, ad or direct-mail campaigns, Web content, and much, much more. For projects like these, where strong graphics are essential, the client will most likely have a graphic designer to professionally produce the piece, which means you'll end up with a good sample.

Another great strategy is to team up with a graphic designer in the same boat as you, starting out, and approach those pro bono entities. Together, you can deliver "turnkey" projects, including coordinating the printing (the designer's job). It can be a pretty attractive offer to the client: free copywriting and design services in return for plenty of samples when it's done.

If you're teaming with a designer, why not just "create" a portfolio? Make 'em up. Show a prospect that you know how to tell a story for even a fictitious business in an ad, brochure, newsletter, direct-mail piece, etc. In this case, because you won't be professionally producing these pieces, you'll need access to a good color printer. This teaming can serve as a wonderful template for future paying collaborations, a crucial strategy for expanding your possible universe of work. And all this, theoretically, can be done while you're employed elsewhere.

Who Will Hire You?

You'll be dealing with two types of clients: the end-user (EU), or a middle-man (MM) who's dealing with the end-user. EU means any company from small to Fortune 100, while MMs include, but aren't limited to, graphic design firms, ad agencies, marketing companies, PR firms, and event production companies. MMs are great "bird dogs" because they rarely staff full-time writers and as they hunt business for themselves, they'll "find" work for you.

With MMs, by definition, your copy is going through two layers of review and approval, theirs and the final EU client, which can result in longer copy cycles. This is one big advantage of dealing with EUs: There is only one layer of communication and copy approval. And if EUs are used to dealing with MMs, that'll work to your advantage as well, since typically they're used to paying inflated rates for copywriting—a normal rate plus the MM's premium.

Established EUs and MMs need little educating about the process. They know what they need, have bought plenty of writing before, and know how the world works. That means things like understanding that you need "concepting" (brainstorming) time and that they don't get twenty-seven rewrites at no extra charge. You'll run into the educating scenario more with smaller firms who are doing their first formal brochure, ad, or marketing campaign.

A caveat about MMs: During tougher economic times, your best bet really is the end-user. As belts tighten, clients who historically used middlemen will be more inclined to hire a low-overhead freelancer. By the same token, MMs are scrambling too and will want to keep as much work in house as possible. Don't ignore the MMs completely, but focus on the end-users first.

End-Users

EUs mean Corporate America plus companies of every size. The larger the company, the broader the spectrum of work. UPS or the Coca-Cola Company, for instance, have countless different departments and wide-ranging needs: ad copy, marketing brochures, POS (point-of-sale) display signage, promotional materials, training videos and manuals, product sheets, sales aids, CD training programs, proposals, internal publications; the list goes on and on. And surprisingly little of it is done in-house.

Your first stop is "MarCom" (Marketing Communications), or "CC" (Corporate Communications). This department, which is essentially an in-house agency for the corporation, turns out a wide array of projects like the ones described above.

In the absence of a MarCom or CC department, contact the marketing department, sales department, and when all else fails, human resources (it's always smarter to go to those with the specific needs, as opposed to those who serve them).

After one or two successful projects, always ask for referrals—to other divisions of the company or elsewhere. A "warm call" is *always* preferable to a cold call.

Middlemen

For any of the following MM categories, start by simply looking in the Yellow Pages for the specific category. Once you reach the firms, your possible contact people are creative director (CD), assistant creative director (ACD), project manager (PM), account executive (AE), producer, and others. With the exception of the big ad agencies and PR firms (which still hire freelancers), most MMs don't staff full-time writers.

♦ *Graphic Design Firms.* I've gotten a huge chunk of my business over the years from graphic design firms. Get to know the talented designers at a particular firm; it's only a matter of time until they go off on their own and if they like you and your work, you'll have a client for a long time.

Speaking of which, don't ignore the "lone rangers." Make a point to forge alliances with three to four talented one-person graphic design shops, and try to become their copywriter of choice. These relationships are likely to be much more long-term, stable, and lucrative than ones you develop with larger firms, where things and people always change. Midway through one year, my number-one account in billings was a one-woman design shop. Don't let size fool you.

❖ *Advertising Agencies.* The average freelancer is unlikely to land the juicy, high-end, big-name Fortune 100 advertising work for the big ad agencies. The agencies will be keeping that work for themselves. Your best bet with ad agencies is "collateral"—brochures, internal campaigns, and other peripheral supporting projects. Try smaller advertising agencies for more opportunities to do fun, creative concepting and headlining projects. Because they're more likely to view you as an expert (and not just the "hired help"), you've got a much better chance of having your efforts see the light of day. That means more job satisfaction and creative fulfillment.

❖ *Marketing Firms.* While these entities (which also rarely have staff writers) often specialize in a particular industry (high-tech, healthcare, real estate, etc.), occasionally they're broad-based. A marketing firm might help a growing company that has made its mark locally but is looking to have a national presence. It might mean designing a comprehensive and strategic campaign involving ad/media campaigns, public relations, direct mail, Web site, etc.

❖ *Public Relations Firms.* PR firms, like ad agencies, span the gamut in size, with a healthy number of huge ones in any large market. As with ad agencies, freelancers aren't likely to see too much of the high-profile PR work, but chances are, there's plenty of collateral work here as well.

❖ *Event Production Companies (EPCs).* EPCs work with large corporations to produce annual conferences, trade shows, product launches, etc. Most handle absolutely everything: design and construction of all tradeshow exhibits, all printed literature before, during, and after the show, conference signage, speaker support, meeting rooms, catering, entertainment, all the shipping, and much more.

By definition, EPCs operate mostly in major convention centers like Las Vegas, Chicago, New York, Boston, Washington, D.C., Atlanta, and others, but of course, they travel anywhere. If you can't locate these companies in the Yellow Pages, contact the management of the big conventions that come to your area and ask who's producing the event. At EPCs, contact producers, creative directors, or account executives for proposals (the first step to landing these huge contracts), conference literature, speaker support, event scripting, etc.

Don't put these bigger brand-name EUs or marquis MM clients on a pedestal and think you're not good enough to work with them. You'd be surprised. They're just people—usually overworked and often ill fitted to their roles. If you're good and reliable, I promise you, they can use your help.

Getting Started

Start with the Yellow Pages (especially for MMs) to build a calling list of companies, looking up categories directly: advertising agencies, public relations firms, graphic designers, etc.

Another great source for prospects is the *Book of Lists,* published by your city's weekly business publication (check out *www.amcity.com* for a complete listing of these publications). Also, check with your library for local business listing directories.

One reader of mine, a writer with a healthy amount of high-tech writing experience, simply got the Fortune 1000 list of companies from the *www.fortune.com* Web site, started at the bottom and worked his way up. Between that and another list, he made about 350 calls before landing about $35,000 in about four months.

Make sure your list is long enough to keep you busy for a while. You don't want any excuses to stop calling (except maybe that it's Saturday). Here are a few tips for successful prospecting:

❖ *Dumb down.* Check the analytical side of your brain at the door: the side that filters and second-guesses every name on the list, asking pointless questions, beginning with, "Should I . . . ," "Would they . . . ," and "I wonder if. . . "

❖ *Reality check.* 75 to 80 percent of the people you talk to won't be interested in your services. That's roughly four out of five. But don't worry; they're almost invariably nice about it.

❖ *Your script.* Know exactly what you're going to say and write it out word-for-word on a 3 × 5 card and keep it in front of you. It's a highly effective tool for staying focused and reducing anxiety. Keep it brief (fifteen seconds or less), simple and to the point. My basic version is: "Good morning, my name is Peter Bowerman, and I'm a freelance writer, making contact with local banks [for instance], to determine whether you have any ongoing or occasional needs for a good freelance writer to help create marketing collateral material: brochures, newsletters, ads, etc. Who might be the best person to talk with?" Ideally, you'll have a name, but if not, this is always enough to get some reaction, which then drives the rest of the call.

❖ *How to talk.* Speaking slowly, clearly, and evenly allows your prospects—who weren't expecting your call—to switch gears and catch up.

- *Get your mind right.* Set a goal to simply have some nice conversations and gather some information. If you feel there's less at stake, you'll come across to prospects as relaxed and confident—a great attitude to project.
- *Keep a log.* Track your calling efforts with a printed log or contact management program.
- *Harness the law of averages.* It absolutely, positively works every time. Make enough calls and you'll find the business. Making fifty calls a day for a month is a thousand calls. This may sound scary, but I can't think of a better way of kick-starting this business. When I started my business, I made close to seven hundred calls in a month. That's called critical mass. I don't care what you're selling. Make that many calls, and something's bound to happen.
- *Provide samples.* There are three main ways to provide samples to a client: (1) via an online portfolio on your Web site (highly recommended); (2) by fax (text only or copies of samples) or e-mail (text-only or PDF files); and (3) by copying and snail-mailing clips along with résumés/cover letters. *Never* send a package to anyone who isn't expecting one. Whichever strategy you use, the next step is always the same: follow up, follow up, follow up, follow up, follow up, and follow up some more.
- *Get out and meet your market.* Early in my career, I heard this statistic: you'll get hired by one of ten prospects to whom you send information but one of three who meet you. *Always* try and get a face-to-face appointment, even if you're also sending samples.

Follow Up!

To get the business, you have to get your name (and usually yourself) in front of a lot of people. The cold calling, sending out of information (mailed, faxed, e-mailed, or steered to a Web site), and follow-up has to happen. Make the process simple and you'll do it. Do this personal marketing on a consistent basis and you'll put yourself ahead of about 95 percent of the competition.

Every time you talk or meet with prospects for the first time, send them something to remind them of you again. Sit down and create a series of form follow-up/cover letters. Each letter should be a separate computer file and should address the following situations:

- You've met with a prospect who's excited about working with you, but no work is immediately pending.
- You've met with a new client and are starting work on a new job.
- An expanded version of the above, reiterating a few key points about your skills that were discussed in your meeting.
- You've talked to a prospect who's a long shot for work, but you're sending out a letter, résumé, and business cards.

- ❖ You've spoken with a new prospect who regularly hires freelancers, and this letter accompanies a mailed package.
- ❖ You receive a call from an assistant to a creative director or communications manager requesting you send his boss a package, accompanied by this letter.

After each meeting, use the appropriate form letter as a template to generate a personalized version and send it out.

Given the capabilities of computers, there's no excuse not to have multiple versions of résumés. In the beginning, I was glad to have even one good one, but as my business grew I created specialized versions (with many items common to all) weighted to ad-copy writing, video/CD, technical projects, brochure/collateral work, speeches, articles/editorial, PR, as well as several general versions. Always limit your résumé to one page.

Unless you're blessed to be in a market bursting with work, you'll probably have to remind your prospect base periodically that you're out there. Yes, you'll be following up with calls, samples, and links to your Web site, but a simple direct-mail campaign two to four times a year can effectively and inexpensively keep you in front of your market.

Design the front and reverse sides of postcards in a program like Microsoft® Publisher. Lay them four-up (4¼" × 5½" each) on an 8½" × 11" page on your computer screen or two-up for an oversize version (8½" × 5½" each). Print out clean laser copies of these front and back pages and then copy them on a brightly colored card stock (yellow is a good choice), cut 'em up, stamp 'em, and mail them to your growing list of prospects who told you they use freelancers. Do it twice (January and June) or four times (add April and September) annually. Again, do this and you'll set yourself apart from the lion's share of your competition.

How Much Should You Charge?

While you'll ultimately be pricing most of your work by the job—i.e., a flat rate—you first need to establish your hourly rate. For creative writing, such as marketing work, ad copy, descriptive collateral, the range is about $50 to $125 an hour with $60 to $80 the average in good-sized metropolitan areas.

I started at $50 an hour. You won't make anyone flinch—except yourself—with a $50-an-hour rate unless it's someone who's never hired a writer before. In fact, $50 is actually going to sound too low to seasoned copywriting buyers. As your portfolio and reputation grow, bump your rates up $10 to $15 an hour.

If You're Fast, Go "Flat"

As clients come to trust you more, they'll be more likely to let you bill by the hour. If you know you work fast, you may prefer to work on a flat rate. If the client signs off on a flat fee bid and it takes you fewer hours then that flat fee was based on, you win. Unethical? Not at all. It'd only be wrong if you quoted a number of hours, used less, but still charged them for the original higher number.

Contracts? (Use the "Bid Letter")

In nearly a decade in the business, I've only signed about six formal contracts, most of which came from the client side. What I have used a lot more often (but by no means on every job) is what I call a "bid letter," in which I spell out the details:

- ❖ The specific parameters of the project.
- ❖ What fee you're quoting (a range is acceptable; i.e., 20 to 23 hours).
- ❖ What hourly rate that fee is based on.
- ❖ What's included for that fee: meetings, background reading/research (if there is any), copywriting, revisions (I include two rounds; additional are billed at my hourly rate).
- ❖ Time frame for delivery.
- ❖ Up-front money expected (usually one-third to one-half for new clients and big jobs).

You send it to the client, have him or her sign it and fax it back to you. Posterior covered.

Keep Your Word

Woody Allen once said something to the effect that, "Ninety percent of success in life is a matter of just showing up." You don't necessarily have to be the best, brightest, fastest, or sharpest. But "show up": Do what you say you're going to do. Be where you say you're going to be. Make your word count for something. Deliver more than you promise. Put this simple no-cost strategy to work and you'll put yourself ahead of about 95 percent of the pack. The work is out there. Why not get your share?

CHAPTER 31

Becoming a Full-Time Freelancer

B y this point, you may be thinking: Wouldn't it be great to quit the rat race? To leave bosses and time clocks behind, skip the commute, ditch the heels or tie, and work in the same clothes you wear to weed the garden?

It's called "taking the plunge," and if you're at all serious about writing, you've probably dreamed about it. But you may also have regarded that dream as, at best, nothing more than an improbable fantasy. Writing may be the career you love, but chances are it's not the career that's keeping food on the table and a roof over your head.

I can't tell you whether you can make that dream a reality. But I can offer a few tips on making the decision: to plunge or not to plunge!

When to Plunge—and When Not to

The first question to ask when considering "the plunge" is: Where is your writing career today?

If the answer is "just getting started," stop right there. If you have only a few clips to your résumé, or no clips at all, you're unlikely to be able to support yourself with your craft.

I hear from many writers who say they would like to quit their jobs and "start writing." To such writers, I say: "Start writing now. Quit later." If you haven't started yet—or if you're just starting—you simply won't know enough about this complex business to earn a living. So start writing. Get your feet wet. Find out what you can and can't do, what you enjoy, what you don't enjoy. Discover your strengths, and the areas that could use improvement. Find out whether you really wish to pursue writing as a business, or whether you'd rather pursue it as an avocation.

Writing can be a career or hobby, or anything you care to make it. *Writing for a living* is a business, pure and simple. If you wouldn't dream of quitting your day job to run, say, an auto-repair shop without any training as a mechanic, then don't dream of quitting your day job to become a writer without a comparable level of experience.

But how much experience *is* enough? Should one have been writing for a year, or three, or five? Can writing experience even be measured in terms of "years"?

I suspect it can't. The real question is "where you are," not how long it has taken you to get there. The following checklist may help you determine whether you are ready to consider "plunging".

A Writer's Checklist

☐ *I write more than 5 hours per week, every week.*
You have discipline. It's tough to find five hours a week for writing when working a day job. You've already passed one of the biggest hurdles writers face.

☐ *I submit at least one new query or article per week.*
You have a high output. Clearly you don't spend those five hours a week (or whatever) repolishing old material, or stuffing your work in a drawer. You're already "in the marketplace."

☐ *More than 50 percent of my queries and/or articles are accepted.*
You know how to target markets effectively, and you obviously write well enough to impress the majority of the editors to whom you submit. (With that kind of acceptance rate, there's a good chance that your rejections aren't due to poor quality.)

☐ *More than 50 percent of my markets pay more than $100 per article.*
You've found the guts to break out of the low-paying "ghetto." You have confidence that your work is worth more. You won't be held back by self-esteem issues.

☐ *I have at least one "regular" market that has accepted several of my articles.*
You have a steady source of income.

☐ *I have at least one "regular" market that contacts me with assignments (i.e., ideas generated by the editor rather than in response to a query from me).*
You are reliable and dependable. You meet deadlines and produce quality work. Otherwise, editors wouldn't come to *you* with ideas.

☐ *I am familiar with the practices and terminology of the publishing marketplace (e.g., I know what "FNASR" and "SASE" mean, and I know how to format a manuscript).*
You know the basics, and won't waste precious time "gearing up."

☐ *I own at least one current market guide.*
You know the importance of obtaining the tools of the trade.

☐ *I subscribe to two or more writing publications.*
You keep current with your field.

☐ *I know how to cope with rejection.*
You won't be daunted by the inevitable disappointments of this type of career.

☐ *I earned more than $5,000 from writing activities last year.*
It won't keep a roof over your head, but it's more than many freelancers make in a year. It's one of those invisible lines: If you know how to earn this much, you know how to earn more. Probably the only thing holding you back is lack of time.

☐ *I currently report writing income for tax purposes, and know how to maintain proper business/tax records of income and expenses.*
You know that "writing" isn't just putting words on a page. It's also a matter of records, accounting, and good business practices.

☐ *I keep a household budget.*
You already have an idea of what it will take to support your household—which means you know how close you are to being able to go full-time.

While scoring 100 percent on this checklist is no guarantee that you're ready to quit your day job, a low score is a pretty good indication that you need to build up more of a foundation for your writing career before attempting to rely on it for a paycheck.

Making a Plan

So you've scored a perfect 13, you're totally fed up with your day job, and you're sure this is what you want to do. What next?

For most writers, the answer is *not* "quit your day job today." The answer is "make a plan." Typically, if you hope to become a full-time writer, you'll need to plan at least six months to a year ahead before actually "taking the plunge."

What will you do during that year? Lots! Here are some of the steps you'll need to take before saying farewell to a regular paycheck and "hello" to the joys and uncertainties of the freelance life.

✤ *Discuss your desire to become a full-time freelancer with everyone in your life who will be affected by that decision (e.g., spouse, significant other, children).* Presumably, your desire to write won't be a total surprise. However, family members who supported your "hobby" may not be as enthusiastic about losing a significant chunk of family income. They may not be happy about making adjustments, such as providing extra income themselves or accepting cutbacks and lifestyle changes. Don't be surprised if you encounter resistance or even sabotage. (I've heard of some wacky "conditions" imposed by spouses.) Don't dismiss those concerns as unfeeling; if your decision will affect others, the needs of those others should be a part of the decision-making process.

❖ *Evaluate your household income requirements.* If you don't track your monthly expenses, this is a good time to start. Before you can make an effective plan, you need to know exactly where every penny of your income goes. Try tracking expenses on a simple spreadsheet, with categories such as:

- Rent/mortgage
- Groceries
- Utilities
- Insurance
- Auto (gas and repairs)
- Medical
- Household expenses (e.g., maintenance)
- Clothes
- Children's expenses
- Meals and entertainment (e.g., restaurants and movies)
- Miscellaneous

It's also wise to break "miscellaneous" into more detailed categories, such as "books, CDs, videos, pets, crafts, subscriptions," etc. A good rule of thumb is to establish a separate listing for every category that exceeds $50 (or even $20) per month.

If you've never tracked your expenses in such detail before, you could be in for a shock. You didn't know you spent $100 a month on books? Or that those twelve magazine subscriptions (that you never have time to read) cost more than $300 per year? Your budget may be a rude awakening, but it can also be a welcome one, as certain categories emerge as ripe for cost cutting.

❖ *Create a projected budget.* It's "trim the fat" time. Go over your current expense list and determine what you can cut and what you can't. Be realistic: Don't imagine that you can go a year without buying a new CD or book, or without eating out even once. (By resolving to buy those CDs or books used instead of new, however, you can cut those categories in half!) Be sure to budget for unexpected expenses: You can bet that sometime in the next year, the car will need repairs, the dog will get sick, or the roof will leak.

❖ *Determine the difference between your projected budget and your current take-home income.* If, for example, you can trim $10,000 in expenses, and you normally take home $30,000, you'll need to earn $20,000—one way or another.

❖ *Save.* Most writers suggest having a full year of income saved (or at least enough to cover a full year of expenses). You need a cushion to pay those regular bills while waiting for irregular checks. Savings will be easier once you trim the budget, however. For example, if you've determined that you can cut $10,000 in expenses, you can save that over the next year. You can also ramp up your writing (by producing more articles or seeking higher-paying markets), and bank every penny of that income as well. If your shortfall is $20,000, and you save $10,000 in expenses and earn another $10,000 in writing over the next year, you'll have covered the difference for the first year.

❖ *Create a business plan.* Determine your existing income sources, and explore ways to increase that income. Should you pitch more articles to your regular customers? Should you seek new, higher-paying markets? Should you focus on a specialty or expand your range?

❖ *Be realistic.* Nothing will sabotage your dream faster than setting impossible or unsatisfying goals. One writer I know attempted to increase her regular workload in order to build up her savings, *and* triple her writing output to gain more clients at the same time. Needless to say, this didn't work, and her "plunge" has been postponed indefinitely. Another common cause of failure is "plunging without a net"—with no savings backup. It only takes one missed rent check to get you back behind that hated office desk.

Your goal is to improve your life, not ruin it. Many writers take the plunge so that they can spend more time with loved ones—so don't create a schedule that shuts those loved ones out of your life! Many also want to find more time to do what they love—so don't create a plan that forces you to give up the types of writing you love in favor of higher-paying projects that bore you to tears. In short, don't sabotage your plan—or your life—in your attempt to make that life more rewarding. Writing is a rewarding activity in itself; writing full-time can be the icing on the cake.

Online Resources

nline resources come and go with lightning speed. Thus, rather than try to provide links to all the wonderful Web resources for writers, I will leave you with a link to mine: Writing-World. com, a site that currently hosts more than 350 articles and columns, and over 1,000 links.

On this site, you'll find additional information on the following topics:

* Getting Started/General Writing Tips—*www.writing-world.com/basics/ index.shtml*
* Business, Finance, Rights and Contracts—*www.writing-world.com/rights/ index.shtml*
* Columns and Syndication—*www.writing-world.com/freelance/index.shtml* (see "Columns")
* Freelancing Techniques and Markets (tips on general freelancing and specialized markets)—*www.writing-world.com/freelance/index.shtml*
* International Writing Markets and Tips—*www.writing-world.com/international/index.shtml*
* Book Publishing—*www.writing-world.com/publish/index.shtml*
* Self-Publishing—*www.writing-world.com/selfpub/index.shtml*
* Author and Book Promotion Tips (including Web site development, public speaking, and more)—*www.writing-world.com/promotion/index. shtml*
* Technical and Business Writing—*www.writing-world.com/tech/index.shtml*

Writing-World.com also offers sections on general fiction, children's writing, romance, mysteries, science fiction and fantasy, poetry, greeting cards, and screenwriting.

Check Writing-World.com's links section (*www.writing-world.corn/links/ index.shtml*) for links to agents, book publishers, business tips, Christian writing, classes and critiquing, dictionary and language resources, essays and journaling, fiction writing, job sites, magazine and newspaper sites, photography tips, promotion tips and resources, publications for writers, rights and contract information, scams and warnings, syndicates, travel writing, writers' guidelines, and much more! Additional resources are available in the e-book *1500 Online Resources for Writers,* also available on the site. An expanded version of this e-book, offering more than 2000 links for writers, is available free with a copy of the second edition of *Writing.com: Creative Internet Strategies to Advance Your Writing Career* (Allworth Press, 2003).

Contributors

About the Author

MOIRA ALLEN has been writing professionally for nearly twenty-five years, and has written more than one hundred articles on the business of writing. She is the author of several published books, including *Writing.com: Creative Internet Strategies to Advance Your Writing Career* (Second Edition: Allworth Press, 2003) and *The Writer's Guide to Queries, Pitches, and Proposals* (Allworth Press, 2001). She has served as a magazine editor, business/technical editor, and online editor, and now hosts the writing Web site Writing-World.com (*www.writing-world.com*).

About the Contributors

SUE FAGALDE LICK, a longtime newspaper reporter, photographer, and editor, has been freelancing full-time for more than a decade. In addition to newspaper and magazine articles, she has published three nonfiction books and a novel. A recent graduate of Antioch University's MFA program in creative nonfiction, she has taught workshops for writers at Writing-World.com, at Oregon Coast Community College, and at numerous writers conferences. For more information, see her Web page at *www.geocities.com/suelick*.

PETER BOWERMAN is the author of the award-winning book, *The Well-Fed Writer: Financial Self-Sufficiency as a Freelance Writer in Six Months or Less*, which is considered by many to be the definitive how-to guide to business freelancing. He has been a freelance commercial writer in Atlanta, Georgia, since 1993, with a corporate-client list that includes Coca-Cola, MCI, BellSouth, IBM, UPS, Holiday Inn, GTE, American Express, Mercedes-Benz, The Discovery Channel, Junior Achievement, Georgia-Pacific, The Cartoon Network, and The American Heart Association, just to name a few. Over 250 of his editorials and articles have appeared in such publications as

Writer's Digest, the *Atlanta Journal-Constitution, The Atlanta Business Chronicle, HOMEBusiness Journal, Money and Profits,* and others, as well as numerous Web sites. He currently leads seminars on writing. For more information on business freelancing, visit his Web site at *www.wellfedwriter.com.*

Index

Books from Allworth Press

Allworth Press is an imprint of Allworth Communications, Inc. Selected titles are listed below.

Writing.com: Creative Strategies to Advance Your Writing Career, Revised Edition
by Moira Allen (paperback, 6 × 9, 288 pages, $19.95)

The Writer's Guide to Queries, Pitches, and Proposals
by Moira Allen (paperback, 6 × 9, 288 pages, $16.95)

The Author's Toolkit: A Step-by-Step Guide to Writing and Publishing Your Book, Revised Edition
by Mary Embree (paperback, 5½ × 8½, 192 pages, $16.95)

The Writer's Legal Guide: An Authors Guild Desk Reference, Third Edition
by Tad Crawford and Kay Murray (paperback, 6 × 9, 320 pages, $19.95)

Business and Legal Forms for Authors and Self-Publishers, Revised Edition
by Tad Crawford (paperback, 8½ × 11, 192 pages, includes CD-ROM, $22.95)

The Journalist's Craft: A Guide to Writing Better Stories
edited by Dennis Jackson and John Sweeney (paperback, 6 × 9, 256 pages, $19.95)

Making Crime Pay: The Writer's Guide to Criminal Law, Evidence, and Procedure
by Andrea Campbell (paperback, 6 × 9, 304 pages, $19.95)

The Copyright Guide: A Friendly Guide for Protecting and Profiting from Trademarks
by Lee Wilson (paperback, 6 × 9, 208 pages, $19.95)

Marketing Strategies for Writers
by Michael Sedge (paperback, 6 × 9, 224 pages, $16.95)

Writing for Interactive Media: The Complete Guide
by Jon Samsel and Darryl Wimberly (paperback, 6 × 9, 320 pages, $19.95)

The Writer's Guide to Corporate Communications
by Mary Moreno (paperback, 6 × 9, 192 pages, $19.95)

Please write to request our free catalog. To order by credit card, call 1-800-491-2808 or send a check or money order to Allworth Press, 10 East 23rd Street, Suite 510, New York, NY 10010. Include $5 for shipping and handling for the first book ordered and $1 for each additional book. Ten dollars plus $1 for each additional book if ordering from Canada. New York State residents must add sales tax.

To see our complete catalog on the World Wide Web, or to order online, you can find us at **www.allworth.com**.